	DATE		

THE WOMEN'S HISTORY OF THE WORLD

The Women's History of the World

Rosalind Miles

Harper & Row, Publishers, New York
Grand Rapids, Philadelphia, St. Louis, San Francisco
London, Singapore, Sydney, Tokyo, Toronto

A hardcover edition of this book was published in 1989
by Salem House Publishers.

THE WOMEN'S HISTORY OF THE WORLD. Copyright © 1988 by
Rosalind Miles. All rights reserved. Printed in the United States of
America. No part of this book may be used or reproduced in any
manner whatsoever without written permission except in the case of
brief quotations embodied in critical articles and reviews. For
information address Harper & Row, Publishers, Inc., 10 East 53rd
Street, New York, N.Y. 10022.

First PERENNIAL LIBRARY edition published 1990.

LIBRARY OF CONGRESS CATALOG CARD NUMBER 88-39598
ISBN 0-06-097317-X

91 92 93 94 FB 10 9 8 7 6 5

For all the women of the world
who have had no history

CONTENTS

Woman *is* and *makes* history.

MARY RITTER BEARD

PREFACE

"What is history?" brooded Gibbon, the great historian of the Roman Empire. "Little more than a register of the crimes, follies and misfortunes of men." At last the hand that rocks the cradle has taken up the pen to set the record straight. In history, there were women too.

It would be hard to find much support for this proposition from the historical record. When a memorial stone was carved into the quay at Plymouth to commemorate the Founding Fathers who made the historic Mayflower voyage of 1620, there was no mention of the seventeen women who sailed with them to build the new world. In general, the historians of every era have shown little interest in the female sex. In 1238, only one maidservant, "awake by night and singing psalms" saw the assassin who gained entry to the bedchamber of the king of England, knife in hand. She changed the course of history—and the chronicler, Matthew de Paris, did not even get her name.

Yet the women of the world have had a history, and the full story has been far more rich and strange than we are ever led to think. The chief aim of this book is to assert the range, power and significance of women's contribution to the evolution of the human race, its huge variety in both the public and the private spheres, and the massive female achievement on every level—cultural, commercial, domestic, emotional, social and sexual. Our world past is packed with countless stories of Amazons and Assyrian war queens, mother goddesses and Great She-Elephants, imperial concubines who rose to rule the world, scientists, psychopaths, saints and sinners, Brunhild, Marie de Brinvilliers, Mother Teresa, Chiang Ch'ing.

The lives of unsung heroines also have the fascination of the greatest story never told. Every historical period and place has brought a new slant on the old saga of the re-creation of the human race. From the empress undergoing a month-long accouchement attended by doctors, midwives, ladies-in-waiting, astrologers and poets laureate, to the peasant fieldworker stepping aside to give birth crouched over a hole under a hedge, then returning to work with her newborn child swaddled at her back, the renewal of the species has always been the sole, whole, unavoidable and largely unacknowledged gift to the future of the female sex worldwide.

All this is lost when our view of history concentrates on men only, claiming a universal validity for the actions of less than half the human race. That view is a one-eyed sham—fractured, partial and censored. Historians have made a fetish of ferreting around in pipe rolls and laundry lists to track down the dirty linen of great men in preference to the great deeds of unfamous women. Society has glorified golden balls, orbs, swords and maces as symbols of worshipful masculinity, flashy phallic shows to elevate what men most valued about themselves. Each generation has bamboozled posterity for a thousand years with fancy-dress fictions and hollow bluster; among a forest of historical phallacies, the so-called "Holy Roman Empire of the German People," for instance, was *none* of these things. As Jane Austen demurely remarked, "I often think it odd that history should be so dull, for a great deal of it must be invention."

Women's history by contrast has only just begun to invent itself. Males gained entry to the business of recording, defining and interpreting events in the third millennium BC; for women, this process did not even begin until the nineteenth century. Early women's history was devoted to combing the chronicles for queens, abbesses and learned women to set against the equivalent male figures of authority and ability, creating heroines in the mirror image of heroes: Joan of Arc, Florence Nightingale, Catherine the Great. This pop-up, cigarette-card version of women's history, though it has some value in asserting that women can be competent and powerful, had two weaknesses— it reinforced the false effect of male domination of history, since there were always many more male rulers and "geniuses" than female; and it failed to address the reality of the majority of women's lives who had neither the opportunity nor the appetite for such activities.

What then should a women's history of the world do? It must fill the gaps left by conventional history's preoccupation with male doings, and give attention and dignity to women's lives in their own right. Women's exclusion from the annals represents a million million stifled voices. To recover the female part of what we have called history is no mean achievement. Any women's history therefore has to be alert to the blanks, the omissions and the half-truths. It must listen to the silences and make them cry out.

The second task is to confront the story of women as the greatest race of underdogs the world has ever known. "Women live like bats or owls, labour like beasts, and die like worms," wrote an English duchess, Margaret of Newcastle, in the seventeenth century. Both women and men have to accept the violence and brutality of men's systematic and sustained attacks on the female sex, from wife-beating to witch-hunting, from genital mutilation to murder, as the first step towards righting history's ancient and terrible wrongs.

As this argues, it is essential to acknowledge that the interests of women have very often been opposed to, and by, those of men. It is no paradox that historical periods of great progress for men have often involved losses and setbacks for women. If there is any truth in Lenin's claim that the emancipation of its women offers a fair measurement of the general level of the civilization of any society, then received notions of "progressive" developments like the classical Athenian culture, the Renaissance, and the French Revolution, in all of which women suffered severe reversals, have to undergo a radical revaluation: for, as the American historian Joan Kelly drily observes, "there was no Renaissance for women—at least in the Renaissance."

A women's history, then, must hope to explain as well as narrate, seeking the answer to two key questions: How did men succeed in enforcing the subordination of women? And why did women let them get away with it? At the origin of the species, it is suggested, Mother Nature saddled women with an unequal share of the primary work of reproduction. They therefore had to consent to domination in order to obtain protection for themselves and their children. The historical record shows, however, that women in "primitive" societies have a better chance of equality than those of more "advanced" cultures. In these, male domination has been elaborated into every aspect of life, indeed strenuously re-invented in every epoch with a battery of religious, biological, "scientific", psychological and economic reasons succeeding one another in the endless work of justifying women's inferiority to men. Traditionalist arguments of masculine supremacy have been remarkably resilient over time—all democratic experiments, all revolutions, all demands for equality have so far stopped short of sexual equality—and women, seen as biologically determined, continue to be denied the human right of full self-determination.

Given that men have sought control, why did women let them have it? As with the "inevitability" of male dominance, the explanations interlock. Handed over as children by one man (their father) to another (as husband), they were legally, financially and physically subject to the power of males in its undisguised form for thousands of years— until very recently within the great time-span of history, men of all cultures had the right to kill a wife suspected of adultery, as some still do today. Backing up physical force, and successfully superseding it as a technique of control, came mental violence. Commandeered in mind as well as in body, women have always been subjected to a barrage of psycho-sexual conditioning to shape them up to the demands of their males. As Dora Russell remarked, "the astonishing fact of human history is that religion, philosophy, political, social and economic thought have been reserved as the prerogative of men. Our world is the product of male consciousness." How then could women think the unthinkable, in Virginia Woolf's words, of "killing the Angel at the hearth"? Finally, and this cannot be dodged, women have colluded in their own subordination—too comfortable with the accommodations they had made, too locked into the ways they had found to live with men and with themselves, too wedded to their own often pathetically ingenious and resourceful solutions, they have not only helped to sustain the systems of male dominance but have betrayed their children, male and female, into them too.

Yet—and this is the final paradox of women's history—women have not ultimately been victims either of men or history, but have emerged as strong, as survivors, as invincible. Now, freed at last from the timeless tyranny of enforced childbearing, they are moving onto the offensive to correct these antediluvian imbalances. For patriarchy has run its course, and now not only fails to serve the real needs of men and women, but with its inalienable racism, militarism, hierarchical structures and rage to dominate and destroy, it threatens the very existence of life on earth. "We women are gathering," declared the American women's Pentagon Action Group of 1980, "because life on the precipice is intolerable." As long as women go on allowing men to make history, we are responsible for the material and moral consequences of our evasion.

The effort then must be to free women from their historical shackles—from the tyranny of ancient customs like bride-burning and genital mutilation still horrifically alive in the twentieth century—and to combat those newly minted in our own time. For the struggle to set women free is far from over, as Westerners like to think. In this century, the new technologies, advances in medical science and urbanization have offered women unparalleled freedoms—but each has carried within it the seeds of its use against women, bringing new opportunities for degradation and exploitation, new forms of drudge labor, new attacks on life and hope. The amniocentesis test, for example, devised as a means of promoting the birth of healthy babies, is now regularly, if illegally, used to establish the sex of a child as a preliminary to aborting unwanted females. This abuse has been reported worldwide, acknowledged in China, for instance, by the official government organ, the China People's Daily (*Sunday Times*, 6/19/88). In India, one Bombay clinic alone performed 16,000 abortions of female fetuses in 1984–5 (*Guardian* 11/4/86). Nor is this practice confined to the East. Fee-paying clinics in all the major western capitals will perform the amniocentesis test privately and take no cognizance of, nor responsibility for, the use parents make of this information.

With a subject of this magnitude, there could have been as many different histories as there are women to write them. This book does not try to be comprehensive, nor does it purport to have solved all the problems of writing women's history. Many people will feel that they could have done better. Please try—we need as much women's history as we can get. This version makes no pretense to the traditional historical fiction of impartiality. Accordingly, as with any work on women, some good ol' boy somewhere is bound to object that it is unfair to men. There is no better reply to this than the spirited self-defense of the pioneer women's historian Mary Ritter Beard: "There is sure to be an overemphasis in places, but my apology is that when conditions have been long weighted too much on one side, it is necessary to bear down heavily on the other."

It will also be objected that women should not be singled out for special pleading, since both sexes suffered alike. When both men and women groaned under backbreaking labor with the ever present scourge of famine and sudden death, the women's afflictions, it is argued, were no worse than those of men. This is another widely held belief that will not stand up to any examination of the real differences between the lives of women and men. The male peasant, however poor and lowly, always had the right to beat his wife; the black male slave, though he labored for the white master by day, did not have to service him by night as well. Nor have changing social conditions had the same impact on men's and women's lives—the industrialization of Europe and America in the nineteenth century that improved the material quality of so many people's lives, itself depended upon the introduction of the ferocious consumerism that more than anything else has devalued women in twentieth-century society.

The future of the world, then, has to be better than its past. In finding the way to the future, our understanding of our past has a crucial part to play. As Lord Acton observed, "history convinces more people than philosophy." Historians create explanations, rationales, symbols and stereotypes that guide us from one era to another. Consequently, history will lead us all astray if it continues to look asquint. Women have been active, competent and *important* through all the ages of man, and it is devastating for us if we do not understand this. But history is also without meaning for men if the centrality of women is denied. Like racist myths, these one-sided accounts of the human past are no longer acceptable: intellectually spurious and devoid of explanatory power, they more and more betray the void of unknowing at their heart.

Can human beings learn from the lessons that history teaches? To move towards a fairer society in the ideal of full humanity for all, men must be ready to dispense with patriarchy's rigid orthodoxies and life-denying hierarchical systems. Women in return have to take up their share of the responsibility for the public organization of their societies, and in the private sphere, learn to love men as partners, not in the insulting traditional combination of domineering father and overgrown child. All future developments from now on must be assessed from the perspective of both sexes, since both men and women are equally important to the making of history. The hope for the future, like the triumph of the past, lies in the cooperation and complementarity of women and men.

ROSALIND MILES

I
IN THE BEGINNING

The key to understanding women's history
is in accepting—painful though it may be—
that it is the history
of the majority of the human race.

GERDA LERNER

1
THE FIRST WOMEN

The predominant theory [of] human cultural evolution has been "Man-the-Hunter." The theory
that humanity originated in the club-wielding man-
ape, aggressive and masterful, is so widely accepted
as scientific fact and so vividly secure in popular
culture as to seem self-evident.

PROFESSOR RUTH BLEIER

For man without woman there is no heaven in the
sky or on earth. Without woman there would be
no sun, no moon, no agriculture, and no fire.

ARAB PROVERB

The story of the human race begins with the female. Woman carried
the original human chromosome as she does to this day; her evolutionary adaptation ensured the survival and success of the species; her
work of mothering provided the cerebral spur for human communication and social organization. Yet for generations of historians, archaeologists, anthropologists and biologists, the sole star of the dawn
story has been man. Man the Hunter, man the tool-maker, man the
lord of creation stalks the primeval savannah in solitary splendor through
every known version of the origin of our species. In reality, however,
woman was quietly getting on with the task of securing a future for
humanity—for it was her labor, her skills, her biology that held the
key to the destiny of the race.

For, as scientists acknowledge, "women are the race itself, the strong
primary sex, and man the biological afterthought."[1] In human cell
structure, woman's is the basic "X" chromosome; a female baby simply
collects another "X" at the moment of conception, while the creation
of a male requires the branching off of the divergent "Y" chromosome,
seen by some as a genetic error, a "deformed and broken X." The
woman's egg, several hundred times bigger than the sperm that fer-
tilizes it, carries all the genetic messages the child will ever receive.
Women therefore are the original, the first sex, the biological norm
from which males are only a deviation. Historian Amaury de Riencourt

sums it up: "Far from being an incomplete form of maleness, according to a tradition stretching from the biblical Genesis through Aristotle to Thomas Aquinas, *femaleness is the norm, the fundamental form of life.*"[2]

How are we going to tell Father? For Nigel Calder, "the first lords of the universe were globules of coloured slime"[3]—they may only have been protoplasmal molecules or start-up bacilli, but they were male. Yet in contradiction to this age-old bias of biology is the startling discovery, debated by the American Anthropological Association in 1987, that every single person on this planet is descended from the same primitive hominid, and that this common ancestor was a woman. Using the latest techniques of gene research into DNA, the molecular structure of gene inheritance, scientists working independently at Oxford, Yale, the University of California at Berkeley, and Emory University in Atlanta have succeeded in isolating one DNA "fingerprint" that is common to the whole of the human race. This has remained constant for millennia despite the divergence of races and populations throughout the world—and it is incontrovertibly female. This research points directly to one woman as the original "gene fount" for the whole of the human race. She lived in Africa about 200,000 years ago, and her descendants later migrated out of Africa and spread across the face of the globe, giving rise to all the people living today.[4]

This work on the woman who could have been our grandmother Eve is still in its infancy, and controversial in its implications. Not least of the problems it poses for the sons of Adam is its implicit dismissal of the Christian myth—for the "gene fount mother" necessarily had a mother herself, and the identity or numbers of her sexual partners were irrelevant, since hers was the only cell that counted. Indisputable, however, is the central role of women in the evolution of the species. In terms of the DNA messages that a new individual needs in order to become a human being, the essential genetic information is only ever contributed by and transmitted through the female. In that sense, each and every one of us is a child of Eve, carrying within our bodies the living fossil evidence of the first women who roamed the African plain side by side with their men.

As this suggests, nothing could be further from the truth of the role played by early woman than the "hunter's mate" stereotype of the dim huddled figure beside the fire in the cave. From around 500,000 BC, when *femina erecta* first stood up alongside *homo erectus* in some sun-drenched primordial gorge, many changes took place before both together became *sapiens*. And there is continuous evidence from a number of different sites throughout the Pleistocene age of women's critical involvement in all aspects of the tribe's survival and evolution generally thought of, like hunting, as reserved to men.

The early woman was in fact intensively occupied from dawn to dusk. Hers was not a long life—like their mates, most hominid females, according to scientific analysis of fossil remains, died before they were twenty. Only a handful survived to thirty, and it was quite exceptional to reach forty.[5] But in this short span, the first women evolved a huge range of activities and skills. On archaeological evidence, as well as that of existing Stone Age cultures, women were busy with and adept in:

- food gathering
- child care
- leatherwork
- making garments, slings and containers from animal skins
- cooking
- pottery
- weaving grasses, reeds and bark strips for baskets
- fashioning beads and ornaments from teeth or bone
- construction of shelters, temporary or permanent
- toolmaking for a variety of uses, not simply agricultural—stone scrapers for skins, and sharp stone blades for cutting out animal sinews for garment making
- medicinal application of plants and herbs for everything from healing to abortion.

Of women's duties, food gathering unquestionably came at the top of the list, and this work kept the tribe alive. *At no point in prehistory did women, with or without their children, rely on their hunting males for food.* Certainly the men hunted, as in many "primitive" societies they still do. Anthropologists have now surveyed around 175 hunter/gathering cultures in Oceania, Asia, Africa and America. In 97 percent of these, the hunting was exclusively dominated by the males of the tribe; in the remaining 3 percent it was totally and invariably a male preserve. But these wide-ranging and well-documented studies also show how inefficient hunting is as a means of providing food. Meat from the kill comes in irregularly and infrequently—the !Kung bushmen of Botswana, for instance, hunt strenuously for a week, then do no more work for the rest of the month—and the meat, especially in hot climates, cannot be stored. As a result, only women's gathering, not men's hunting, sustains the tribe. Working unceasingly during the daylight hours, women regularly produce as much as 80 percent of the tribe's total food intake, on a daily basis. One interpretation of these figures is that in every hunter/gatherer society, the male members were and are doing only one-fifth of the work necessary for the group to survive, while the other four-fifths is carried out entirely by the women.[6]

In earliest times, women's gathering served not only to keep the tribe alive—it helped to propel the race forward in its faltering passage towards civilization. For successful gathering demanded and developed skills of discrimination, evaluation and memory, and a range of seeds, nutshells and grasses discovered at primitive sites in Africa indicate that careful and knowledgeable selection, rather than random gleaning, dictated the choice.[7] This work also provided the impetus for the first human experiments with technology. Anthropologists' fixation on man the hunter has designated the first tools as weapons of the hunt.[8] But since hunting was a much later development, earlier still would have been the bones, stones or lengths of wood used as aids to gathering for scratching up roots and tubers, or for pulverizing woody vegetation for ease of chewing. All these were women's tools, and the discovery of digging sticks with fire-hardened points at primitive sites indicates the problem-solving creativity of these female dawn foragers, who had worked out that putting pointed sticks into a low fire to dry and harden would provide them with far more efficient tools for the work they had to do.[9]

Unlike the worked flint heads of axes, spears and arrows, however, very few of the earlier tools have survived to tell the tale of women's ingenuity and resourcefulness. Sticks also lacked the grisly glamour of the killing-tools in the eyes of archaeologists, and had no part to play in the unfolding drama of Man the Hunter. Archaeology is likewise silent on the subject of another female invention, the early woman gatherer's "swag bag," the container she must have devised to carry back to the camp all she had found, foraged, caught or dug up in the course of her day's hunting.[10]

For the volume of food needed, and the range of food sources available, make it impossible that the women gatherers could have carried all the provender in their hands or inside their clothing. Their haul would have included not merely grasses, leaves, berries and roots, but also vital protein in the form of lizards, ants, slugs, snails, frogs and grubs. Eggs and fish were rare treats but not unknown, and for shore dwellers the sea presented a rich and bottomless food store.

Whatever presented itself, from dead locust to decomposing snake, the woman gatherer could not afford to pass it up; nor, with the burden of sustaining life for all on her shoulders, could she return to the homesite until her bag was full, when she faced the day's final challenge, that of converting these intimidating raw materials into something resembling a palatable meal.

Woman's work of gathering would inevitably take on a wider and more urgent dimension when she had infants to feed as well as herself. Her first task as a mother would have been to adapt her gathering bag into a sling to carry her baby, since she had to devise some means of taking it with her when she went out to forage. As most early women did not live beyond their twenties, there would be no pool of older, post-menopausal women to look after the next generation of infants once their own were off their hands. Hominid babies were heavy, and got heavier as brains, and therefore skulls, became larger. Similarly, evolving bodies of mothers presented less and less hair for their infants to cling to. Whether she slung her baby diagonally across her breasts, or on her back in the less common papoose style of the native mothers of the New World, sling her she did. How? If only archaeology could tell us that.

Mothering the young had other implications too, equally crucial both to early women and to the future of the race. Two factors made this work far more demanding than it had been to their primate grandmothers. First, human young take far longer to grow and become self-supporting than baby apes—they consequently need far more care, over an extended period of time, and cannot simply be swatted off the nipple and pointed at the nearest banana. Then again, the mothering of human babies is not just a matter of physical care. Children have to be initiated into a far more complex system of social and intellectual activity than any animal has to deal with, and in the vast majority of all human societies this responsibility for infants has been women's primary work and theirs alone. How well the first mothers succeeded may be seen from the world history of the success of their descendants.

The prime centrality of this work of mothering in the story of evolution has yet to be acknowledged. A main plank of the importance of Man the Hunter in the history of the human race has always been the undisputed claim that cooperative hunting among males called for more skill in communication and social organization, and hence provided the evolutionary spur to more complex brain development, even the origins of human society. The counterargument is briskly set out by Sally Slocum:

> The need to organize for feeding after weaning, learning to handle the more complex socioemotional bonds that were developing, the new skills and cultural inventions surrounding more extensive gathering—all would demand larger brains. *Too much attention has been given to skills required by hunting, and too little to the skills required for gathering and the raising of dependent young* [italics inserted].[11]

Similarly women's invention of food sharing as part of the extended care of their children must have been at least as important a step towards group cooperation and social organization as the work of man the hunter/leader running his band. Women's work as mothers of human infants who need a long growing space for postnatal development also involves them in numerous other aspects of maternal care (sheltering, comforting, diverting), in play, and in social activity with other mothers and other young. All these are decisively shown by modern psychology to enhance what we call IQ, and must have been of critical value in assisting our branching away from the great apes in mental and conceptual ability. Female parents are not the only ones who can comfort, stimulate or play. But all these activities are very far removed from the supposed role of hunting, killing, primitive man.[12]

Nor does the significance of the mother-child bond end there. In the myth of Man the Hunter, he invents the family. By impregnating his mate and stashing her away in the cave to mind the fire, he creates the basic human social unit which he then maintains by his hunting/killing. The American journalist Robert Ardrey, chief exponent of the hunting hypothesis, naïvely pictures the sexual division of the average primeval working day: "the males to their hunting range, the females to their homesite (we think of it today as the office and the home)."[13] But in contradiction to this Big Daddy scenario, a mass of evidence shows that the earliest families consisted of females and their children, since all tribal hunting societies were centered on and organized through the mother. The young males either left or were driven out, while the females stayed close to their mothers and the original homesite, attaching their males to them. In the woman-centered family, males were casual and peripheral, while both nucleus and any networks developing from it remained female. These arrangements continue to operate in a number of still-existing Stone Age tribes worldwide, the so-called "living fossils." As anthropologist W. I. Thomas stresses, "Children therefore were the women's and remained members of her group. The germ of social organization was always the woman and her children and her children's children."[14]

In fact the human debt to the first women goes on and on, the more we unravel the biological evidence. It is to early woman that we owe the fact that most of us are right-handed, for instance. As Nigel Calder explains, "handedness, the typical right-handedness of modern humans, is a female phenomenon."[15] From time immemorial woman has made a custom of carrying her baby on the left side of the body, where it can be comforted by the beating of her heart. This frees the right hand for action, and would have been the spur towards the evolution of predominant right-handedness in later human beings. Support for the "femaleness of handedness," Calder shows, comes in the fact that to this day infant girls develop handedness, like speech, very much more quickly and decisively than boys.

One last biological legacy of woman to man deserves more gratitude than it seems to have received. At primate level, the male penis is an unimpressive organ. So far from terrorizing any female, the average King Kong can only provoke sympathy for his meager endowment in relation to his vast bulk. Man, however, developed something disproportionately large in this line, and can truly afford to feel himself lord of creation in the penile particular. And he owes it to woman. Quite simply, when *femina* aspiring to be *erecta* hoisted herself on to her hind legs and walked, the angle of the vagina swung forward and down, and the vagina itself moved deeper into the body. The male penis then echoed the vagina's steady progress, following the same evolutionary principle as the giraffe's neck: it grew in order to get to something it could not otherwise reach.[16] This need also dictated the uniquely human experimentation with frontal sex. The future of the species demanded that man gained entry somehow. But the ease with which most couples move between frontal and rear-entry positions during intercourse is a constant reminder of the impact of woman's evolutionary biology.

The biology of woman in fact holds the key to the story of the human race. The triumph of evolution occurred in the female body, in one critical development that secured the future of the species. This was the biological shift from primate estrus, when the female comes into heat, to full human menstruation. Although generally unsung, indeed unmentioned, female monthly menstruation was the evolutionary adaptation that preserved the human species from extinction and ensured its survival and success.

For female estrus in the higher primates is a highly inefficient mechanism. The great female primates, chimpanzees, gorillas and orang-utans, come on heat rarely, and produce one infant every five or six years. This puts the whole species dangerously at risk of extinction, and the great apes today survive only in small numbers and in the most favorable environments. With twelve chances of conceiving in every year, instead of one every five years, the human female has a reproductive capacity *sixty times higher than that of her primate sisters*. Menstruation, not hunting, was the great evolutionary leap forward. It was through a female adaptation, not a male one, that "man" thrived, multiplied and conquered the globe.

And female menstruation was not merely a physical phenomenon like eating or defecation. Recent commentators have argued that women's so-called curse operated to cure not only man's shortage of off-spring, but also his primeval mental darkness. In their pioneering work on menstruation, *The Wise Wound*, Penelope Shuttle and Peter Redgrove stress the connection made in primitive societies between the lunar and menstrual cycles, suggesting that woman first awakened in humankind the capacity to recognize abstracts, to make connections and to think symbolically. For Elise Boulding, these mental functions arise from an earlier stage in which women taught men the principles of number, calendar organization and counting: "Every woman had a 'body calendar'—her monthly menstrual cycle. She would be the first to notice the relationship between her own body cycle and the lunar cycle."[17] Other female authorities have expressed their amusement at the naïvety of one professor, the celebrated Jacob Bronowski, who on the TV series "The Ascent of Man" solemnly described a prehistoric reindeer bone with 31 scratches on it as "obviously a record of the lunar month." Commenting on "The Ascent of You Know Who," Vonda McIntyre demurred: "Do tell. A 31-day lunar month? I think it a good deal more likely that the bone was a record of a woman's menstrual cycle."[18]

Objectively, this carefully notated silent witness of an irretrievably lost transaction could have been either of these; or both; or neither. But in the routine, unconscious denial of women's actions, experiences, rhythms, even of their ability to *count*, the possibility that it could have been a woman's record of her own intimate personal life was not even considered.

No attention at all, in fact, has been given to the implication for women when light and infrequent estrus gave way to full menstruation, with bleeding in varying but substantial amounts for one week in every four. What did early woman do? Did she simply squat on a pile of leaves and leak? This is uncomfortably close to the passive female fire watcher of the Man the Hunter myth—and it is out of the question that the tribal food gatherers, so vital to survival, could have been out of action for 25 percent of their time. But if the women moved around at all, an unchecked menstrual flow would have resulted in badly chapped and painful inner thighs, especially in colder or windy weather, with the added risk of infection in hot climates. Skin scabbing so caused would hardly have had a chance to heal before the menstrual flow was on again.

A number of indicators point to the solution. In the wild, female monkeys are observed to bunch up pads of leaves to wipe off estrus spotting. From still surviving Stone Age cultures it is recorded that the women weave or fashion clothes, slings for their babies, and rough bags to carry what they scavenge or garner. The first women must have devised menstrual slings or belts, with some kind of pad to absorb the heaviest flow. Even today both Maori and Eskimo women contrive pads of a fine soft moss, while Indonesian women make tampon-type balls of a soft vegetable fiber. The Azimba women of Central Africa use the same fiber as pads, which are held in place by an oval sling of soft goatskin fastened to a belt of twisted thong.[19] It is difficult to avoid the conclusion that the women capable of bringing the infant human race forward into the future could also have found the way to deal efficiently with their own bodies.

But one thing is certain: that any such object, along with other examples of early woman's technology, would not have survived. Even if it had, would it have been deemed worthy of attention? Wide-ranging consideration at every level from academic investigation to wild surmise has been devoted to all aspects of the life of early man. But no attention in either scholarly or popular work has been given to what anthropologist Donald Johanson, discoverer of the early female hominid "Lucy," dismissed as "the estrus argument"—that is, the importance of the female's biological shift to menstruation. As Johanson explained, "I don't believe anything I can't measure, and I've never seen an estrus fossil."[20] Well, he wouldn't, would he?

Like Johanson, generations of male commentators have blinded themselves both to the facts and the significant implications of the evolution of early woman. They have insisted instead on rewriting primitive woman as no more than a sexual vehicle for man. "They were fatted for marriage, were these Stone Age squaws," wrote H. G. Wells. "The females were the protected slaves of the old male, the master of all

the women"—a wistful Wellsian fantasy of women on tap.[21] For Robert
Ardrey, menstruation only evolved as a bonanza for the boys. When
a female primate came into heat, burbled Ardrey, she "hit the sexual
jackpot," providing "fun for all . . . and for herself a maximum of
male attention."[22] But estrus episodes are brief and infrequent—there
had to be something more to bring the hunter home from the hill.
Accordingly, the first woman learned to convert primate heat into
menstruation. This made her sexually available and receptive to man
all the year round, as a reward for her share of his kill, in history's
first known example of the time-honored convention of *quim pro quo*.
The "fun for all" theory of women's early sexual evolution also accounts
for the physical arrangement of the modern woman's body. When
Man the Hunter began to walk upright, he naturally wanted frontal
sex. As Desmond "Naked Ape" Morris so engagingly explains, woman
obliged this desire "to make sex sexier" by growing breasts. Realizing
that her "pair of fleshy hemispherical buttocks" were now quite passé
as a means of attracting men's attention, she "had to do something to
make the frontal region more stimulating."[23] Any connection between
the increase in women's breast size and the increasing size of the human
baby at birth must have been purely coincidental.

For in this androcentric account of woman's evolution, every aspect
of her bodily development took place for man's benefit, not her own.
For him she evolved the female orgasm, as a well-earned bonus for
the trail-wearied meat-provider at the end of the day. "So female
invention went on," rejoices Ardrey. "The male might be tired; female
desire would refresh him."[24] In the last of his evolutionary incarnations
Man the Hunter now becomes sexual athlete and rutting ape while
woman, receptive and responsive for 365 days of the year, awaits his
return to display her new-found repertoire of fun tricks with breasts
and clitoris, the Pleistocene Playmate of the Month.

In the light of all the evidence, from a wealth of scientific sources,
of the centrality of woman, how do we explain the dominance and
persistence of the myth of Man the Hunter? Charles Darwin's concept
of the origins of the human race included no such creature—his early
man was a social animal working within "the corporate body" of the
tribe, without which he would not survive. But later Darwinians like
Thomas Huxley and Herbert Spencer ("the greatest ass in Christendom," according to Carlyle) reinterpreted the evolutionary battle for
survival as taking place not between *genes,* but *individuals.* By 1925
academics were treating this idea as fact, Professor Carveth Read of

London University excitedly proposing that early man should be re-named *Lycopithecu* for his wolvish savagery, a suggestion enthusias-tically taken up by another thriller-writer manqué, the South African professor Raymond Dart:

> Man's predecessors differed from living apes in being confirmed killers; carnivorous creatures, that seized living quarries by violence, battered them to death, tore apart their broken bodies, dismembered them limb from limb, slaking their ravenous thirst with the hot blood of their victims and greedily devouring living, writhing flesh.[25]

As this suggests, the notion of Man the Hunter unpacks to reveal a number of other elements that feed and flatter male fantasies of violence and destruction. "We are Cain's children," droned Ardrey. "Man is a predator whose natural instinct is to kill with a weapon." Lots of the boys have taken up this theme, from Konrad Lorenz to Anthony Storr: "The simple fact is that we [*who we?*] are the cruellest and most ruthless species that has ever walked the earth."[26] Man's natural aggression found its natural outlet in subordinating those around him: "women, boys and girls," wrote H. G. Wells, "all go in fear of the old male." For Ardrey, "dominance, a revolutionary social ne-cessity even in the carefree forest life, became a day-to-day survival institution in the lives of the hunters."[27] Man's "hunting pedigree" can thus be used to justify every act of male aggression from business chicanery to wife-battering and rape, while the "right to dominate" of "early boss man" has proved far too serviceable to his successors to be cast aside.

In fact there is almost no aspect of modern human society, no self-flattering delusion about man's "natural" instinct to dominate and destroy, that "Man the Hunter" cannot be said to originate and explain. Generations of academics have joined their respectful voices to the paean of praise for him and his pals: "our intellects, interests, emotions and basic social life," chirped American professors Washburn and Lancaster, "all these we owe to the hunters of time past." Needless to say, Man the Hunter did not carry all before him: Donald Johanson has described the hunting hypothesis as the product of Ardrey's "vivid imagination," and "an embarrassment to anthropologists." In profes-sional circles now the whole theory has been consigned to the wasteland between revision and derision, and psychologist Dr. John Nicholson is not the only academic to admit to being "still annoyed that I was once taken in by it."[28]

But once up and running through the great open spaces of popular belief, Man the Hunter has proved a hard quarry to bring down, and few seem to have noticed that for millennia he has traveled on through the generations entirely alone. For woman is nowhere in this story. Aside from her burgeoning sexual apparatus, early woman is taken to have missed out completely on the evolutionary bonanza. "The evolving male increased in body size, muscular strength and speed, as well as in intelligence, imagination and knowledge," pronounced a leading French authority, "in all of which the female hardly shared."[29] Countless other historians, anthropologists, archaeologists and biologists worldwide all make the same claim in different ways. Man, it seems, singlehandedly performed all the evolving for the rest of the human race. Meanwhile early woman, idle and dependent, lounged about the home base, the primordial airhead and fully evolved bimbo.

Yet in celebrating the achievement of early woman, and dismissing the farrago of flattering fictions that make up the myth of hunting man, it is essential not to substitute a denial of his real activities for the historic denial of hers. Man's part in the survival of the species becomes more normal, more natural, and paradoxically more admirable once the essentially cooperative nature of early human life is reasserted.

Hunting was a whole-group activity, not a heroic solo adventure. As Myra Shackley explains, "successful hunting, especially of large animals traveling in herds such as reindeer, horses, mammoth, bison and woolly rhinoceros meant cooperation in bands."[30] To this day, all members of hunting societies, including women and children, join in hunting/beating activities as a matter of course. In their own right, too, women have long been known to hunt smaller, slower or safer animals. An eighteenth-century trader of the Hudson Bay Company in Canada discovered an Eskimo woman who had kept herself alive for seven months on the mid-winter ice-cap by her own hunting and snaring "when there was nothing but desolation for 1000 miles around."[31]

Hunting did not mean fighting. On the contrary, the whole purpose of group organization was to ensure that primitive man did *not* have to face and do battle with his prey. The first humans, as Shackley shows, worked together to avoid this, "driving animals over cliffs to their deaths (as certainly happened at the Upper Paleolithic site of Solutre) or using fire to stampede them into boggy ground (the method used at Torralba and Ambrona)."[32] Cro-Magnon cave paintings from the Dordogne region of France vividly depict a mammoth impaled on stakes in a pit, a practice known worldwide. This method of hunting did not even involve killing, as the animal could be left to die. Most forms of hunting did not in fact involve direct aggression, personal combat or a struggle to the death, but involved preying on slow-moving creatures like turtles, on wounded or sick animals, on females about to give birth or on carcasses killed and abandoned by other, fiercer predators.

Men and women relied on each others' skills, before, during and after the hunt. The anthropologist Constable cites the Stone Age Yukaghir of Siberia, whose men formed an advance party to check out the traps for prey, while the women came up behind to take charge of dismembering the carcass and transporting it to the home site.[33] Since carcasses were used for food, clothes, shelter, bone tools and bead ornaments, most of which the women would be producing, they had a vested interest in the dismemberment. As Myra Shackley reminds us:

> Apart from their use as food, animals were hunted for their hides, bones and sinews, useful in the manufacture of clothing, tents, traps, and the numerous odds and ends of daily life. Suitable skins would have been dried and cured and softened with animal fats. Clothes could be tailored by cutting the hides with stone tools and assembling the garment by lacing with sinews through holes bored with a stone tool or bone awl . . . There is no reason to suppose that Neanderthal clothes were as primitive as many illustrators have made them out to be . . . The remains of ostrich shells on Mousterian sites in the Neger desert suggest the Neanderthal was using them as water containers, as Bushmen do today . . . what use was made of the exotic feathers? There is no need to suppose that because there is a lack of archaeological evidence for personal adornment no attention was paid to it.[34]

Hunting man, then, was not a fearless solitary aggressor, hero of a thousand fatal encounters. The only regular, unavoidable call on man's aggression was as protector: *infant caring and group protection are the only sexual divisions of labor that invariably obtain in primate or primitive groups.* When the first men fought or killed, then, they did so *not* for sport, thrill or pleasure, but in mortal fear, under life-threatening attack, and fighting for survival.

Because group protection was so important a part of man's work, it is essential to question the accepted division by sex of emotional labor, in which all tender and caring feelings are attributed to women, leaving men outside the circle of the camp-fire as great hairy brutes existing only to fight or fornicate. In reality the first men, like the first women, only became human when they learned how to care for others.

A skeleton discovered in the Shanidar caves of what is now Iraq tells an interesting story, according to anthropologist John Stewart:

> The man . . . had been crippled by a useless right arm, which had been amputated in life just above the elbow. He was old, perhaps forty in Neanderthal years, which might be the equivalent of eighty today, and he suffered from arthritis. He was also blind in the left eye, as indicated by the bone scar tissue on the left side of the face. It is obvious that such a cripple must have been extensively helped by his companions . . . the fact that his family had both the will and ability to support a technically useless member of the society says much for their highly developed social sense.[35]

Whatever became of "man the hunter striding brutally into the future"?[36] Isn't he beginning to sound like a real human being?

This is not to say that the women of prehistory were not subjected to violence, even death. A female victim of a cannibalistic murder which took place between 150,000 and 200,000 years ago was discovered at Ehringsdorf in Germany. She was an early Neanderthaler who had been clubbed to death with a stone axe. After death her head was separated from her body, and the base of her skull opened to extract the brains. Near her lay the remains of a ten-year-old child who had died at the same time.[37]

Nor was prehistory any stranger to sexual violence. An extraordinary bone carving in the shape of a knife from Isturitz in the Basses-Pyrénées shows a harpooned bison graphically vomiting blood as it wallows in its death throes. On the other side of the blade a woman similarly harpooned crawls forward on her hands and knees while a male figure crouches lecherously behind her, clearly intent on sexual penetration from the rear, although the droop of her breasts and the swelling of her belly show that she is pregnant. In a bizarre definition of primitive man's idea of foreplay, the French anthropologist G-H Luquet interprets this gruesome object as a "love charm"![38]

But interestingly, women of primitive societies are often far less subjugated than a modern, particularly a Western, observer might expect. Far from being broken-down slaves to their men's drives and needs, women in early societies often had a *better* chance of freedom, dignity and significance than many of their female descendants in more "advanced" societies. The key lies in the nature of the tribe's relation to its surroundings. Where sheer subsistence is a struggle and survival is the order of the day, women's equality is very marked. Women in these cultures play too vital a role to be kept down or out of action, and their knowledge and experience are a cherished tribal resource.

As the major food providers, holding the secret of survival, women have, and know they have, freedom, power and status.

Men in hunter/gatherer societies do not command or exploit women's labor. They do not appropriate or control their produce, nor prevent their free movement. They exert little or no control over women's bodies or those of their children, making no fetish of virginity or chastity, and making no demands of women's sexual exclusivity. The common stock of the group's knowledge is not reserved for men only, nor is female creativity repressed or denied. Today's "civilized" sisters of these "primitive" women could with some justice look wistfully at this substantial array of the basic rights of women.

And there was more. Evidence from existing Stone Age cultures conclusively shows that women can take on the roles of counsellors, wise women, leaders, storytellers, doctors, magicians and lawgivers.[39] Additionally, they never forfeit their own unique power based on woman's special magic of fertility and birth, with all the *mana* attendant upon that. All the prehistoric evidence confirms women's special status *as women* within the tribe. Among numerous representations of women performing religious rituals, a rock painting from Tanzoumaitak, Tassili N'Ajjer, shows two women dancing ceremonially among a flock of goats, richly ornamented with necklaces, bracelets and bead headdresses, while in one of the most famous of prehistoric paintings, the so-called "White Lady" of the Drakensberg Mountain caves of South Africa leads men and women in a ritual tribal dance.[40]

From the very beginning then, the role of the first women was wider, their contribution to human evolution immeasurably more significant, than has ever been accepted. Dawn woman, with her mother and grandmother, her sisters and her aunts, and even with a little help from her hunting man, managed to accomplish almost everything that subsequently made *homo* think himself *sapiens*. There is every sign that man himself recognized this. In universal images ranging from the very awakening of European consciousness to the Aboriginal "Dreamtime" myths on the other side of the world, woman commands the sacred rituals and is party to the most secret mysteries of tribal life.

For woman, with her inexplicable moon rhythms and power of creating new life, *was* the most sacred mystery of the tribe. So miraculous, so powerful, she had to be more than man—more than human. As primitive man began to think symbolically, there was only one explanation. Woman was the primary symbol, the greatest entity of all—a goddess, no less.

2
THE GREAT GODDESS

The Great Goddess is the incarnation of the Feminine Self that unfolds in the history of mankind
as well as in the history of every individual woman.

ERICH NEUMANN, *The Great Mother*

The Mother of songs, the Mother of our whole
seed, bore us in the beginning. She is the Mother
of all races of men, and all tribes. She is the Mother
of the thunder, of the rivers, of the trees and of
the grain. She is the only Mother we have, and She
alone is the Mother of all things, She alone.

SONG OF THE KAYABA INDIANS OF COLOMBIA

Around 2300 BC, the chief priest of Sumeria composed a hymn in
praise of God. This celebration of the omnipotent deity, "The Exal-
tation of Inanna," is a song of extraordinary power and passion, and
it has come down to history as the world's first known poem. But it
has another claim to world attention—both the first God and this first
known priest-poet were female.

For in the beginning, as humankind emerged from the darkness of
prehistory, God was a woman.[1] And what a woman! The Sumerian
inhabitants of what is now Iraq worshipped her in hymns of fearless
eroticism, giving thanks for her tangled locks, her "lap of honey," her
rich vulva "like a boat of heaven"—as well as for the natural bounty
that she "pours forth from her womb" so generously that every lettuce
was to be honored as "the Lady's" pubic hair. But the Supreme Being
was more than a provider of carnal delights. Equally relished and
revered were her warlike rages—to her first priest-poet Enheduanna
she was "a dragon, destroying by fire and flood" and "filling rivers
with blood." Enheduanna herself enjoyed temporal power as the
daughter of Sargon I. But it was in her role as chief "moon-minister
to the Most High" that her true authority lay. For as poet, priest and
prophet of Inanna, Enheduanna was the voice of a deity whose power
and worship spanned the whole world and was as old as time itself,
the first divinity, the Great Mother.[2]

The power and centrality of the first woman God is one of the best-kept secrets of history. We think today of a number of goddesses, all with different names—Isis, Juno, Demeter—and have forgotten what, 5000 years ago, every schoolgirl knew; no matter what name or guise she took, there was only one God and her name was woman. The Roman lawyer Lucius Apuleius was skillfully recycling the whole compendium of contemporary clichés in his portrait of "the Goddess" as she spoke to him in a vision:

> I am nature, the universal mother, mistress of all the elements, primordial child of time, sovereign of all things spiritual, queen of the dead. . . . Though I am worshipped in many aspects, known by countless names, propitiated with all manner of different rites, yet the whole round earth venerates me.[3]

Later ages dismissed accounts of Goddess-worship as "myths" or "cults." But since Sir Arthur Evans, discoverer of the lost Minoan civilization at the turn of this century, stated that all the innumerable goddess-figures he had discovered represented "the same Great Mother . . . whose worship under various names and titles extended over a large part of Asia Minor and the regions beyond," modern scholarship has accepted that "the Great Goddess, the 'Original Mother without a Spouse,' was in full control of all the mythologies" as "a worldwide fact."[4]

Nor was this an isolated or temporary phenomenon. Commentators stress the prominence and prevalence of the Great Mother Goddess as an essential element from the dawn of human life. From its emergence in the cradleland of the steppes of Southern Russia her worship ranged geographically throughout the Mediterranean, the Indus Valley, and Asia as far as China, to Africa and Australia. Historically the span is even more startling:

- 25,000—15,000 BC—with the so-called "Venus figurines" of stone and ivory in Europe, of Nile mud in Egypt, "the Great Mother . . . bursts on the world of men in overwhelming wholeness and perfection."[5]
- 12,000—9000 BC—in Dolní Věstonice, Czechoslovakia, and Shanidar, Iraq, ceremonial burials of bodies coated in red ochre, commonly associated with Goddess worship.
- 7000 BC—in Jericho, the first shrines to the Mother Goddess.
- 6000 BC—the village settlement of Çatal Hüyük in Turkey, a site of only 32 acres, contained no less than 40 shrines to the Goddess, in three incarnations as maiden, mother and crone.

- 5000 BC—a statuette from Hacilar in Turkey shows the Goddess in the act of making love.
- 4000 BC—the first written language appears on the temple of the Goddess under her title of Queen of Heaven at Erech (modern Uruk) in Sumeria.
- 3000 BC—she now appears everywhere in the known world, in statues, shrines and written records.
- 200 BC—tribal Celts sent their own priests of the Goddess to the great sacred festival of Cybele in Anatolia.
- AD 200—at Tralles, in western Anatolia, a woman called Aurelia Aemiliana erected a carving at the temple of the Goddess, recording that she had duly performed her sexual service (sacred intercourse in honor of the Goddess) as her mother and all her female ancestors had done before her.

AD 500—Christian emperors forcibly suppressed the worship of the Goddess and closed down the last of her temples.

As this shows, the sacred status of womanhood lasted for at least 25,000 years—some commentators would push it back further still, to 40,000 or even 50,000. In fact there was never a time at this stage of human history when woman was *not* special and magical.[6]

For as the struggle for survival eased by degrees into the far harder struggle for meaning, woman became both focus and vehicle of the first symbolic thought. The French archaeologist Leroi-Gourhan solved a riddle of the early cave paintings that had defeated anthropologists of more puritanical cultures when he revealed that the recurrent and puzzling "double-eye" figure was a symbol of the vulva. Similarly in a remarkable sculpted frieze of animal and human figures at Angles-sur-l'Anglin, the female forms are represented by pure abstract triangles of women's bodies, with the sexual triangle prominently emphasized.[7]

How did woman assume from the first this special status? One source of it was undoubtedly her moon-linked menstruation and the mystery of her nonfatal yet incurable emission of blood. Another was her close and unique relation to nature, for as gathering gave way to planned horticulture, women consolidated their central importance as the principal food producers. But the real key lies where the exaggerated breasts and belly of the earliest images of woman direct us to look, in the miracle of birth. Before the process of reproduction was understood, babies were simply born to women. No connection was made with intercourse (to this day Australian Aboriginals believe that spirit children dwell in pools and trees, and enter any woman at random when they wish to be born). Men, so it seemed, therefore had no part in the chain of generation. Only women could produce new life, and they were revered accordingly: all the power of nature, and over nature, was theirs.[8]

So arose the belief that woman was divine, not human, gifted with the most sacred and significant power in the world; and so was born the worship of the Great Mother. The birth of new life out of woman's body was intricately related to the birth of new crops out of the body of the earth, and from the very first both were interlocked in the concept of a female divinity far more complex and powerful than conventional accounts suggest. The most ancient incarnation of the Goddess was as mother—but the number of local and national variations on this apparently straightforward archetype in itself testifies to the maverick vigor of "the God-Mother of the country" as Tibetans called her, and her refusal to submit to stereotypical sentimentalization. So in India, Mata-Devi is the traditional mother, depicted as squeezing milk for humankind from her ample breasts. But other creation myths as far apart as Assyria and Polynesia have the Great Mother delivering not a race of men and women, but one mighty once-and-for-all "world egg." And in Greece at the most sacred climax of the most secret mysteries of Eleusis the Goddess (or her earthly representative) yearly "gave birth" to a sheaf of corn, in an explicit link between woman's fertility and nature's, as the archetypal "Mother Earth."

In some versions of the Great Goddess, however, her worshippers were anxious to stress that no matter how ancient she was, the feminine principle was there before her. So Gaea, the Roman Mother Earth, emerges from a primal vagina, the abyss of all-feeling and all-knowing, while Ishtar of the Babylonians *is* the cosmic uterus, the stars of the zodiac her raiment. The historical softening or bowdlerization of the Goddess's mother role has obscured the briskly functional nature of her motherhood—Ymir, the wind god of Norse legend (i.e., the breath of life) comes "out of the cunt of the All-Mother Ginnungagab." And paradoxically the denial of the unblushingly physical denies also the ascent into the realms of the metaphysical, a key element of the Great Mother's godhead: "I was pregnant with all power," boasted the goddess Vac in a song of the Vedic nature-religion of India. "I dwell in the waters of the sea, spread from there through all creatures, and touch the sky with my crown; I roar through all creation like the wind." The proclamation carved on the temple of "the Holy One,"

Nut of Egypt, makes an even stronger claim: *"I am what is, what will be, and what has been. No man uncovered my nakedness, and the fruit of my birthing was the sun."*[9]

Overemphasis on the good mother, procreative and nurturing, also denies the bad mother, her dangerous, dark and destructive opposite. These early civilizations, however, understood very well the strong association of the divine woman with death, and stress that the Goddess who brings humankind into the world is also she who kindly (or not so kindly) commands the way out of it. In the Ireland of 1000 BC a sinister triad of goddesses, the Morrigan, haunted battlefields, collecting severed heads and showing themselves to those about to die. In other cultures the Goddess rounds up the dead rather like a sheepdog, and takes them below; to the Greeks the dead were simply "Demeter's people."

In her darkest incarnation the bad mother did not simply wait for people to die, but demanded their deaths. The Persian Ampusa, her worshippers believed, cruised about the world in a blood bubble looking for something to kill. Her blood thirst might be propitiated by sacrifice—around 1500 BC at Hal Tarxien in Malta, the ministers of a seven-foot goddess, her belly obesely pregnant above pear-shaped legs of massive stone, caught the blood of victims in a deep vessel symbolic of the divine vagina. But the mother, and her blood-anger, endured, as in this vivid eyewitness account of the "Black Mother" of the Hindu religion, Kali-Ma:

> And Kalee-Ma'ee, the Dark Mother is there. She is luminous-black. Her four limbs are outstretched and the hands grasp two-edged swords, tools of disembowelment, and human heads. Her hands are blood-red, and her glaring eyes red-centred; and her blood-red tongue protrudes over huge pointed breasts, reaching down to a rotund little stomach. Her *yoni* is large and protuberant. Her matted, tangled hair is gore-stained and her fang-like teeth gleam. There is a garland of skulls about her neck; her earrings are the images of dead men and her girdle is a chain of venomous snakes.[10]

Wedded as we are to an all-loving, all-forgiving stereotype of motherhood, it is at first sight difficult to reconcile this terrifying image of bad mother with the good. But both "life" and "death" sides of the Goddess come together without strain in her primary aspect, which is in fact *not* motherhood pure and simple, but her *sexuality*. As her primary sexual activity she created life; but in sex she demanded man's essence, his self, even his death. Here again the true nature of the

Goddess and her activities have fallen victim to the mealymouthed prudery of later ages. Where referred to at all, they are coyly labelled "fertility" rituals, beliefs or totems, as if the Great Goddess selflessly performed her sexual obligations solely in order to ensure that the earth would be fruitful. It is time to set the historical record straight. *The fruitfulness of crops and animals was only ever a by-product of the Goddess's own personal sexual activity.* Her sex was hers, the enjoyment of it hers, and as all these early accounts of her emphasize, when she had sex, like any other sensible female, she had it for herself.

But not *by* herself. In every culture, the Goddess has many lovers. This exposes another weakness in our later understanding of her role as the Great Mother. To the children of patriarchy, "mother" always includes "wife"; mother is the woman who is married to father. That puts a further constraint on the idea of the *good* mother. The good mother does not sleep around. She does not even choose the one man she does have, but is chosen by father. Hence the insoluble paradox of the Goddess for the custodians of succeeding moralities—she was *always* unmarried and *never* chaste. Among the Eskimos, her title was "She Who Will Not Have a Husband." But there was more to her sexual freedom than this. As the source and force of life, she was timeless and endless. In contrast males came and went, their only function the service of the divine "womb" or "vulva," which is the Goddess's name in most cultures.[11]

Yet the lover of the Goddess did not simply have the kind of crudely functional experience that this might suggest. Some representations of her sexuality stress its power and terror: on seal-engravings from Babylon she puts scorpions to flight with the ritual display of her awe-inspiring pudenda, while in the Sumerian epic of Gilgamesh from before 2000 BC, the goddess Ishtar, thwarted in her unbridled sensuality, threatens to burst gates, tear down houses and "make the dead rise and overwhelm the living."[12] Far more common, however, are the tender, almost girlish poetic tributes to the skill of the lover and the delights of his body, like this song of Inanna, over 4000 years old, yet as fresh as this morning's loving:

> My brother brought me to his house,
> Laid me down on a fragrant honey bed,
> My precious sweet, lying on my heart,
> My brother did it fifty times,
> One by one, tongue-making.[13]

Further north in the legendary city of Nineveh, the unknown poet made the goddess Ishtar croon like a mother as she beds the Assyrian king Ashur-bani-pal:

> My face covers thy face
> As a mother over the fruit of her womb.
> I will place thee as a graven jewel between my breasts
> During the night will I give thee covering,
> During the day I shall clothe thee,
> Fear not, oh my little one, whom I have raised.[14]

Brother? Little one? Who were these lovers of the Goddess, and why are they described in such terms? The answer to this question leads to the clearest indication of the undisputed power of the Goddess that historical evidence affords.

For the Great Mother originally held the ultimate power—the power of the undisputed ruler, that of life and death. Where woman is the divine queen, the king must die. Mythologically and historically, too, the rampant sensuality of the Great Goddess and her taste for blood unite in the archaic but undisputed practice of the killing of the king. "King" is in fact an honorary title for the male chosen to have intercourse with the Queen-Goddess in a simple reenactment of the primal drama subsequently described by historians and anthropologists as "the sacred marriage," with the male "acting as divine consort" to the Goddess. But the savage, inexorable logic of the ritual could hardly be more opposed to this weak and anachronistic attempt to dignify the male's part in the proceedings. For when *all life* was thought to flow into, through and out of the female, the highest hope of the male was to escape the fate of all the other disposable drones and associate with the deity, even at the price of then being returned to earth.

Mythologically, the ritual sacrifice of the young "king" is attested in a thousand different versions of the story. In these the immortal mother always takes a mortal lover, not to father her child (although children often result) but essentially in exercise and celebration of her womanhood. The clear pattern is of an older woman with a beautiful but expendable youth—Ishtar and Tammuz, Venus and Adonis, Cybele and Attis, Isis and Osiris. In the story of Demeter, the functional motif of the story is even clearer: the bold Iasion "lies with" the corn goddess in the furrow of a cornfield, and dies by thunderbolt immediately afterwards. The lover is always inferior to the Goddess, mortal where she is immortal, young where she is ageless and eternal, powerless where she is all-powerful, and even physically smaller—all these elements combine in the frequent representation of the lover as the

Goddess's younger brother or son. And always, always, he dies. The fate of the lovers of the Great Goddess was well known when Gilgamesh resisted the command of "glorious Ishtar" with the reproach, "Which of your lovers did you love for ever? What shepherd of yours pleased you for all time? . . . And if you and I should be lovers, should not I be served in the same fashion as all these others whom you loved once?"[15]

Within recorded history, versions of the killing of the king frequently occur. The goddess Anaitis of Nineveh annually demanded the most beautiful boy as her lover/victim: beautified with paint, decked with gold ornaments, clothed in red and armed with the double axe of the goddess, he would spend one last day and night in orgiastic sex with her priestesses under a purple canopy in full view of the people, then he was laid on a bed of spices, incense and precious woods, covered with a cloth of gold, and set on fire. "The Mother has taken him back to her," the worshippers chanted.[16] In Ireland, the chief priestess of the Great Goddess of the Moon killed the chosen male with her own hands, decapitating him over a silver "regeneration" bowl to catch his blood. The "Jutland cauldron," one of these vessels now in the Copenhagen Museum, gives a graphic illustration of the goddess in action at the height of the sacrificial ceremony.[17]

Historic survivals of the killing of the king continued up to the present day. As late as the nineteenth century, the Bantu kingdoms of Africa knew only queens without princes or consorts—the rulers took slaves or commoners as lovers, then tortured and beheaded them after use. The last queen of the Ashanti, according to the outraged reports of British colonial administrators of the Gold Coast, regularly had several dozen "husbands" liquidated, as she liked to wipe out the royal harem on a regular basis and start again. Even where kingship was established, African queens had the power to condemn the king to death, as Frazer recorded, and the right to determine the moment of execution. Other cultures, however, gradually developed substitute offerings: first, the virility of the young male in place of his life, in a ritual castration ceremony widely practiced throughout Asia Minor (though note that the Aztecs in Meso-America never made this an either/or, until the end of their civilization insisting on *both*); then in place of men, taking children, animals, even doll-figures of men like the "mannikins" the Vestal Virgins drowned in the Tiber every spring.[18]

In real terms, however, the average man does not seem to have had much to fear from the Goddess or her worship. In a culture where the supreme deity is female, the focus is on women, and society draws its structures, rhythms, even colors from them. So, for instance, the special magic of women's sexuality, from her mysterious menstruation to her gift of producing new life, is expressed in the widespread practice throughout the period of Goddess-worship of treating certain sacred grave-burials with red ochre. Strong or bright red is associated in many religions with female genital blood, while the link between red ochre and blood is clearly indicated by its other name of "haematite." With the red ochre, then, the worshippers of the Goddess were invoking for their dead a symbolic rebirth through the potent substance of menstruation and childbirth. The literal as well as symbolic value of women's menstrual blood, their "moon-gift from the Goddess," is demonstrated in the ancient Greek custom of mixing it with seed-corn for the annual sowing, to provide "the best possible fertilizer."[19]

This open veneration of women's natural rhythms and monthly flow contrasts strangely with the secret shame and "curse" they later became. But when God was a woman, all women and all things feminine enjoyed a higher status than has ever been seen since in most countries of the world. Where the Goddess held sway, women did so too. Does this mean then that there was ever a time when women ruled men—when the natural and unquestioned form of government was matriarchy?

"The age of queens"—what is the historical truth behind the persistent myths of women holding power over men? Approaches to this question have been dogged by historians' search for societies where women had total control, and where the men were downgraded and oppressed as an inevitable consequence—for a mirror-image of every patriarchy, in fact. Not surprisingly, this process of going backwards through the looking glass has failed to produce any concrete results. Another will o' the wisp was the conviction of nineteenth-century scholars that matriarchy had once been a *universal* stage in world culture, when, the argument ran, as human society emerged from animal promiscuity, women succeeded in bringing about matriarchy through the defeat of their lustful males. In the social order thus created, woman held primacy at every level from human to divine, and the excluded males, uncivilized and violent, lurked about on the fringes of each individual "gynocracy" plotting furious revenge. For matriarchy was only a *stage* of the human ascent towards civilization. Ultimately (and quite logically to the mind of the male historian) the males contrived to overthrow matriarchy and institute patriarchy, the ultimate stage of civilization and its finest flower.[20]

Feminist historians could hardly be expected to take all this in the missionary position. Simone de Beauvoir explosively attacked the idea as early as 1949:

> The Golden Age of woman is only a myth. . . . Earth, Mother, Goddess—she was no fellow creature in his eyes; it was beyond the human realm that her power was confirmed, and she was therefore outside that realm. Society has always been male; political power has always been in the hands of men.[21]

Recent orthodoxy dismisses any idea of a primeval rule of women, stressing that the myth of women in power is nothing but a useful tool for justifying the domination of men.

But in the nature of things, matriarchy could not be a system of political rule like that developed later by men, since patriarchy evolved subsequently and from previously unknown ideological roots. Nor can we reasonably look for any one universal system in a world whose societies were developing at such a wildly divergent rate that one might have stone, iron, pottery or village organization some 30,000 years ahead of one another. To return to our indisputable mass of evidence both on the Goddess and on the social systems of which she was the prop and pivot, "matriarchy" is better understood as a form of social organization which is woman-centered, substantially egalitarian, and where it is not considered unnatural or anomalous for women to hold power and to engage in all the activities of the society alongside the men. On that definition, in the 4000 years or so between the emergence of the first civilizations and the coming of the One God (as Buddha, Christ or Allah), matriarchies abounded; and even societies clearly under the rule of men displayed strong matriarchal features in the form of freedoms since lost and never regained by the vast number of women in the state of world "advancement" that we know today.

What were these freedoms? The commandment carved on the base of the giant statue of the Egyptian king Rameses II in the fourteenth century BC is quite uncompromising on the first: "See what the Goddess-Wife says, the Royal Mother, the Mistress of the World."[22]

Women held power to which man habitually deferred. As women, they "were" the Goddess on earth, as her representative or descendant, and little distinction was made between her sacred and secular power—the Greek historian Herodotus describing the real-life reign of the very down-to-earth Queen Sammuramat (Semiramis), who ruled Assyria for forty-two years during which she irrigated the whole of Babylon and led military campaigns as far as India, interchangeably calls her "the daughter of the Goddess" and "the Goddess" herself. As this indicates, the power of the Goddess was *inherited*, passed from mother to daughter in a direct line. A man only became king when he married the source of power; he did not hold it in his own right. So in the eighteenth dynasty of the Egyptian monarchy, the Pharaoh Thutmose I had to yield the throne on the death of his wife to his teenage daughter Hatshepsut, even though he had two sons. The custom of royal blood and the right to rule descending in the female line occurs in many cultures: among the Natchez Indians of the Gulf of Mexico, the high chief of Great Sun only held rank as the son of the tribe's leading elder, the White Woman. When she died, her daughter became the White Woman and it was *her* son who next inherited the throne, thus retaining the kingly title and descent always in the female line. This tradition was still evident in Japan at the time of the Wei dynasty (AD 220–264) when the death of the priestess-queen Himeko led to a serious outbreak of civil war that ended only with the coronation of her eldest daughter.

The power of the queen was at its most extraordinary in Egypt, where for thousands of years she was ruler, goddess, wife of the god, the high priestess and a totem object of veneration all in one. Hatshepsut, who like Sammuramat fought at the head of her troops, also laid claim to masculine power and prerogative, and was honored accordingly in a form of worship that lasted for 800 years after her death: "Queen of the north and south, Son of the Sun, golden Horus, giver of years, Goddess of dawns, mistress of the world, lady of both realms, stimulator of all hearts, the powerful woman."[23] But the frequent appearance of the queen as ruler, not simply consort, was by no means confined to the Egyptian dynasties. Queenhood was so common among the Celtic Britons that the captured warriors brought in triumph before Claudius in AD 50 totally ignored the Roman emperor and offered their obeisance instead to his empress, Agrippina. Perhaps the most interesting of all, however, is Deborah, leader of the Israelites around 1200 BC; in *Judges* 4 and 5, she holds evident and total command over the male leaders of the tribe, whose dependency on her is so total that their general, Barak, will not even take to the field of battle without her. Early Jewish history is rich in such powerful and distinguished women:

A Jewish princess? Judith, who saved the Jewish people; she flirted with the attacking general, drank him under the table; then she and her maid (whose name is not in the story) whacked off his head, stuck it in a picnic basket and escaped back to the Jewish camp. They staked his head high over the gate, so that when his soldiers charged the camp they were met by their general's bloody head, looming;

and ran away as fast as their goyishe little feet could run. Then Judith set her maid free and all the women danced in her honor. *That's* a Jewish princess.[24]

Nor was female power and privilege at this time confined to princesses and queens. From all sides there is abundant evidence that "when agriculture replaced hunting . . . and society wore the robes of matriarchy," *all* women "achieved a social and economic importance,"[25] and enjoyed certain basic rights.

In Sparta, the women owned two-thirds of all the land. Arab women owned flocks which their husbands merely pastured for them, and among the Monomini Indians, individual women are recorded as owning 1200 or 1500 birch bark vessels in their own right. Under the astonishingly egalitarian Code of Hammurabi which became law in Babylon about 1700 BC, a woman's dowry was given not to her husband but to her, and together with any land or property she had it remained her own and passed on her death to her children. In Egypt, a woman's financial independence of her husband was such that if he borrowed money from her, she could even charge him interest![26]

A number of Codes akin to that of Hammurabi explicitly contradict the "chattel" status that marriage later meant for women. In Babylon, if a man "degraded" his wife, she could bring an action for legal separation from him on the grounds of cruelty. If divorce occurred, women retained care and control of their children, and the father was obliged to pay for their upbringing. The Greek historian Diodorus records an Egyptian marriage contract in which the husband pledged his bride-to-be:

> I bow before your rights as wife. From this day on, I shall never oppose your claims with a single word. I recognise you before all others as my wife, though I do not have the right to say you must be mine, and only I am your husband and mate. You alone have the right of departure . . . I cannot oppose your wish wherever you desire to go. I give you . . . [here follows an index of the bridegroom's possessions][27]

Another, stronger indication of the warm intimacy and forbearance that an Egyptian wife could expect from her husband is to be found in the "Maxims of Ptah Hotep," at more than 5000 years old possibly the oldest book in the world:

> If you're wise, stay home, love your wife, and don't argue with her.
> Feed her, adorn her, massage her.
> Fulfil all her desires and pay attention to what occupies her mind.
> For this is the only way to persuade her to stay with you.
> If you oppose her, it will be your downfall.[28]

The respect accorded to women within marriage mirrors the autonomy they frequently enjoyed before it. In the early classical period Greek girls led a free, open-air life, and were given athletic and gymnastic training to promote both fitness and beauty. In Crete, chosen young women trained as *toreras* to take part in the ritual bull-leaping, while Ionian women joined in boar-hunts, nets and spears at the ready. Across thousands of Attic vases ("Grecian urns" to Keats), girl jockeys race naked, or dance and swim unclothed through millennia of silence and slow time. The freedom of the young unmarried women was so marked in Sparta that it even caused comment in the other city-states of Greece. Euripides was not the only Athenian to be scandalized:

> The daughters of Sparta are never at home!
> They mingle with the young men in wrestling matches,
> Their clothes cast off, their hips all naked,
> It's shameful!

The strength and athletic ability of these young women was not simply fostered for fun, as the story of the Roman heroine Cloelia shows. Taken hostage by the Etruscan king Lars Porsenna during an attack on Rome in the sixth century BC, she escaped, stole a horse and swam the Tiber to get back safely to Rome. Even though the Romans promptly handed her back, Cloelia's courage won the day; for Lars Porsenna was so impressed by this feat that he freed her and all her fellow hostages as a mark of honor.[29]

The hardening of young women's bodies by sport and the regular practice of nudity had wider implications than these sporadic acts of personal daring. Throughout the ancient world there is scattered but abundant evidence of women under arms, fighting as soldiers in the frontline engagements that conventional wisdom decrees have always been reserved for men. Ruling queens led their troops in the field, not as ceremonial figureheads but as acknowledged and effective war leaders: Tamyris, the Scythian warrior queen and ruler of the Massagetae tribe of what is now Iran, commanded her army to victory over the invading hordes of Cyrus the Great, and had the great king put to death in revenge for the death of her son in battle. Ruling women also commanded military action at sea, as the Egyptian queen Cleopatra did at the battle of Actium, where her uncharacteristic failure of nerve cost her the war, her empire, her lover Antony and her life. Warrior queens were particularly celebrated in Celtic Britain, where the great goddess herself always bore a warlike aspect. The pre-Chris-

tian chronicles contain numerous accounts of female war leaders like
Queen Maedb (Maeve) who commanded her own forces, and who,
making war on Queen Findmor, captured fifty of the enemy queen's
women warriors single-handed at the storming of Dun Sobhairche in
County Antrim.[30]

The fighting women of the Celts were in fact legendary for their
power and ferocity—an awestruck Roman historian, Dio Cassius, describes Boudicca, queen of the Iceni, as she appeared in battle, "wield-
ing a spear, huge of frame and terrifying of aspect."[31] The same
belligerence was remarked in the female foot soldiers; another Roman
chronicler who had seen active service warned his compatriots that a
whole troop of Roman soldiers would not withstand a single Gaul if
he called his wife to his aid, for "swelling her neck, gnashing her
teeth, and brandishing sallow arms of enormous size she delivers blows
and kicks like missiles from a catapult."[32]

Stories of women fighters have always been most persistent around
the Mediterranean and the Near East, and from earliest times written
and oral accounts record the existence of a tribe of women warriors
who have come down to history as the Amazons. The absence of any
"hard" historical data (archaeological remains of a city, or carved
inscriptions detailing famous victories, for instance) means that these
accounts have been treated as pure myth or legend, "nothing more
than the common travellers' tales of distant foreigners who do everything the wrong way about," as the Oxford Classical Dictionary dis-
missively explains. Feminist historians of the twentieth century have
also been uneasy with the Amazon story, finding it an all-too-conve-
nient reinforcement of history's insistence on the inevitability of male
dominance, as the Amazon women were *always* finally defeated and
raped/married by heroes like Theseus. Another problem lies in the
evidently false and fanciful interpretation of the name "Amazon," from
Greek *a* (without) and *mazos* (breast). This is now known to be lin-
guistically spurious as well as anatomically ridiculous—how many
women have a right breast so large that they cannot swing their arm?—
and consequently the whole idea of the tribe of women who amputated
their breasts in order to fight has been discredited.

But wholesale dismissal of the subject is to throw out the baby with
the bathwater. The written accounts, ranging from the gossip of storytellers to the work of otherwise reliable historians, are too numerous
and coherent to be ignored; and anything which could engage the
serious attention and belief of writers as diverse as Pliny, Strabo,
Herodotus, Aeschylus, Diodorus and Plutarch holds a kernel of hard

information that later generations have too readily discarded. The body of myth and legend also receives historical support from the numerous rituals, sacrifices, mock battles and ceremonials of later ages confidently ascribed to Amazon origins by those who practiced them, as commemorations of key episodes of their own past history.[33]

As with the wider question of matriarchy, to which the concept of a self-governing tribe of powerful women so clearly relates, the way forward lies in the synthesis of myth and legend with the incontrovertible events of "real" history. Women fought, as war leaders and in the ranks; women fought in troops, as regular soldiers; and the principal symbol of the Great Goddess, appearing widely throughout the Mediterranean and Asia Minor, was the double-headed battle axe or *labrys*. There are, besides, innumerable authenticated accounts like that of the Greek warrior-poet Telessilla, who in the fifth century BC rallied the women of Argos with war-hymns and chants when their city was besieged. The Argive Amazons took up arms, made a successful sally and after prolonged fighting, drove off the enemy, after which they dedicated a temple of Aphrodite to Telessilla, and she composed a victory hymn to honor the Great Mother of the gods.[34] Combine this with the mass of similar evidence of Amazon activity among women, and it is clear that, as with matriarchy, there may have been no *one* Amazon tribe, but the historical reality of women fighting can no longer be doubted.

The physical autonomy expressed by these women through sport and military activity speaks of a deeper freedom, and one that later ages found most difficult to tolerate or even adequately explain. Customs varied from country to country and tribe to tribe, but it is evident that women at the birth of civilization generally enjoyed a far greater freedom from restraint on their "modesty" or even chastity than at any time afterwards. For many societies there was no shame in female nakedness, for instance, and this did not simply mean the unclothed body of a young girl athlete or gymnast. Adult women in fact practiced regular cult-nakedness, frequently disrobing for high ceremonials and important rituals either of a solemn or a joyful kind. The evidence of Attic vases dating from the ninth and eighth centuries BC shows that women mourners and usually the widow herself walked naked in the funeral cortège of any Athenian citizen.

With this physical freedom went certain key sexual freedoms of the sort one would expect to find in a matriarchal society. Where women rule, women woo; and of twenty erotic love songs from the Egypt of the thirteenth century BC, sixteen are by women. One shamelessly records, "I climbed through the window and found my brother in his bed—my heart was overwhelmed with happiness." Another is even more frank: "O my handsome darling! I am dying to marry you and become the mistress of all your property!"[35] Customs elsewhere in the world were less flowery and more basic. When Julia Augusta, wife of the Roman Emperor Severus, quizzed a captive Scots woman about the sexual freedoms British women were reputed to enjoy, the Scot reproved her with, "We fulfil the demands of nature much better than do you Roman women, for we consort openly with the best man, while you let yourselves be debauched in secret by the vilest."[36] Fulfilling the demands of nature did not apply only to human beings, as Elise Boulding explains:

> The free ways in which Celtic women utilised sex come out in the stories of Queen Maedb, who offered "thigh-friendship" to the owner of a bull for the loan of it [to service her cows]. She also offered thigh-friendship in return for assistance in raids and battles. Apparently all parties, including her husband, considered these deals reasonable.[37]

Equally reasonable, apparently, were the rights and dues that women claimed not in pursuit of their own pleasure but for the honor of the Great Goddess. These were extensive, ranging from ritual self exposure to far darker mysteries whose disclosure brought the risk of death to the betrayer. At the simplest level, the worship of the Goddess seems to have been conducted naked or only half clothed: a cave painting from Cogul near Lerida in Catalonia shows nine women with full pendulous breasts clad only in caps and bell-shaped skirts performing a ritual fertility dance around a small male figure with an unpropitiously drooping penis, while Pliny describes the females of ancient Britain as ritually stripping, then staining themselves brown in preparation for their ceremonials.[38] Sacred, often orgiastic, dancing was a crucial element of Goddess worship, and the use of intoxicants or hallucinogens to heighten the effect was standard practice: the Goddess demanded complete abandon.

The Goddess also demanded in some cultures a form of sexual service that has been deeply misunderstood by later historians, who as a consequence have misrepresented it under a frankly misleading label. Writing in the fifth century BC, Herodotus described the ritual as follows:

> The worst Babylonian custom is that which compels every woman of the land once in her life to sit in the Temple of Love and have intercourse with some stranger.

The men pass by and make their choice, and the women will never refuse, for that would be a sin. After this act she has made herself holy in the sight of the goddess, and goes away to her home.[39]

This is the practice which wherever it occurs throughout the Near or Middle East is always described as "ritual prostitution." Nothing could more comprehensively degrade the true function of the *qadishtu*, the sacred women of the Goddess. For in the act of love these women were revered as the reincarnation of the Goddess herself, celebrating her gift of sex which was so powerful, so holy and precious that eternal thanks were due to her within her temple. To have intercourse with a stranger was the purest expression of the will of the Goddess, and carried no stigma. On the contrary the holy women were always known as "sacred ones," "the undefiled," or as at Urek in Sumeria, *nu-gig*, "the pure or spotless."[40]

This unhistorical projection of anachronistic prejudice (sex is sin, and unmarried sex is prostitution) fails to take account of historical evidence supporting the high status of these women. The Code of Hammurabi, for instance, carefully distinguishes between five grades of temple women and protects their rights to continue in the worship of their mothers. It also makes a clear division between sacred women and secular prostitutes—for it is an interesting assumption embedded in the very phrase "ritual prostitute," that somehow these people did not have the real thing.

They did, of course; and the perennial commercialism of the true "working girl" comes through strongly in one recorded anecdote of the most celebrated courtesan of the Egyptians, Archidice. The fame of her sexual skill was so great that men ruined themselves for her favors. One suitor, rejected because he could not afford her price, went home and dreamed that he had enjoyed her instead. The enraged Archidice took him to court, alleging that, as he had had the pleasure of sex with her, he should pay her normal fee for it. The court admitted the legality of her claim, but after much debate finally adjudicated that as the client had only *dreamed* he had enjoyed her, she should *dream* she had been paid.[41]

Poets, priests, queens, mothers, lovers, athletes, soldiers and litigious courtesans, as the first individual women emerge to take their place in human history, they present an impressive spectacle. No one had yet told them that women were physically weak, emotionally unstable or intellectually ill-equipped; consequently they throng the annals of Minoan Crete, for example, as merchants, traders, sailors, farmers, charioteers, hunters and ministers of the Goddess, in apparent ignorance of the female inability to perform these roles that more advanced societies had yet to discover. At every level women made their mark, from the brilliant Aspasia, the courtesan-scholar-politician who partnered Pericles in the Athens of the fifth century BC, to her contemporary Artemisia, the first-known woman sea-captain, whose command of her fleet at the battle of Marathon was so devastating that the Athenians put a huge bounty on her head: sadly, she survived the Persian wars to die of love, throwing herself off a cliff in a passion of grief when rejected by a younger man.

These were real women, then, vividly alive even at the moment of death: women who knew their strengths. These strengths were recognized in the range of social customs and legal rights known to be women's due from a mass of historical evidence: physical and sexual freedom, access to power, education, full citizenship, the right to own money and property, the right to divorce, custody of children and financial maintenance.

The value placed on women in the legal codes and customs of the day traced back to their special female status; and this derived directly from their link with, and incarnation of, the Great Goddess. Though localized, since every country, tribe, town or even village had its own version of "Our Lady," she was universal. To her worshippers, after so many thousand years, she seemed eternal:

> I am Isis, mistress of every land. I laid down laws for all, and ordained things no one may change. . . . I am she who is called divine among women—I divided the earth from heaven, made manifest the paths of the stars, prescribed the course of the sun and the moon. . . . I brought together men and women. . . . *What I have made law can be dissolved by no man.*[42]

Was this the challenge man was driven to take up? For where was man in the primal drama of the worship of the Great Mother? He was the expendable consort, the sacrificial king, the disposable drone. Woman was everything; he was nothing. It was too much. Man had to have some meaning in the vast and expanding universe of human consciousness. But as the struggle for understanding moved into its next phase, the only meaning seemed to lie through the wholesale reversal of the existing formula of belief. Male pride rose to take up the challenge of female power; and launching the sex war that was to divide sex and societies for millennia to come, man sought to assert his manhood through the death and destruction of all that had made woman the Great Mother, Goddess, warrior, lover and queen.

3

THE RISE OF THE PHALLUS

Holy Shiva, Divine Linganaut,
Heavenly Root, Celestial Penis,
Phallus Lord, thy radiant *lingam*
is so large that neither Brahma
nor Vishnu can reckon its extent.

HINDU PRAYER

He let fly an arrow, it pierced her belly,
Her inner parts he clove, he split her heart,
He destroyed her life,
He felled her body and stood triumphant upon it.

King Marduk overthrows the Great Mother in the
Babylonian *Epic of Creation, c.* 2000 BC

Men look to destroy every quality in a woman that
will give her the powers of a male, for she is in
their eyes already armed with the power that brought
them forth.

NORMAN MAILER

"In the beginning," writes Marilyn French, "was the Mother." That
mother, as her "children" saw her, is still with us today—her outsize
breasts, bulging belly and buttocks, flaring vulva and tree-trunk thighs
survive in the familiar figurines found in their tens of thousands in
Europe alone. Against this massive, elemental force the human male
cut a poor figure indeed. Every myth, every song in praise of the Great
Goddess stressed by contrast the littleness of man, often in caustically
satiric terms—the illustrated Papyrus of Tameniu of the twenty-first
Egyptian dynasty (1102–952 BC) shows her naked, over-arching the
whole world, flaunting her star-spangled breasts, belly and pubic zone,
while the boy-god Geb, flat on the ground, reaches up to her in vain
with a phallus that although exaggerated, plainly is not man enough
for the occasion. Nor was this the limit of the sexual humiliations the
Great Mother would exact. Among the Winnepagos of Canada, a brave
who dreamed of the Goddess, even once, knew himself singled out

for a terrible fate, that of becoming *cinaedi*, a homosexual compelled to wear women's garb and to submit in every way to the sexual demands of other males. There are countless similar examples from widely different cultures of the Goddess's dreaded and inexorable power: as Robert Graves explains, "under the Great Mother, woman was the dominant sex and man her frightened victim."[1]

For when all meaning, all magic, all life lay with woman, man had no function, no significance at all. "The baby, the blood, the yelling, the dancing, all that concerns the women," declared an Australian Aboriginal: "men have nothing to do but copulate." Into this vacuum, as consciousness deepened, came envy, the "uterus-envy of female-protest within men awed by the apparently exclusive female power of creation of new life." Resentful of the women's monopoly of all nature's rhythms, men were driven to invent their own. In origin, however, these male-centered rituals consisted of no more than attempts to mimic the biological action of women's bodies, a debt openly acknowledged by many still-surviving Stone Age cultures: "in the beginning we had nothing . . . *we took these things from the women.*"[2]

Typical of numerous such imitations worldwide was the hideous Aztec rite of dressing a sacrificing priest in the skin of his human sacrifice. He would then "burst from the bleeding human skin as the germinating shoot from the husk of the grain," becoming both the new life and the one who gives birth by the power of his magic.[3] More horrific still was the fate that befell every boy initiate in the Aranda tribe of Australia:

> . . . the ritual surgeon seizes the boy's penis, inserts a long thin bone deep into the urethra, and slashes at the penis again and again with a small piece of flint used as a scalpel. He cuts through the layers of flesh until he reaches the bone, and the penis splits open like a boiled frankfurter.[4]

This hideous ceremony, christened "sub-incision" by the white settlers, tormented their civilized minds—what possible purpose could it serve? Had they understood Aranda, all would have been clear. The Aboriginal word for "split penis" derives from the term for the vagina, and the title "possessor of a vulva" is the honorific bestowed on all boys who undergo the ordeal. Later rituals also included the regular re-opening of the wound to demonstrate that the initiate could now "menstruate."[5]

It was, in Margaret Mead's words, "as if men can only become men by taking over the functions that women perform naturally."[6] For Jung, the secret of all male initiation rituals lay in "going through the mother again," embracing the fear, the pain and the blood in order to be born anew not as a child but as a man and a hero. "Through the mother," though, does not imply any sympathetic identification with the female. On the contrary, the key element is the takeover of birth as a male mystery, the first "weapon in the men's struggle to shake off the feminine domination created by the matriarchy."[7] This struggle of men not merely to imitate and outdo, but to usurp women's power of creating new life took place on every level; Zeus giving birth to Athene from his head is a classic reversal of the primal creation myth that finds a parallel in many other mythologies. It was nothing less than a revolution: of the weak against the strong, of the oppressed against their oppression, of value structures and habits of thought.

And human thought was itself progressing along lines that eased the way towards the domination of males. As human beings crossed the mental threshold between interpreting events in symbolic and magical terms, and the dawning realization of cause and effect, man's part in the making of babies became clear. Now women's rhythms were seen to be human, not divine, and the knowledge that man determined pregnancy completed the revolution that his resentment and resistance had already set in train. Historian Jean Markdale sums it up:

> When man began to assert that he was essential to fertilization, the old mental attitudes suddenly collapsed. This was a very important revolution in man's history, and it is astonishing that it is not rated equally with the wheel, agriculture, and the use of metals. . . . As the male had been cheated for centuries . . . equality was not enough. *He now understood the full implications of his power, and was going to dominate . . .*[8]

And what better weapon of dominance was there at hand but the phallus? As man began to carve out some meaning for himself to set against woman's eternal, innate potency, what would serve his turn better than man's best friend, his penis? In its fragile human form, prey to unbidden arousal, stubborn refusal and unpredictable deflation, it could not challenge women's unfailing power of birth. But elevated above reality into symbol, transformed into "phallus" and enshrined in materials known to be proof against detumescence like metal and stone, it would do very well.

At a stroke, then, the power was there at man's bidding. Now he was transformed from an unregarded afterthought of creation whose manhood held no magic for any except himself, to the whole secret and origin of the Great Mother's life force. The power was not hers, but his. His was the sacred organ of generation; and the phallus, not the uterus, was the source of all that lived. Power to the phallus became the imperative (to, from, by, in and of the phallus); and so a new religion was born.

This is not to suggest that the penis and its symbolic equivalent the phallus were unknown to these early societies before the discovery of biological paternity began to sweep the world around the beginnings of the Iron Age, some 3500 years ago. Phallic emblems made their appearance in the earliest recorded living sites, and from the time of the "Neolithic Revolution" (around 9000–8000 BC in the Near East), they occur in impressive size and profusion. At Grimes Grave in Norfolk, England, for example, an altar discovered in the bowels of the abandoned Neolithic flint mine workings bore a cup, seven deer antlers, and a mighty phallus carved in chalk, all set out as offerings to the figure of the Great Goddess reared up before it. For whatever their proportions (and some of the lovingly wrought models in clay or stone display a truly impressive capacity for wishful thinking), these emblems were only fashioned as part of the worship of the Goddess, and were not sacred in themselves.

Paradoxically then, it was the Great Goddess herself who first established the cult of the phallus. In the myth of Isis, whose worship spread from the Near East throughout Asia and into Europe, the Goddess ordered a wooden *lingam* of Osiris to be set up in her temple at Thebes. Subsequently the worship of the Goddess involved making offerings to her of phallic emblems or tokens; the women of Egypt carried images of Osiris in their sacred processions, each one equipped with a movable phallus "of disproportionate magnitude," according to one disgruntled observer, while a similar model in the Goddess-worship of Greek women had a phallus whose movements the celebrants could control with strings. In this state of ecstatic animation, the god was conveyed to the temple, where the most respected matrons of the town waited to crown the phallus with garlands and kisses in honor of the Great Goddess, as a sign that she accepted the tribute of phallic service.[9]

But once promoted from minor bit player to leading man in the primal drama, the penis proved to be hungry for the smell of the greasepaint, the roar of the crowd. In Greece, phalluses sprang up everywhere, like dragon's teeth; guardian Herms (phallus-pillars) flourished their potency on every street corner, while by the third century BC, Delos boasted an avenue of mammoth penises, supported on bulging testicles, shooting skyward like heavy cannon. Across the

Adriatic in Italy, the god Phalles was familiar to every family as one of its regular household deities, and many cities like Pompeii were entirely given over to the worship of the phallus-god, Priapus—a fact that disapproving later sages were quick to connect with its destruction by Vesuvius in AD 79. In Dorset, England, the ancient Britons poured the pride of their creation into the huge hill-figure of the Cerne Abbas Giant—40 feet tall, he glares out to history brandishing a chest-high erection and a massive phallic club to ram home the message of his mightiest member.

No country in the world, however, embraced phallus worship with more enthusiasm than India. There, as its mythologizers insisted, was to be found "the biggest penis in the world," the "celestial rod" of the god Shiva, which grew until it shafted through all the lower worlds and towered up to dwarf the heavens. This so overawed two other principal gods of the Hindu pantheon, Brahma and Vishnu, that they fell down and worshipped it, and ordered all men and women to do likewise. How well this commandment was obeyed for many thousands of years may be gauged from bewildered Western accounts of a long-standing custom. Traders, missionaries and colonial invaders recorded that every day a priest of Shiva would emerge naked from the temple and proceed through the streets, ringing a little bell which was the signal for all the women to come out and kiss the holy genitals of the representative of the god.[10] To the average Victorian Englishman, it must have seemed like phallus in wonderland.

With its rise to sacred status, the phallus increased in significance, as well as in size and sanctity. From this epoch onwards, male superiority becomes vested in and expressed through this one organ, as an ever-present reminder of masculine power. By extension, and the extension was limitless, the phallus then becomes the source not only of power, but of all cultural order and meaning. For men, clasping and invoking the penis validated all greetings and promises; among the Romans the *testes* underwrote every *testament*, while an Arab would declare "O Father of Virile Organs, bear witness to my oath," and as a mark of respect suffer any sheikh or patriarch to examine his genitals on meeting.[11]

Over women the power of the sacred phallus began to make itself felt in a number of ways. In the temples of Shiva, a slave girl specially chosen for her "lotus-beauty" was consecrated to "the divine penis" and tattoed on her breasts and shaven groin with the emblem of the god. Worldwide, both historical records and archaeological evidence confirm women's practices of imprecating, touching, kissing or even

mounting sacred phalluses of wood or stone as a cure for infertility
from the "phallus lord," who may well have been also the original
recipient of their virginity. In the remote villages of southern France,
to the deep embarrassment of the Catholic church, the Provençal
"Saint" Foutin was worshipped in all the pride of his priapic magnificence as late as the seventeenth century. This was under constant
threat from the women's habit of scraping shavings from the wooden
end to boil into a potion to promote conception; but it was always
renewed by the priests, who sustained the saint's reputation as "the
inexhaustible penis" by surreptitious mallet-taps to the other end behind the altar.[12] Perhaps most sinister of all was the Celtic ritual still
in use in Wales as late as the reign of Hywel Dda (Howel the Good),
AD 909–950. There, if a woman wanted to prosecute a man for rape,
she had to swear to the offense with one hand on a relic of the saints,
while with the other she grasped "the peccant member" of her
offender[13]—to prick his conscience, perhaps? This reminder that the
male organ can be a weapon of war as well as an instrument of love
is nowhere more clearly illustrated than in the monumental phallus at
Karnak erected by King Meneptha of Egypt in 1300 BC; its inscription
records that the king cut off all the penises of his defeated enemies
after a battle and brought home a total of 13,240.

As the date of this episode shows, the rise of the phallus did not
mean the immediate overthrow of the Great Goddess. On the contrary
it is fascinating to observe how the myths, stories and rituals of her
worship were adapted over a considerable period of time to accom-
modate the accelerating rhythms of the male principal in its thrust
towards full centrality. The devolution of power from Goddess to God,
from Queen to King, from Mother to Father, took place in stages,
which may be as plainly detected in world mythology as strata in rock.
In the first phase, the Great Mother alone *is* or *creates* the world; she
has casual lovers and many children, but she is primal and supreme.
In the second, she is described or illustrated as having a consort, who
may be her son, little brother or primeval toy-boy; originally very
much her junior, he grows in power to become her spouse. At the
third stage, the God-King-Spouse rules equally with the Goddess, and
the stage is set for her dethronement; finally the Man-God kings it
alone, with Goddess, mother and woman, defeated and dispossessed,
trapped in a downward spiral which humankind has only recently
begun to arrest, let alone reverse.[14]

Mythologies are never static, and even to divide this development
into phases is to suggest an organizational logic that historical processes

rarely possess. Different developments occurred over different times in different places, and even when men had made themselves into kings and held gods and goddesses under their sway, they found it still advisable to honor the old customs and pay the Great Mother her due. "The Goddess Ishtar loved me—thus I became king," declared Sargon of Assyria in the eighth century BC.[15]

Other records of religious and political rituals in these early kingdoms abundantly testify to the fact that the king's power, however great, was not absolute; a king of Celtic Ireland had to perform the *banfheis rígí*, or "marriage-mating," with "the Great Queen," the spirit of Ireland, before he could be accepted as king by the people. For the kings of Babylon, this duty was literal, not symbolic. Their power had to be renewed every year, and was only confirmed when the royal embodiment of the sacred phallus was seen to consummate his "divine marriage" with the high priestess of the Great Mother in a public ceremony on a stage before all the populace.[16]

The Great Goddess still had some power, then, and the evidence suggests that the ruling men neglected the due observances at their peril. On the wider horizon, however, an interlocking series of profound social changes combined to shake these early civilizations to their foundations, and the force of events conspired with the new aggressive phallic impetus to drive out the last remaining elements of the power of the Goddess and the accompanying "mother-right." Broadly, these changes arose from the population growth that resulted from the first successful social organization. They derived from the most basic of imperatives, the need for food. Nigel Calder explains the nature of the development that helped to push women from the center of life to its margins:

> From Southern Egypt 18,000 years ago comes the earliest evidence for cultivation of barley and wheat in riverside gardens . . . feminine laughter no doubt disturbed the water-birds when the women came with a bag of seed to invent crops. Perhaps it was a waste of good food and nothing to tell the men about—yet it took only moments to poke the seeds into the ready-made cracks in the mud. . . . The women knew little of plant genetics, but the grain grew and ripened before the sun parched the ground entirely, and when they came back with stone sickles they must have felt a certain goddess-like pride.[17]

This "goddess-like" control of nature by women continued, Calder judges, for 10,000 to 15,000 years. But from about 8000 years ago, an upsurge in population enforced changes in the way that food was produced. By degrees *agriculture*, heavier and more intensive, replaced

women's *horticulture*. Where previously women had worked with nature in a kind of sympathetic magic as her natural ally, now men had
to tame and dominate nature to make it deliver what they determined.
The new methods involved in agriculture found an equally damaging
symbolic echo in the male/female roles and relationships, as a Hindu
text, *The Institutes of Mana* from around AD 100, makes plain: "The
woman is considered in law as the field and the man as the grain."
Where the Goddess had been the only source of life, now woman had
neither seed nor egg; she was the passive field, only fertile if ploughed,
while man, drunk with the power of his newfound phallocentricity,
was plough, seed, grain-chute and ovipositor all in one.

As planned husbandry and domestication of land replaced casual
cultivation, the more the role of the male strengthened and centralized.
Paradoxically, this was also true of those groups who failed to produce
enough from the land to live on. For those tribes, any shortage or
failure of crops brought enforced migration, which also necessarily
involved warfare, as groups already established on fertile territory
banded together to resist the invaders.[18] Both in the group's nomadic
wanderings and in any fighting which resulted, men had the advantage,
as they had superior muscle power and mobility, over women encumbered with children. All women's earlier hard-won skills of cultivation
became useless when the tribe was on the move. Meanwhile, men
driven by the darker side of phallicism seized the upper hand through
aggression and military organization. As these clashes of force inevitably produced dominant and submissive groups, winners and losers,
determining rank, slavery and subjection, it was not possible for women
to escape from this framework. Caught between the violence of plough-
share *and* sword, women had to lose.

There could be only one outcome. However, wherever, and whenever it came in the millennia immediately before the birth of Christ,
all the mythologies speak of the overthrow of the Great Mother Goddess. In the simplest version of the story, like that of the Semitic
Babylonians, the god-king Marduk wages war on Ti'amat, the Mother
of All Things, and hacks her to pieces. Only after her death can he
form the world, from the pieces of her body, as it rightfully should
be. This motif is astonishingly consistent through a number of widely
separated cultures, as witness this Tiwi creation myth from central
Africa:

Puvi made the country the first time. The sea was all fresh water. She made the
land, sea and islands. . . . Puriti said, "Don't kill our mother." But Iriti went ahead

and killed her. He struck her on the head. Her urine made the sea salty and her spirit went into the sky . . .[19]

In other versions of the story, the Great Goddess is defeated, but lives. Celtic folk myth relates how the Three Wise Ones (the Goddess in her triad form), Emu, Banbha and Fódla, meet the sons of Mil the war god in battle, but after many violent clashes are subdued and humbled to the power of the invader. *Whatever form it takes, the fundamental power-shift from female to male is reflected in all mythologies.* Among the Greeks, Apollo took over the Goddess's most sacred oracle at Delphi; the Kikuyu of Africa still relate how their ancestors overthrew their women by ganging up in a scheme to rape all their women on the same day, so that nine months later they could overmaster the pregnant women with impunity; while for the Axtecs, Xochiquetzel the Earth Mother gave birth to a son Huitzilopochtli, who killed her daughter the Moon Goddess and took her place as the ruler of heaven, killing and scattering all her other children in his rage for domination.

This pattern of defeat and partial survival finds a frequent expression in the motif employed here, the victory of the sun god over the moon, who is always female. In the Japanese version, the goddess Ama-terasu, the supreme deity of the Shinto pantheon, is attacked by the god Susa-nu-wo, who destroys her rice fields and pollutes her sacred places with feces and dead flesh. Although she fights him, he "steals her light," and she only regains half her previous power, and so may only shine by night.[20] Just as in the historical shift from horticulture to agriculture, this apparently natural development masked some profound and irreversible changes in the relations between men and women, even in the ways of thought:

> The divinity of the sun, lord of time and space, was essentially masculine—the phallic sunbeams striking down on Mother Earth—a maleness whose rays impregnate the earth and cause the seeds to germinate. From Spain to China, the prehistoric sun stood for maleness, individual self-consciousness, intellect and the glaring light of knowledge, as against the moon ruler of the tide, the womb, the waters of the ocean, darkness and the dream-like unconscious . . . *solarization*, the victory of the male sun god over the female moon goddess . . . implied the collapse of the female-oriented *cyclical* fertility cults and the rise to supremacy of the male concept of *linear* history, consisting of unrepeatable events . . .[21]

Nor was the overthrow of the female simply a mythological theme. Women of power in real life came under attack, as men sought to wrest from them their authority in a number of different ways. Where royalty passed through the female line, a bold adventurer could commandeer it by enforcing marriage on the queen, or seizing possession by rape—Tamyris the Scythian ruler fought off a "proposal" of this sort from Cyrus the Great of Persia in the sixth century BC. Others were not so lucky. When Berenice II of Egypt refused to marry her young nephew Ptolemy Alexander in 80 BC, he had her murdered. The violence of this outrage is demonstrated by the fact that the loyal Alexandrians then rose up and killed him.[22] But in general, kings were more successful in retaining the powers they usurped. From this period of aggressive male encroachment on female prerogative comes the introduction of royal incest, when the king who was unwilling to vacate the throne on the death of his wife, would marry the rightful heir, her daughter. Alternatively, he would marry one of his sons to the new queen; this had the double benefit of keeping the monarchy under male control, and by degrees weaving sons into the fabric of inheritance until their right superseded that of any daughter.

Under these circumstances, ruling women rapidly became pawns in male power-games, their importance only acknowledged by the lengths men went to in possessing or controlling them. Galla Placida, daughter of the Roman Emperor Theodosius the Great, was captured by the Visigoth Alaric at the sack of Rome, and after his death taken over by his brother. On the murder of the brother, she was handed back to the Romans, and forcibly married to their victorious general Constantius, who designated her Augusta, and as "Augustus" ruled as her co-emperor. When Constantius died, her brother exiled her to Constantinople and took the throne, and only when her son became emperor in AD 425 did she achieve any peace or stability.

There are countless historical examples from all countries of royal women, through whom inheritance or claim to the throne would pass, being exploited as pawns in the power game, and then disposed of. A classic story is that of Almasuntha, queen of the Ostrogoths: made regent on behalf of her son when her father King Theodoric died in AD 526, Almasuntha was forcibly married by the late king's nephew when her son died, and then, as soon as the usurper had secured his power, put to death.

Women of royal blood were not alone in experiencing men's rage to dominate, to downgrade and destroy. With written records come the first in a series of orchestrated attacks on women's nature, their rights in their children, even their right to full human existence. The sun-moon dualism now becomes extended into a cosmic system of polar opposition; whatever man is, woman is not, and with this imposition of the principle of sexual contrast comes the gradual definition of man as commanding all the human skills and abilities, woman as the half-formed, half-baked opposite. By the fourth century BC, Aristotle's summary of the sexual differences in human nature said no more than any man or woman of his age would have accepted as fact:

> Man is active, full of movement, creative in politics, business and culture. The male shapes and moulds society and the world. Woman, on the other hand, is passive. She stays at home, as is her nature. She is matter waiting to be formed by the active male principle. Of course the active elements are always higher on any scale, and more divine. Man consequently plays a major part in reproduction; the woman is merely the passive incubator of his seed . . . the male semen cooks and shapes the menstrual blood into a new human being . . .[23]

Once articulated, the denigrations of women flood forth unchecked as war-leaders, politicians and historians like Xenophon, Cato and Plutarch, worry away at the "woman problem":

> The gods created woman for the indoors functions, the man for all others. The gods put woman inside because she has less tolerance for cold, heat and war. For woman it is honest to remain indoors and dishonest to gad about. For the man, it is shameful to remain shut up at home and not occupy himself with affairs outside.[24]

> You must keep her on a tight rein. . . . Women want total freedom, or rather total licence. If you allow them to achieve complete equality with men, do you think they will be any easier to live with? Not at all. Once they have achieved equality, they will be your masters . . .[25]

> I certainly do not give the name "love" to the feeling one has for women and girls, any more than we would say flies are in love with milk, bees with honey, or breeders with the calves and fowl they fatten in the dark . . .[26]

As Plutarch here reminds us, for the Greeks there was "only one genuine love, that which boys inspire." The homosexuality of ancient Greece in fact institutionalized the supremacy of the phallus, denying women any social or emotional role other than childbearing. But to the emerging male, newly born into consciousness and thinking with his phallus, it seemed inescapable that such a creature should have as little part as possible in his children; and in the famous "Judgement of Apollo" at the climax of Aeschylus' *Eumenides*, the sun god obligingly pronounced:

> The mother is not the parent of that which is called her child: but only nurse of the newly planted seed that grows. *The parent is he who mounts.*

In this simple, brutal *diktat* phallic thought reversed the primeval creation beliefs of thousands of years. Woman was no longer the vessel of nature, creating man. Now man created woman as a vessel for himself. As the sun overthrew the moon, the king beat down the queen, so the phallus usurped the uterus as the source and symbol of life and power.

Under the new dispensation women's rights went the way of their rites, and in cities and states from Peking to Peru women dwindled into little more than serfdom. They became property, and found the truth of Proudhon's statement that property is theft. The new social and mental systems robbed them of freedom, autonomy, control, even the most basic right of control over their own bodies. For now they belonged to men—or rather, to one man. At some unidentified but pivotal point of history, women became subjected to the tyranny of sexual monopoly—for once it was realized that one man only was necessary for impregnation, it was a short step to the idea of *only one man*.

Yet the exclusive possession of a woman and the monopoly of her sexual service could always be waived when a greater need arose. In Eskimo tribes, for instance, wife-lending is endemic. For the Eskimo husband, this is "a wise investment for the future, because the lender knows he will eventually be a borrower," when he needs a woman who "makes the igloo habitable, lays out dry stockings for him . . . and is ready to cook the game he brings back." Nor was this all—the extent of the obligations of the borrowed wife can be judged from the special term by which Eskimo children refer to any man who does business with their father: "he-who-fucks-my-mother."[27]

As their property, women of these early societies were at the disposal of men; and when women were no longer the struggling tribe's prime resource, nor the sacred source of life and hope for the future, nothing inhibited men's use of force against them in the struggle for control. Among the ancient Chinese, the Greek writer Posidippus noted in the second century AD, "even a poor man will bring up a son, but even a rich man will expose a daughter."[28] On the other side of the world, a chieftain of Tierra del Fuego told Darwin during the voyage of *The Beagle* that to survive in a famine they would kill and eat their old women, but never their dogs.[29] From written records, epics and chronicles, and from anthropological and archaeological evidence, come countless examples of sexual hostility in action, frequently carried to extremes: women are traded, enslaved, ravished, sold in whoredom, slaughtered on the death of their lord or husband, and in every way abused at will.

One poignant story from an Anglo-Saxon settlement of pagan England puts some flesh on the bones of this stark generalization. Two female skeletons of the pre-Christian period were discovered lying together in one pit grave. The older woman, in her late twenties, had been buried naked and alive; the position of the skeleton after death showed that she had tried to raise herself as the earth was thrown on to her. The younger of the two, a girl about sixteen years old, had previously sustained injuries "typically the result of a brutal rape, which was strongly resisted by the victim," including a cavity in the bone behind her left knee where she had been prodded with a dagger to make her draw her legs up for the rapist. She had survived for about six months after the attack, and the fact that she was buried naked, bound hand and foot and possibly alive like her sister inhabitant of the same grave suggests that her death was the result of her unchastity coming to light, most probably through pregnancy, as the archaeologists conclude:

> We can only guess what crime and punishment enmeshed the older woman. . . . But for the young girl, naked, bound, lacerated and perhaps still alive, with the howl of human jackals in her ears, her passport to a merciful oblivion is likely to have been the slime and mire of this chalky trench.[30]

No longer sacred, women became expendable. One Aztec ceremony of death was indeed a direct mockery of women's former power; every December a woman dressed up as Ilamtecuhtli, the Old Goddess of the earth and corn, was decapitated and her head presented to a priest wearing her costume and mask, who then led a ritual dance of celebration followed by other priests similarly attired. This was only one of a number of Aztec rituals of this kind. Every June a woman representing Xiulonen, Goddess of the young maize, was similarly sacrificed, while in August a woman representing Tetoinnan, Mother of the Gods, was decapitated and flayed, her skin being worn by the priest who played the role of the Goddess in the ensuing ceremony. The "strike-the-mother-dead" motif is even clearer in one detail of this grisly procedure—one thigh of the woman victim was flayed separately, and the skin made into a mask worn by the priest who impersonated the *son* of the dead "mother."[31] But similar customs obtained worldwide—in pre-feudal China a young woman was annually selected to be "the Bride of the Yellow Count," and after a year of fattening and beautifying, was cast adrift to drown in the Yangtse Kiang (Yellow River).[32] From ritual sacrifice to the enforced suttee of unwanted child-brides, the destruction of women spread like a plague virus through

India, China, Europe and the Middle East to the remotest human settlements—anywhere in fact where the phallus held sway.

As societies evolved, male control through brute force was gradually supplemented by the rule of law. In Rome, the paterfamilias held undisputed power of life and death over all members of his family, of which he was the only full person in the eyes of the law. In Greece, when Solon of Athens became lawgiver in 594 BC, one of his first measures was to prohibit women leaving their houses at night, and the effect of this was to confine them more and more to their homes by day. In ancient Egypt, women became not simply the property but legally part of their fathers or husbands, condemned to suffer whatever their male kindred brought down on their heads. As the horrified Greek historian Diodorus recorded in his *World History* (60–30 BC), innocent women even swelled the ranks of the pitiful slaves whose forced labor built the pyramids:

> . . . bound in fetters, they work continually without being allowed any rest by night or day. They have not a rag to cover their nakedness, and neither the weakness of age nor women's infirmities are any plea to excuse them, but they are driven by blows until they drop dead.[33]

Not all women, however, lived as victims and died as slaves; it would be historically unjust as well as inaccurate to present the whole of the female sex as passive and defeated in the face of their oppressions. Even as Aristotle was earnestly discoursing to his students on the innate inferiority of women, a woman called Agnodice in the fourth century BC succeeded in penetrating the all-male world of learning. After attending medical classes she practiced gynecology disguised as a man, with such success that other doctors, jealous of her fame, accused her of seducing her patients. In court she was forced to reveal her sex in order to save her life, at which new charges were brought against her of practicing a profession restricted by law to men alone. Eventually acquitted of this, too, Agnodice lived to become the world's first known woman gynecologist.[34]

As this suggests, even under the most adverse circumstances, women have never been wholly subordinate. As a sex, the female of the species has taken a lot of treading down, and the greater the efforts of the emerging phallocrat, the more resourceful and sustained was the resistance he produced. It did not take much female ingenuity, for example, to subvert the systems that men had themselves set up: the worldwide system of menstrual taboo, for instance, by which menstruating women were excluded from society so that they should not infect men, pollute food, or, as Aristotle believed, tarnish mirrors with their breath, in fact provided ample and perfect opportunity for women to develop alternative networks of power, all the more effective for being invisible, unseen. What went on in the menstrual huts or women's quarters when the women foregathered to bring food, news or messages to a menstruating sister would be beneath the ken of the males; but it would make itself felt in their lives nevertheless.

Not infrequently women's resistance to masculine control was expressed directly, even violently, as the Roman senators found to their cost in 215 BC, when to curb inflation they passed a law forbidding women to own more than half an ounce of gold, wear multi-colored dresses or ride in a two-horse carriage. As the word spread, crowds of rioting women filled the Capitol and raged through every street of the city, and neither the rebukes of the magistrates or the threats of their husbands could make them return quietly to their homes. Despite the fierce opposition of the notorious anti-feminist Cato, the law was repealed in what must have been one of the earliest victories for sisterhood and solidarity.

For in the game of domination and subordination, women have not always been the losers: the annals of nineteenth-century explorers were rich in accounts of primitive African tribes where the women had fought off the challenge of the phallus and continued to rule the men. Most of these have now vanished, like the Balonda tribe of whom Livingstone noted that the husband was so subjected to his wife that he dared do nothing without her approval. Yet even today records continue to document tribes like that of the cannibal Munduguma of the Yuat River of the South Seas, whose women are as ferocious as their head-hunting men, and who particularly detest having children. This age-old resistance to the traditional wifely role is echoed in a Manus proverb of the same region: "Copulation is so revolting that the only husband you can bear is the one whose advances you can hardly feel."[35]

As this suggests, women did not fall easily into the subservient supporting role for which the lords of every known phallocracy have insisted they are "naturally" fitted. Many and varied in fact have been the ways that women have found to subvert and convert the power of men, asserting their own autonomy and control as they did so. For the new political systems of male domination were not monolithic nor uniform; there were plenty of cracks through which an enterprising female might slip. In addition, the phallus supreme might count himself king of infinite space, but in real life, willy-nilly, men had to marry and father females. Taken together these factors provided a number of bases from which women could operate in much the same way as men.

The classic route to power derived from access to the men who wielded it, in a direct reversal of the previous rule of the matriarchies. One of the clearest indications of its scope comes from the impressive careers of "the Julias," a powerful female dynasty of two sisters and two daughters who ruled in Rome during the third century AD. The elder sister, Julia Domna, first struck into Roman power politics when she married the Emperor Severus. After her death in 217, her younger sister Julia Maesa took over, marrying her two daughters, also Julias, with such skill that they became the mothers of the next two emperors, through whom the three women ruled with great effect until 235. Another mistress of this game was the Byzantine Empress Pulcheria (AD 399–453). Made regent for her weak-minded brother when she was only fifteen, Pulcheria later fought off a challenge to her supremacy from her brother's wife, and after his death ruled in her own right, supported by her husband, the tough General Marcian: husband in name only, Marcian was never allowed to break his wife's vow of chastity which after her death enabled her to be canonized as a saint.

As Pulcheria's story shows, women learned very early on how to operate the machinery of power, how to maneuver successfully within frameworks which may have constricted their actions but never prevented them from achieving their deeper goals. So the magnificent Theodora, one-time bear-keeper, circus artiste and courtesan who fulfilled every Cinderella fantasy when she married the Prince Justinian, heir to the Byzantine Empire in AD 525, proposed her measures to the Councils of State, "always apologizing for taking the liberty to talk, being a woman."[36] Yet from behind this façade Theodora pushed through legislation which gave women rights of property, inheritance and divorce, while at her own expense she bought the freedom of girls who had been sold into prostitution, and banished pimps and brothel-keepers from the land.

Unlike Theodora, who used her borrowed power with magisterial altruism, other women displayed an appetite for *realpolitik* in its cruellest forms. The Roman empresses Drusilla Livia (c. 55 BC–AD 29) and Valeria Messalina (AD 22–48) were among many who engaged in endless violent intrigues, including the free use of poison on any obstacles to their designs. Poison was also one of the weapons of the legendary beauty Zenobia. This Scythian warrior queen routed the Roman army, went on to capture Egypt and Asia Minor, and, when finally defeated by the Romans, escaped death by seducing a Roman senator. She later married him, and lived on into a gracious retirement until her death in AD 274.

Unquestionably though, the female Bluebeard of dynastic power games must be Fredegund, the Frankish queen who died in AD 597. Beginning as a servant at the royal court, she became the mistress of the king, whom she induced to repudiate one wife and murder another. When the sister of the dead queen, Brunhild, became her mortal enemy as a result, Fredegund engineered the death of Brunhild's husband and plunged the two kingdoms into forty years of war. Fredegund's later victims included all her stepchildren, her husband the king, and finally her old enemy Queen Brunhild, whom she subjected to public humiliation and atrocious torture in the face of the army for three days before Brunhild's death put an end to her sport: after which she died at last peacefully in her own bed.

The work of many gifted women known to history by name is a salutary reminder that, as the majority of the human race, women have always commanded over half of the sum total of human intelligence and creativity. From the poet Sappho, who in the sixth century BC was the first to use the lyric to write subjectively and explore the range of female experience, to the Chinese polymath Pan Chao (Ban Zhao), who flourished around AD 100 as historian, poet, astronomer, mathematician and educationalist, the range is startling. In every field, women too numerous to list were involved in developing knowledge, and contributing to the welfare of their societies as they did so: the Roman Fabiola established a hospital where she worked both as nurse and doctor, becoming the first known woman surgeon before she died in AD 399.[37] In various fields, too, women emerged not simply as respected authorities, but as the founding mothers of later tradition: Cleopatra, "the alchemist of Alexandria," an early chemist and scholar, was the author of a classic text *Chrysopeia* (Gold-making), which was still in use in Europe in the Middle Ages, while the Chinese artist Wei Fu-Jen, working like Cleopatra in the third century AD, is still honored today as China's greatest calligrapher and founder of the whole school of the art of writing.

Not all women everywhere were destined to make their mark on history. This does not mean, however, that they were inevitably lost in the great silence of the past. Folk stories from all cultures preserve accounts of the heroines of ordinary life who tamed brutal or stupid husbands, outwitted rapacious lords, schemed for their children and lived to rejoice in their children's children. Occasionally these tales have a peculiarly personal ring, like the Chinese folk tale of the early T'ang dynasty (AD 618–907), in which the little heroine, desperate for education, is presented as setting out for her first day's schooling disguised as a boy, "as happy as a bird freed from its cage." Even more poignant is the earlier story, "Seeking her Husband at the Great Wall" (*c.* 200 BC), which tells of a wife who succeeded in making a long and terrible journey in order to find her husband, surviving every danger and disaster in vain, since her beloved had been dead all along.[38]

For there was love between men and women; the new lords of creation may have been engaged in urging that "a man is just a life-support system for his penis,"[39] but no man is a phallus to his wife. In the mysterious intimacy of the marriage bed, bonds were formed which outlasted time, like this extended grieving epitaph erected by a distraught Roman husband, which almost 2000 years later reads as directly as a letter to his dead wife:

> It was our lot to be harmoniously married for 41 years. . . . Why recall your wifely qualities, your goodness, obedience, sweetness, kindness . . . why talk of your affection and devotion to your relatives when you were as thoughtful with my mother as with your own family? . . . When I was on the run you used your jewels to provide for me . . . later, skilfully deceiving our enemies, you kept me supplied . . . when a gang of men collected by Milo . . . attempted to break into our house and pillage it, you successfully repulsed them and defended our home . . .[40]

Set this against the mysogynistic posturing of the majority of Roman commentators, and it is difficult to believe that the subjects under discussion are one and the same creature—woman. It becomes in fact increasingly clear that experience on the micro-level of what real women were doing, contradicts the macro-dimension of what men were insisting should and did happen.

Yet there is no denying the growth of the threat of women, as phallus-worship swept the world from around 1500 BC. The accumulated force of men's resentment of women, their struggle for significance and the recognition of the male part in reproduction had brought an irresistible attack on women's former prerogative. The Mother Goddess lost her sacred status and the power that went with it; and in this violent downgrading queens, priestesses and ordinary women at every stage of their lives, from birth to death, shared in the loss of the "mother-right." The phallus now separating out from the rites of mother-worship becomes a sacred object of veneration in itself, then the center of all creative power, displacing the womb, and finally both symbol and instrument of masculine domination over women, children, Mother

Earth and other men. When all life flowed from the female, creation had been a unity; when the elements became separated out, male became the moving spirit, and female was reduced to matter. With this god-idea of manhood, Mesopotamian males fought through their fears of being slaves of the woman-god by destroying her godhead and making slaves of women.

What this meant for women may be illustrated by the story of Hypatia, the Greek mathematician and philosopher. Trained from her birth in about 370 BC to reason, to question and to think, she became the leading intellectual of Alexandria where she taught philosophy, geometry, astonomy and algebra at the university. She is known to have performed original work in astronomy and algebra, as well as inventing the astrolabe and the planisphere, an apparatus for distilling water, and a hydroscope or aerometer for measuring the specific gravity of liquids. Adored by her pupils, she was widely regarded as an oracle, and known simply as "The Philosopher" or "The Nurse." But her philosophy of scientific rationalism ran counter to the dogma of the emerging religion of Christianity, as did her womanhood and the authority she held. In a terrorist attack of the sort with which women were to become all too familiar, Cyril, the patriarch of Alexandria in AD 415, incited a mob of zealots led by his monks to drag her from her chariot, strip her naked and torture her to death by slicing her flesh from her bones with shells and sharpened flints.[41]

Hypatia's infamous murder signified more than the death of one innocent middle-aged scientist. In Cyril and his bigots, every thinking woman could foresee the shape of men to come. The aggressive rise of phallicism had revolutionized thought and behavior; but it was not enough. Domination was not absolute, systems were imperfect, there was still too much room for maneuver—control could not be based on an organ that men could not control. There had to be more—an idea of immanent, eternal maleness that was not physical, visible, fallible; one that was greater than all women because greater than man; whose power was omnipotent and unquestionable—one God, God the Father, who man now invented in his own image.

> All men allow women to have been the founders of religion.
>
> STRABO (64 BC–21)

> Behind man's insistence on masculine superiority there is an age-old envy of women.
>
> ERIK ERIKSON

II
THE FALL OF WOMAN

Is it perhaps in a spirit of revenge
that man has for so many centuries
made woman his slave?

EDWARD CARPENTER

4

GOD THE FATHER

The birth of a man who thinks he is God is nothing
new.

TURKISH PROVERB

As a man is, so is his God—this word
Explains why God so often is absurd.

GILES AND MELVILLE HARCOURT,
Short Prayers for the Long Day

Blessed art Thou, O Lord our God, King of the
Universe, that Thou hast not made me a woman.

DAILY PRAYER OF HEBREW MALES

"In the beginning was the Word," declared St. John, "and the word
was God." In fact the word was a lie. In the beginning, God was not.
But as history unfolded in different nations and at different times it
became necessary to invent him.

For the assumption of divinity and power from a purely physical
base had certain crucial limitations. The human penis, even when
inflated to magico-religious status, falls short of godhead. Up to a
point, the rising phallocrat had carried all before him. Women's traditional power based on creation and nature had been systematically
whittled away. The Sacred King had stolen from the Great Queen her
selective technique of man-management on the Kleenex principle of
"use and throw away," and applied it wholesale to the female sex. But
brute force could only go so far. So long as women still retained their
atavistic power of giving new life, they could not be stripped of all
association with the divine.

Additionally, with the discovery of agriculture and the consolidation
of tribes into townships, human societies became increasingly sophisticated, requiring structures, systems and administration. Once survival was assured, surplus became *property*, and man awoke to the
glory of being lord and master. To secure ownership and protect rights
of inheritance in a more complex society called for something subtler
than the indiscriminate deployment of man's bluntest instrument. And

with the increase of organizational structures came greater opportunities for subversion or resistance; every tribe, township, throne-room or temple held women of ingenuity and resource eager to demonstrate that, whatever men's claim to power, it would not automatically be accepted. These women could not all be destroyed like Berenice or Boudicca, thrown to the dogs and ravens, or hurried to unmarked graves. Achieving *power*, man reached out for the secret of *control*; and as he began to look beyond the end of his penis, he found a stronger lord, a greater master—God.

Male divinity, of course, was nothing new. Isis had her Osiris, and Demeter had been forced to bow to the vengeance of the Lord of the Underworld. Indeed, as phallomania swept the world, male godhead found a new measurement in lost maidenhead; Zeus, king of the immortals, demonstrated his supremacy by the numbers of young women he raped. The new gods of power were equally aggressive and rapacious. The difference was that now each one insisted that he *alone* was God—he was the *One* God, the *only* God, and no one else could play.

For within the short millennium or so that separates the forging of Judaism from the birth of Islam, all the world's major religions made their début one by one. Immediately each set about the twin tasks of carving out their own community of believers, and annihilating all opposition. Where other male deities were targeted for extinction, what price female divinity? Walking in the garden that had been Eden, Mother Nature met Father God and her doom. In the duel for possession of the soul of humanity she lost her own, as the father god, in Engels' phrase, brought about, "the world historic defeat of the female sex."

Not all these new religions were god-systems. Judaism offered the paternalistic prototype, once it had succeeded in elevating the petty tribal godlet Yahweh into quite a different order of being after the trauma of the Exile just before 600 BC. Islam likewise patented the slogan "There is no God but God" following the birth of its prophet Muhammad just before AD 600. And straddling the period between the two, lodged at its pivotal midpoint, was the reformed Judaism called Christianity formulated when the old God of the Jews gave birth to a son in whom, as a junior version of himself, he was naturally well pleased.[1]

Equally important, though, to India and China respectively, were Buddhism and Confucianism, both of which arose with the birth of their human founders and spread far and fast from these deceptively modest origins. Neither Buddha nor Confucius ever claimed to be divine, and their teachings are properly understood as value-systems rather than as religions proper. But the foundation of their beliefs was uncompromisingly patriarchal; the founders themselves have been worshipped as gods by their followers throughout history; and the ideologies of both these systems have had a remarkably similar impact on women's lives to that of religions organized around a central concept of a Father God. To women, therefore, the effect was broadly the same, however the message of male supremacy came packaged. All these systems—Judaism, Confucianism, Buddhism, Christianity and Islam—were presented to them as holy, the result of divine inspiration transmitted from a male power to males empowered for this purpose, thereby enshrining maleness itself as power.

Historians, both male and female, have not always resisted the temptation to see the rise of monotheism as a plot against women, since the aftereffects have been so uniformly disastrous for the female sex. But attractive though the notion of a cosmic conspiracy is to women's learned feelings of weakness and helplessness, it overlooks the fact that many of the elements of these early religions held a strong appeal for both sexes, and often for women in particular. Organized religion may have been a root cause of the historic defeat of womankind—Eve did not fall, she was pushed—but it did not begin with that aim. Seen in the wider context of the struggle of human beings of different races towards a deeper understanding of the meaning of their lives and of their growing spirituality, these five patriarchal systems readily reveal why in the first instance they were so attractive.

To begin with, each offered a clarity, a certainty, a synthesized world view that carried a fresh and profound conviction after the pluralistic muddle and overlap of the old gods, and of goddess-worship too. An Athenian woman in labor praying for a safe delivery in the fifth century BC, for example, had to choose between the Great Mother Cybele, Pallas Athene, or even the virgin huntress Artemis (Diana to the Romans), all of whom had a special care of women in childbirth. Her husband, sacrificing for the birth of a son, could propitiate Ares for a little warrior or Apollo for a poet or musician, but neglected Zeus the king of the gods at his peril. Once all these rival divinities had been caught up into one all-powerful father, whose eye was on every sparrow let alone each of his human creations, or into a firm framework of "the Enlightenment," "the One Path," there was a security that had previously been sought in vain.

For the newcomers were wonderfully confident. "I am the Lord your God," Jehovah told the Jews, "and thou shalt have none other gods before me"—the same message, delivered with the same assurance, as that of the gods of Christianity and Islam. But this apparent simplicity masked a rich complexity that succeeded in harmonizing the universe, offering its believers a patterned metaphysical framework in which each individual, however lowly, was guaranteed their own snug niche. In this confidence, not previously available to them, women could find a terrible strength. The Christian slave Felicitas, martyred with her mistress Perpetua in the Roman persecutions of AD 203, on the night before her ordeal gave birth to a baby in prison. When she cried out in labor, the guards mocked her with the taunt, "You suffer so much now—what will you do when you are tossed to the beasts?" But when Felicitas faced the lions in the amphitheatre the next morning she was calm, even joyful, and died without a sound.[2]

As this shows, these early believers could find through pain and suffering an answer to the pain of the human predicament itself, a meaning to the apparent meaninglessness of life. With belief came, therefore, an enhanced sense of self as the faithful were liberated from being the helpless slaves either of the Mother Goddess or of her phallic supplanters, the petty, disputatious male divinities. Now the individual mattered, to a god who cared about her and her potential: "I am thy God," declared Jehovah, "walk before me and be thou perfect." And for the believer—but *only* for the believer—the reward was nothing less than paradise. This is the triumphant boast of the virgin martyr Hirena in a play of the first European dramatist, the Saxon writer Hrotsvitha, who as a woman seems to identify strongly with her tough, jeering heroine:

> Unhappy man! Blush, blush Sisinnius, and groan at being vanquished by a tender little girl. . . . You shall be damned in Tartarus; but I, about to receive the palm of martyrdom and the crown of virginity, shall enter the etherial bedchamber of the eternal king.[3]

This combination of revenge psychology with the satisfaction of sublimated sensuality must have been intensely comforting to downgraded women. In a reward-and-punishment system, too, the more women submitted and suffered, the greater the final payoff.

Interestingly, the more sophisticated of the women under the early monotheisms speedily grasped that her God in fact offered a post-dated check, and no one had ever come back to complain that it had bounced. Consequently they plunged into less-than-godly behavior with extraordinary vigor, only making sure to build into their lives a final phase of high-profile godliness to ensure their passage to eternity. Mistress of this technique was the Russian Queen Olga. Becoming regent after the assassination of her husband Igor I, she first instituted a reign of terror in revenge for his murder, scalding the leading rebels to death and executing hundreds of others. After twenty years of iron-hearted cruelty she devoted herself to Christianity with such good effect that she became the first saint of the Russian Orthodox church.

The confidence with which the women of the early churches adopted, even manipulated, the dictates of the new patriarchies provides another pointer to the reason for their success. At their origins, they were all only a breath or two away from the goddess-religions they had usurped, and there is abundant evidence that for many hundreds of years women worshippers of the Father Gods continued with their traditional female rituals alongside the new observances. The prophet Ezekiel, a founder of the elevation of Judaism from its scattered tribal beginnings, was horrified to witness Jewish women of the fifth century BC "weeping for Tammuz," mourning the death of the sacrificial king, who as Tammuz, Attis or Adonis was remembered every year on the Day of Blood at the end of March (later colonized by Christianity as Good Friday). And not only the women: to the scandalized eyes of the prophet Jeremiah, every man, woman and child was guilty of the same offense:

> Seest thou not what they do in the cities in Judah and the streets of Jerusalem? The children gather wood, and the fathers kindle the fire, and the women knead their dough to make cakes to the Queen of Heaven [the Great Goddess] that they may provoke me to anger.[4]

All patriarchies, in fact, only succeeded by colonizing, indeed cannibalizing the forms, emblems and sacred objects of the Goddess they were purporting to root out. Much recent theological scholarship has been devoted to recovering what in ages past every schoolgirl knew: that the Great Goddess in her threefold incarnation (maiden, mother and wise woman) lies behind the Christian trinity, that her immature aspect of moon maiden became the Virgin Mary, and so on. To this day modern events like May Day and Lady Day commemorate her special festals, especially the first, when at the celebration of the vernal equinox, maidens wreathed in flowers symbolizing the Earth Mother's powers of fecundity and growth dance round a maypole, a phallic evocation of the boy-king/sacrificial lover of the woodland (Tammuz, Attis, Adonis, Virgius) who has been cut down. This continuity is even to be observed in the ethical systems that make no overt use of the Father God; the Chinese character denoting "ancestor" had an earlier meaning of "phallus" which, even earlier, found on the most ancient and sacred bronzes and oracle bones, had meant "earth." Chinese ancestor-worship, then, embodying patriarchal supremacy (only a son can perform the ritual sacrifices which set his father's soul free to join his ancestors) grows out of the Great Goddess/Mother Earth worship which promoted fertility and secured offspring for the first male "ancestors."[5]

Of all religions, however, Islam most clearly reveals this hijacking process at work. From the crescent moon on its flag to the secret of its most sacred shrine, the Goddess is omnipresent, as Sir Richard Burton observed on his travels:

> Al-Uzza, one aspect of the threefold Great Goddess of Arabia, was enshrined in the Ka'aba at Mecca, where she was served by ancient priestesses. She was the special deity and protector of women. Today the Ka'aba still survives and is the most holy place of Islam.[6]

Even when the priestesses of the Great Goddess were replaced by priests, her power lingered on. These male servitors were called *Beni Shaybah*, which means "Sons of the Old Woman," one of the Great Mother's more familiar nicknames. In an even clearer link, what they guard is a very ancient black stone, sacred to Allah, and covered with a black cloth called "the shirt of the Ka'aba." But underneath the "shirt" the black stone bears on its surface a mark called "the impression of Aphrodite," an oval cleft signifying the female genitals: to one eyewitness "it is the sign of . . . the Goddess of untrammelled sexual love, and clearly indicates that the Black Stone at Mecca belonged originally to the Great Mother."[7] When her women worshippers knew that "the Lady" was still in her stone, and her stone was still in her shrine, it would not at first have mattered that she gained another name, she who had 10,000 appellations, nor that now she was served by different acolytes. In embracing the new father gods, therefore, women did not have to abandon all contact with their first mother, and this undoubtedly enabled the struggling patriarchies to consolidate their hold.

In these early struggles of each of the male-centered systems lies another reason for their initial success with women. In the fight for recognition and survival, any ideology seizes on and makes use of whatever recruits come to hand—it is no accident that the first devotees of both Buddha and Muhammad were their wives. Women were, as a result, well to the fore in all these foundations, which offered them a central role and opportunity. It seems clear, for instance, that Khadijah, the brilliant businesswoman and prominent member of the leading Meccan tribe of the Quraish, actually discovered Muhammad when at the age of forty she gave the ill-educated, epileptic shepherd boy of twenty-five regular employment, took him as her husband and encouraged his revelations.

The early annals of Judaism are similarly stiffened with strong-minded women, even in extremes of terror, pain and loss. A well-known figure is that of the mother of the Maccabees, who stood by her seven sons while each in turn was tortured and burned to death in the holocaust of 170 BC, urging them to stand firm. But for this, it is agreed, the God of the Jews could have been wiped out: "the blood of the Maccabean martyrs . . . saved Judaism."[8] In early Christianity likewise, women found not merely a role, but an instrument of resistance to male domination; in choosing to be a bride of Christ they inevitably thumbed a nose at lesser male fry. Thousands of young women helped to build the church of God with their body, blood and bones when frenzied fathers, husbands or fiancés preferred to see them die by fire, sword or the fangs of wild beasts rather than live to flout the duty and destiny of womanhood.

Just as important as the fearless witness of the virgin martyrs was the work of the women who put their time, their money, their enthusiasm, their houses and their children freely at the disposal of the struggling founders. Even St. Paul, later the unregenerate prophet of female inferiority, was forced to acknowledge the help he received from Lydia, the seller of purple dyes in Philippi. Indeed the very first Christian churches in Rome and elsewhere were houses donated by wealthy widows, and all the Christian communities in the Acts of the Apostles are recorded as meeting under a woman's roof: "the church in the house of Chloe, in the house of Lydia, in the house of Mary, the mother of Mark, in the house of Nympha, in the house of Prisca . . ." Most significant of all, as a leading theologian shows, of the common offices of the church in its pioneer days (teaching, prayer and prophecy, thanksgiving over bread and wine, and administering the gifts and discipline of the faith), *there is none that a woman could not do.*"[9]

Early Christianity, in fact, claimed through its prophets that it liberated women from their traditional subservience and gave them complete sexual equality with men. "In Christ," wrote St. Paul, "there is neither bond nor free, neither male nor female . . ." Buddhism, too, at its beginnings held out to its female adherents a delusive promise of equality; the threefold reality, "all is suffering, all is impermanence and there is no soul," was as available to women as it was to men. Additionally, Buddha taught that life, or form, was only one of twenty-two faculties that composed a person; sex, therefore, was of minimal importance. And, like Christianity, Buddhism also had its early heroines, idealized examples of passion, purity and sublime faith:

> Subhā puts the thought [of Buddha] into action [when] a rogue inveigles her into the forest and tries to seduce her. Subhā responds by preaching the doctrine to him. But the rogue sees only the beauty of her eyes and ignores her lofty words. So to demonstrate the irrelevance of both her beauty and sex to the inner life, Subhā plucks out one of those lovely eyes and offers it to him. He is converted at once . . .[10]

Of all the early patriarchies, though, perhaps the most surprising in its attitude to women is Islam; the gross oppressions which later evolved like veiling, seclusion, and genital mutilation (the so-called "female circumcision") were brought about in the teeth of the far freer and more humane regime of former times. From pre-Islamic society, for instance, women had inherited the right to choose their own husbands—husbands in the plural, for the old "mother-right" still flourished throughout the tribes and townships of the Arab states, as the feminist historian Nawal El Saadawi explains:

> Before Islam a woman could practise polyandry and marry more than one man. When she became pregnant she would send for all her husbands. . . . Gathering them around her, she would name the man she wished to be the father of her child, and the man could not refuse . . .[11]

When a Bedouin woman wanted to divorce one of these spare husbands, she simply turned her tent around to signal that her door was no longer open to him. In later generations Muslim women must have considered folk tales or memories of those freedoms either a cruel joke or the purest fantasy. Yet the proof that they existed lies in the marriage story of the founder of Islam, the prophet Muhammad himself. When the self-assured Khadijah wanted him, she despatched a woman with instructions for Muhammad to propose to her—and he did.

Even more remarkable than this free right of sexual choice was the readiness with which the women of early Islam took up arms and fought in pitched battles alongside the men. One honored heroine and warleader was Salaym Bint Malhan, who with an armory of swords and daggers strapped round her pregnant belly fought in the ranks of

Muhammad and his followers. Another is credited with turning the tide in a fierce fight against the Byzantines, when the wavering forces of Islam were rallied by a tall knight muffled in black and fighting with ferocious courage. After the victory, the "knight" was reluctantly exposed as the Arab princess Khawlah Bint al-Azwar al-Kindiyyah.

Even losing in battle could not defeat Khawlah's spirit. Captured at the battle of Sabhura, near Damascus, she rallied the other female captives with the passionate challenge, "Do you accept these men as your masters? Are you willing for your children to be their slaves? Where is your famed courage and skill that has become the talk of the Arab tribes as well as the cities?" A woman called Afra' Bint Ghifar al-Humayriah is said to have returned the wry reply, "We are as courageous and skillful as you describe. But in such cases a sword is quite useful, and we were taken by surprise, like sheep, unarmed." Khawlah's response was to order each woman to arm herself with her tent-pole, form them into a phalanx, and lead them in a successful fight for freedom. "And why not?" as the narrator of their story concludes, "if a lost battle meant their enslavement?"[12]

Another woman warrior of Islam, as potent with her tongue as with a sword, was the celebrated 'A'ishah. Although the youngest of the twelve wives of the polygamous prophet, married to the aged Muhammad when she was only nine and widowed before her eighteenth birthday, 'A'ishah became famous for her courageous intelligence and resistance to the subordination enjoined on virtuous Islamic wives. She had no hesitation in opposing or correcting Muhammad himself, arguing theology with him in front of his principal male followers with such devastating logic and intellectual power that Muhammad himself instructed them, "Draw half your religion from this ruddy-faced woman." Her courage extended even to resisting the will of the Prophet when it came through the hot-line of a revelation from Allah himself. When in answer to his desire to take another wife Muhammad was favored with a new batch of Koranic verses assuring him that Allah permitted his prophet to marry as many women as he wished, she hotly commented, "Allah always responds immediately to your needs!"[13]

What else would a father god do? And how were women to respond? 'A'ishah, still only a girl of eighteen when Muhammad died, outgrew this rebellion and went on to become a leading figure in Islam, where her active political power and influence on Muslim evolution and tradition were enormous. But the challenge she had thrown down remained unanswered. It could only gain in immediacy and urgency in the years that followed.

For whatever needs were answered by the new patriarchies as they grew, throve and put on beef, they were not the deeper needs of the female sex. Of course there were attractions—there had to be, for women to swallow the ideological bait without perceiving either the hook or the poisonous lead weighting it down. None of these systems could have been imposed on women against their will. There had to be consent from the women members of each tribe, township or race proselytized by the zealots of the new gods, at some level. Which of them, though, presented with the first appealing package of function and freedom, could have known what she was consenting to for herself and all her female descendants for the next 2000 years? In the whole of the vast fun-house of history's jokes and tricks, there can be few greater ironies than the spectacle of women embracing and furthering the systems which would all too soon attack their autonomy, crush their individuality, and undermine the very reason for their existence.

From the unknown moment in history when the secret of birth became known, women were doomed to decline from their goddess-like eminence. But man's self-elevation to a god did more than cut woman down to normal human size; it succeeded in subordinating her to a lower form of being. Each in its own way, the five major belief systems of Judaism, Buddhism, Confucianism, Christianity and Islam *by their very nature* insisted on the inferiority of women and demanded their subjection to values and imperatives devised to promote the supremacy of men.

How did this come about? Buddha, Jesus, Muhammad and other prophets of the cause in fact taught the love of women—the latter in particular was famous for his enthusiastic interpretation of his revelation from Allah that women were the greatest gift of God to man. Theoretically, too, women were not specifically debarred from the spiritual fruits of the new faiths. Buddha categorically laid down the doctrine that women just as much as men could destroy "the five fetters" of sinful humanity and achieve enlightenment, while the emphasis of Christianity and Islam on the individual soul placed a value upon the youngest child, let alone its mother. Muhammad taught his followers to revere worthy women, and even after his death women continued to command respect: Zubaidah, the glamorous queen of the *Thousand and One Nights*, in real life saved her country from civil war by her refusal to take revenge after the murder of her son. This, coupled with her pioneer work in civil engineering (she pushed through a continuous water supply on the 900-mile pilgrim route from Iraq to Mecca) made her a national heroine.

Individual patriarchs may indeed wriggle off the charge of woman-hating; the key to the gross inflictions laid on women in their names lies in the nature of the system itself. For a monotheism is not merely a religion—it is *a relation of power*. Any "One God" idea has a built-in notion of primacy and supremacy; that One God is god above all others and his adherents are supreme over all non-believers. In a multiple pantheon, by contrast, all jostle for primacy. Even the king of the immortals, Zeus himself, could be challenged or outwitted by his angry wife and jealous sons. The ancient world rejoiced in a plethora of such myths and beliefs whose gods, goddesses and godlets were widely tolerated by rulers throughout Mesopotamia, India, Egypt, Rome and Greece—Alexander the Great exemplified as he so often did his country's highest form of wisdom in his assertion that no one system, no one god held a monopoly on truth.

Patriarchy changed all that. With a genuine belief in the One God came the inescapable duty to enforce it upon others; with the claim to a patent on truth came for the first time ideas of orthodoxy, habits of bigotry and the practice of persecution. Any opponents of the born-again zealots were to be destroyed without mercy, as in the covenant of the Jews, "that whoever would not seek the Lord God of Israel should be put to death, whether small or great, whether man or woman." As the Jews persecuted other tribes and their hated idols who challenged the One God, so Christians were to hound them down the ages. Islam in its turn warred on Jews and Christians alike, Muhammad whipping up to wholesale slaughter bloodthirsty hordes who killed or died equally cheerfully to win the paradise he held out to them. "Saracens" thus joined "Israelites" on Christianity's hit-list, to be massacred in the name of the Lord our God . . . ah, men.

As a power-relation, then, monotheism inevitably creates a hierarchy—of one god over others, of stronger over weaker, of believer over unbeliever. In addition, the new concept of a personal relationship between man and his god, since God had chosen to create him in his own image, led to the idea of the Father God as vested in every human patriarch. So men suffered in two ways, as enemies and as subordinates: the patriarchal ordinances of Ecclesiasticus prescribe "bread, correction and work for a servant" and unremitting oppression for any sons—"bow down their neck from their youth."

Men, however, were persecuted for extrinsic reasons, not simply because they were men. And in the nature of things, the system afforded opportunities for them to improve upon, or even reverse, their lowly position in the patriarchal pecking order. Enemies of the faith could convert, and did, in huge numbers, hence the worldwide success of the father god religions. With even less difficulty young men turned into old men; sons became fathers; servants became senior servants; and even slaves could become free. None of these options was open to the female of the species. Under patiarchal monotheism, womanhood was a life sentence of second-order existence.

For woman could never recover from one primal, overwhelming disability—she was not male. The ensuing syllogism represented a triumph of masculine logic. If God was male and woman was not male, then whatever God was, woman was not. St. Augustine spelled it out: "For woman is not the image of God, whereas the man alone is the image of God." As man stands beneath God in the hierarchy, so the woman, as further removed, comes below him: in practical terms, then, setting every man over every woman, father over mother, husband over wife, brother over sister, grandson over grandmother. In every one of these new systems, God freed man from slavery and took him into partnership for eternity, while women were never even apprenticed to the celestial corporation. Man could progress to become each-his-own paterfamilias while women remained trapped in their perpetual inferiority. Muhammad explained it with his usual clarity, along with the traditional patriarchal penalties for disaffected subordinates:

> Men are in charge of women because Allah has made one to exceed the other. So good women are obedient, guarding in secret that which Allah has guarded. As for those from whom you fear rebellion, admonish them, banish them to beds apart and scourge them.[14]

Under the father god, only man attains to full adult freedom and control. Woman in diametric contrast is sentenced to a double subordination, to God and to man, as St. Paul instructed the Corinthians; because "man is the image and glory of God, but the woman is the glory of man . . . neither was the man created for the woman, but the woman for the man."

As this shows, male supremacy does more than imply female inferiority: it demands it. How then was that demand brought home to each and every woman? The first step had to be the eradication of all traces of women's previous superiority. This meant a wholesale onslaught on the worship of the Mother Goddess, on her devotees, and by extension on women's right to rule or command. A laconic account in II Chronicles gives us a gynoclast at full tilt:

> And also concerning Maachah the mother of Asa the king, he removed her from

being queen because she had made an idol in a grove: and Asa cut down her idol
and stamped on it and burned it at the brook Kidron . . . and the heart of Asa
was perfect all his days.[15]

This was only one of many such attacks on the Goddess, her temples,
scriptures, rituals and followers. These are detailed in both Old and
New Testaments of the Bible, since Christianity no less than Judaism
declared from the outset that the Great Goddess "whom Asia and all
the world worshippeth" must be persecuted, "and all her magnificence
destroyed" (Acts 19, 27).

The women resisted, of course. Over a thousand years after the
events related by the chronicler, Muhammad almost paid with his life
for his insistence that his "One God" should usurp "the Lady," "the
Queen of Heaven," "the Mother of Life and Death." Indeed, barri-
caded in his house by a raging mob of Goddess-worshippers, he was
favored with the timely revelation that the trinity of the old goddesses
Al-Uzza, Al-Manat and Ul-Uzzat, the Great Goddess in her three-fold
incarnation, still existed alongside the new boy, his Allah. As indeed
she did—but only for as long as it took Muhammad to regroup his
forces, cancel that revelation, and renew the assault.

Countless women took up arms against this tyranny. Foremost among
them was the Arab leader Hind al Hunnud, Known as peerless, the
"Hind of Hinds," she led the opposition of her tribe, the wealthy and
powerful Quraish, to the forced imposition of Islam. The climax of
her campaign came at the terrible battle of Badr in AD 624 where she
engaged directly with Muhammad himself, but her father, uncle and
brother were killed. For a time she directed a guerrilla war of vengeance
against the enemy, but eventually, outnumbered and surrounded, she
was compelled to submit and convert to Islam. In her military heyday
Hind had been not only a war-leader but a priestess of "the Lady of
Victory," inspiring the women to sacred chants for valor and victory.
After she bowed to the will of Allah, nothing more was heard of this
brilliant and unusual woman.

In his dealings with the Mother Goddess and her worshippers,
Muhammad was content with nothing less than "the historical liqui-
dation of the female element," in the words of the Muslim historian
Fatnah A. Sabbah. Even this, though, was not enough to ensure the
perpetuation of the father god's victory. Women and men too had to
be brought to believe in women's inferiority, to know that her rightful
place was, in every sense, beneath the male. Accordingly the patriarchs
of the One God embarked on a strenuous and hysterical myth-campaign

to account for and enforce the subjection of women. Its essence is neatly summed up by St. Ambrose: "Adam was led to sin by Eve, and not Eve by Adam. It is just and right then that woman accept as lord and master him whom she led to sin."[16] Women's world-without-end obligation to pay for the sin of Eve was also enshrined, indeed elaborated, in Islam: the Muslim sage Ghazali declared that "when Eve ate the fruit which He had forbidden to her, the Lord, be He praised, punished her with *eighteen things.*" These included menstruation, childbirth, separation from her family, marriage to a stranger and confinement to her house—plus the fact that out of the 1000 components of merit, women had only one, while men, however sinful, were gifted with the other 999.

The Adam and Eve myth, possibly the single most effective piece of enemy propaganda in the long history of the sex war, had other crucial implications. It performed the essential task of putting man first in the scheme of things; for in all the father god religions, Judaism, Christianity and Islam, God creates man first: woman is born after man, framed of an insignificant and expendable lump of his bony gristle, and taken out of him like a child from its mother. Essentially this is just one of the countless attempts of womb-envious men to usurp women's power of birth: with a swift piece of patriarchal prestidigitation, God reverses biology and stands nature on its head with the birth of his man-child, in defiance of evolution, where men and women evolved together, and of life itself, where woman gives birth to man. God now assumed the power of all new life—all the monotheisms taught that God alone created and breathed life into each fetus, using the woman in whom he lodged it simply as an "envelope," in the Islamic phrase.

Yet still the fathers of the early religions were not done with downgrading women. Alongside this notion of women's inferior status flourished a conviction of women's inherent and inescapable inferiority. Among the Jews a husband was felt to be so much at the mercy of his wife's innate baseness that he was empowered to proceed against her any time "the spirit of jealousy come upon him," whether or not he had any evidence of misconduct on her part. Hauling her to the temple, he handed her over to the priest who uncovered her head in token of her humiliation, forced her to drink "bitter water" mixed of the dirt from the temple floor and gall, and cursed her, so that "her belly shall swell and her thigh shall rot." Vindicated, the husband received an unequivocal thumbs-up from God: "then shall the man be guiltless from iniquity, and this woman shall bear her iniquity."[17]

For his part the messenger of Allah received a personal verification of female turpitude in one of his revelations: "I stood at the gate of Hell," he reported. "Most of those who entered there were women."[18]

As this shows, under the rule of the father god the male has become the arbiter, type and supreme *exemplum* of the human race, the female merely a defective instrument, the vehicle designed by God to carry it on. Yet despite the enormous weight of the propaganda, it must have been hard for individual men to see the women they loved as mere "cauldrons" to "contain their hell of lustfulness," in St. Augustine's phrase. And how readily women took to the Jewish ordinance that they should address their husbands only as *ba'al* (master) or *'adon* (lord) as slaves did, may be gauged from the enormous stress appearing now in all written texts upon women's silence, obedience and total, passive submission to her husband, as in this rather frantic injunction from the Hindu *Kama Kalpa:*

> There is no other god on earth for a woman than her husband. The most excellent of all good works she can do is to seek to please him by manifesting perfect obedience. . . . Be her husband deformed, aged, offensive, choleric, debauched, blind, deaf or dumb . . . a woman is made to obey at every stage of her existence.[19]

Nor was submission merely a spiritual exercise. For a grotesque exercise of obedience to the lord and master, see this "Advice to a Wife" from a Japanese pillow-book of the eighth century:

> The most important thing is the respect that the woman shows her husband. . . . She will draw on her imagination for anything that might increase his pleasure, without refusing him anything. If he has a taste for little boys, let her imitate them by kneeling down so that he can take her from behind. Let her not forget that the man does not realise the delicate nature of a woman's anus, and will try to enter with as much vigour as usual. She had better prepare herself slowly and use *sizishumi* cream . . .[20]

Afterwards, whatever her condition, the Japanese wife had not concluded her obligations: "You will always say of his *membrum virile* that it is huge, wonderful, larger than any other; larger than your father's when he used to go naked to take his bath. And you will add, 'Come and fill me, O my wonder!', and a few other compliments of the same kind."[21]

This blind obedience and dumb submission became, in the eyes of the patriarchs, the only way that a woman could atone for her existence. The Koran makes it clear that the only virtuous woman was a mother: "When a woman conceives by her husband, she is called in Paradise a martyr, and her labor in child-bed and her care of her children protect her from hellfire."[22] Woman, once sacred for her mysterious power of life, is now reduced to nothing more than an obliging uterus; once the Mother of all, she is now a mere container; and the Great Goddess, "She of the Thousand Lovers," is forced to present an obliging orifice to every conscienceless cock.

Yet by a bizarre and limiting paradox, the emphasis on women's duty of procreation carries no connotations of female sexuality. As women were denied any full part in the process of reproduction, so they were likewise denied any pleasure of participation in the act. In fact, the less they knew about sex, the better, decreed their fathers and keepers; and thus in another reversal of the old mother-centered ways of thought, the highest value shifted from adult womanhood and the pride of fecundity to maiden ignorance. Now the child bride, the unspoiled female, not-yet-woman, became the finest type; and a small film of atavistic membrane, the hymen, casually deposited by evolution in the recess of every woman's body, was discovered to be her prize possession. Virginity came in with a vengeance as every budding patriarch suddenly realized his divine right to a vacuum-sealed, factory-fresh vagina with built-in hymeneal gift-wrapping and purity guarantee.

So powerful was this fetish of virginity that a new ideal gathered momentum, that of preserving it in perpetuity. One early Christian father, St. Jerome, was active in persuading fathers to dedicate their daughters to nunneries *at birth,* while another, St. Martin of Tours, constantly compared the "pure ungrazed field of virginity" to "the field of marriage torn up by the pigs and cattle of fornication." As this shows, the Christian church had from its origins a particular problem with women's sexuality: "to embrace a woman," wrote Odo of Cluny in the twelfth century, "is to embrace a sack of manure." The "sack of manure" metaphor for women's bodies was an obsession with the early Christians: "If a woman's bowels were cut open," pronounced the monk Roger de Caen, "you would see what filth is covered by her white skin. If a fine crimson cloth covered a pile of foul dung, would anyone be foolish enough to love the dung because of it?"[23]

Yet Christ was born of woman. The solution to this embarrassment was found only after protracted doctrinal councils, when the gruesome hilarity of debating how the divine seed could penetrate the Virgin's hymen, or how Christ could have emerged from her uterus without rupturing the said hymen with His sacred infant feet, appears to have gone unnoticed. But one thing was clear. Our Lord, the Son of God, the Redeemer of Man, could not have been born from a "sack of manure." The Christian fathers had to protect Mary's purity in order to protect his. The Blessed Virgin Mary, it was decreed, remained a virgin not only before the birth of Christ, but *afterwards* as well. She was unravaged by the bloody mess and pain of childbirth; He was hermetically sealed off from any contact with her filthy and disgusting innards. Nor was this merely a Christian perversion. The compulsive drive of the patriarch not simply to occupy and possess a pure and unspotted vagina but also to emerge from one may be demonstrated from the fact that in addition to Jesus, Buddha, Plato, Quetzalcoatl, Montezuma and Ghenghis Khan all claimed to be virgin-born.

With womanhood reduced to its most immature aspect, man therefore saddles himself with the problem of her regulation and control. What this boils down to, in every case, is a withdrawal of the previous freedoms of adult women, which then traps them in a permanently arrested state of adolescent dependency and as such fulfils all the prescriptions of the patriarch. Confucianism, spreading rapidly through China and the Far East after the death of its founder K'ung Fu-tsze, "the master king," in 478 BC, is a case in point. In feudal times, the people of China celebrated an annual spring festival when young men and women from the surrounding villages met in a woodland hung with wine gourds and refreshments, to play the time-honored game known in Shakespeare's England as "making green backs." These uncomplicated sexual liaisons were only translated into marriage in the autumn if the girl became pregnant and wanted a husband: and her free right of choice in the whole process is illustrated by this girl's song composed around 800 BC in the feudal state of Cheng:

> On the heath there is creeping grass,
> Soaked in heavy dew
> There was a handsome man
> With clear eyes and a fine brow
> We met by chance
> And my desire was satisfied
> We met by chance
> And together we were happy.[24]

Chinese history also records countless women of power, like the seventh-century Empress Wu of the T'ang dynasty. An imperial concubine at 13, Wu Chao ruled China for over half a century, in AD 696 proclaiming herself "supreme god." Many ordinary women throughout China worked as merchants, traders, farmers and manufacturers, as women have always done, everywhere. Yet when "the great sage," Confucius, drew up his "five fundamental relationships, which together compose "the order of natural harmony" (the relationship between a man and his wife, between father and son, between older and younger brother, between friend and friend and between sovereign and minister), women were excluded from every single one except the first.

The achievement of patriarchy, as here, is the creation of a system in which women are excluded by divine warrant from everything that counts, forever. All monotheisms are built on the idea of men and women as two complementary *opposites*, forming two sides of one coin. In this lies the very root of women's inequality—for if males embody one set of characteristics, and if with characteristic modesty they abrogate to themselves all the strength and virtues, then women are necessarily opposite *and lesser* creatures: weak where men are strong, fearful where men are brave, and stupid where men are intelligent. This dualistic opposition is neatly summed up in the teaching of Zoroaster:

> The two primal spirits who revealed themselves in vision as the twins are the Better and the Bad, in thought, word and action. And between these two, the wise knew to choose aright, the foolish not so.[25]

Translated into human terms, the impact of this on women is summed up in the laconic Arab proverb, "Man is heaven, woman is hell." The effect has been to constitute the whole race of women as an out-group in perpetuity, the largest and most long-standing out-group in the history of the human race. A summary of the disabilities imposed on women in the name of these false gods fatuously posturing as loving fathers can hardly do justice to their crippling nature or extent:

Women were stripped of any choice in marriage. Where previously the Mother had chosen freely her many lovers, now throughout all of India and China, as well as the lands under the sway of Judaism, Christianity and Islam, the woman became a passive participant, *chosen* by her husband, *given* in marriage by her male guardian. Women were also denied security even within marriage. Like choice, divorce became a solely male prerogative, to be evoked at will, as in the contemptuous Islamic formula. Another innovation to promote insecurity and deny women any chance of an equal partnership in marriage was polygamy.

Women were forced to live within marriage. Access to the world outside the home was banned: women were confined to a permanent house arrest, intensified in the Eastern religions by the imposition of veiling, seclusion, *purdah*, and the harem or *zenana* battery-hen existence. In the West, women were frozen out of any public activity: Irish laws against using women in military operations of the seventh century overthrew a Celtic tradition of female fighters going back at least 3000 years.[26]

Women were victimized by patriarchal laws. All so-called "laws of God" express in reality the will of man. In a worldwide blitz of new legislation males became the owners and holders of *everything*, including women and their children. Women now lost rights of property and inheritance, even the right to control their own bodies or to have any stake in their offspring. In a famous Chinese test case of the ninth century, a woman had been left seven-tenths of her father's estate, on condition that she reared the lesser beneficiary, his little son. The state intervened to reverse the will, leaving the daughter with only three-tenths—plus the task of rearing the boy who had supplanted her.

Women were deprived not simply of human rights, but of humanity. They were reduced to less than full personhood, systematically defined as inferior, perpetually doomed to adverse comparisons with the masculine norm, the whole, the ideal, the perfect image of the incomparable male, his God. Under Islam women are "mutilated beings," in the phrase of Fatna A. Sabbah; she adds, "I feel nauseated whenever I hear the tedious introductory phrase, 'Since the seventh century Islam has given a privileged place to woman . . .' You have to be a man to decode the Koranic message as positive to woman."[27] And in Japan, while the wife was accepting with cries of rapture her husband's rape of her anus, her newborn daughter, according to the very same pillow-books, was to be left for three days and three nights untended on the ground, "because woman is Earth and man is Heaven": "This is the law that grants the man, not the woman, the right to have the final word, and to make all the decisions. . . . In the hands of man, the woman is only an instrument. Her submission is total, and will last right up to her death."[28]

What escape was there for the individual woman from this violent and sustained onslaught of masculine lust for possession and the rage to destroy? The new father gods who arose in the East during the crucial millennium spanning the birth of Christ were very different from their phallic predecessors, though no less equipped with mindless aggression and manic drive. Now God was no longer in the thunder, or far away in the clouds veiling the peak of the distant mountain range—he was in every male authority figure from priest to judge to king; he was in every woman's father, brother and uncle; he was in her husband; he was at her board and in her bed. Finally, and most important of all, he was in her head.

For arraigned at the bar of history, the gods of the patriarchs had many crimes against women to answer for. They had attacked and demolished the worship of the Great Goddess, colonizing only what served their ends, reducing the former Earth Mother to child-bride and exploited virgin. Woman's sexuality had been inverted or denied, her body reduced to a sexual vessel of God's will, belonging to her husband who in his own person was God, and who was therefore to be obeyed and adored. In the first and greatest act of discrimination, of deliberate *apartheid* in human history, women were made into *untermenschen*, a separate and inferior order of beings. But worse than all these, they were made to believe in their own downgrading and debasement.

Not every woman submitted to the relentless ideological bombardment of the new patriarchal systems; not every system was as snugly jointed and watertight as those who put to sea in it liked to think. The gods of the patriarchs tightened their grip only slowly, and the gap between what the authorities prescribed and what human beings actually did allowed women of skill and resource more room for maneuver than the historical record has often been prepared to show. But women's resistance henceforth was to be localized, sporadic and all too frequently shortlived. In the struggle for supremacy, the budding ideologues hit upon the happy inspiration of shifting the battleground to an area where to this day women feel exposed and vulnerable—the female body. Viciously attacked for and through their breasts, their hips and thighs and above all for their "insatiable cunt," all too many women were lost beyond all hope of recovery.

> A woman's heaven is under her husband's feet.
> BENGALI PROVERB

5

THE SINS OF THE MOTHERS

Three things are insatiable—the desert, the grave
and a woman's cunt.

ARAB PROVERB

The body of a woman is filthy, and not a vessel for
the law.

BUDDHA

We are dealing with an existential terror of women
. . . men have deep-rooted castration fears which
are expressed as horror of the womb . . . These
terrors form the substrata of a myth of feminine
evil which in turn justified several centuries of gynocide . . .

ANDREA DWORKIN

When man made himself God, he made woman less than human. "A
woman is never truly her own master," argued Luther. "God formed
her body to belong to a man, to have and to rear children." In the
grand design of the monotheistic male, woman was no more than a
machine to make babies, with neither the need nor the right to be
anything else: "let them bear children till they die of it," Luther
advised. "That is what they are for."[1] But this reduction of the whole
sex to the one basic function of childbearing did not make women
more acceptable to the patriarchal opinion-makers. On the contrary,
downgraded from human being, woman stood revealed as "a most
arrogant and intractable *animal*"[2]—and this monster, born of the father
gods' sleep of reason, came to threaten their days and haunt their
nights for a thousand years and more. The consequent campaign of
hate against women's animal physicality, pursued from the dawn of
Judaism to the birth of the early modern world, has now emerged as
one of the most decisive historical facts in the story of women.

For women's history is not composed of the history of external
events in linear progression. Wars, dynasties and empires have come
and gone within a shorter span of time, and with less impact on

women's lives, than the practice of menstrual taboos, for instance, or female infanticide. Such themes shape women's lived experience far more than dates and deeds; and the patterns they create are continuous, circular, unchanging over many generations. The attack on women's bodies that was one of the most marked consequences of the imposition of patriarchal monotheism has no convenient onset or conclusion— but it was a principal determining factor of every woman's history over an extended period of time. It signaled, precipitated even, the decline of women into their long night of feudal oppression and grotesque persecution. Only the accelerating descent to the lowest pitch of physical misery could produce the momentum required for the slow climb back to full humanity.

Why did women's bodies become such a crucial battleground in the sex war? The answer to this lies at the heart of the masculine struggle for supremacy. By denoting women as separate, different, inferior and therefore rightly subordinate, men made women the first and largest outgroup in the history of the race. But it is impossible to exclude women totally from all the affairs of men. No other subordinated class, caste or minority lives as closely integrated with its oppressor as women do; the males of the dominant culture have to allow them into their homes, kitchens, beds. Control at these close quarters can only be maintained by inducing women to consent to their own downgrading. Since women are not inferior, they had to be bombarded with a massive literature of religious, social, biological and more recently psychological ideology to explain, insist, that women are secondary to men. And to make women believe that they are inferior, what better subject for this literature of religious teaching, cautionary folk tales, jokes and customs, than the female body? By destroying the basic site of human confidence and sense of self, by dumping in sexual guilt and physical disgust, men could ensure women's insecurity and dependence. There is no mistaking the true nature and purpose of the worldwide, orchestrated, rising crescendo of onslaughts on women during these centuries. Every patriarch fulminating in denigration of the sex was engaged in as brutal a bid for women's abject capitulation as the gangraping Mundurucu of the South Seas whose tribal boast was, "We tame our women with the banana."[3]

Yet the sheer volume of prescriptive material, the huge battery of devices aimed against women, while they argue the high level of male anxiety, imply too the strength of women's resistance. For woman was an "intractable animal," and she displayed her brute unreason nowhere more clearly than in her refusal to acquiesce in her own subjection. The violence and continuance of the denunciations imply a consistency and continuance of the prohibited behavior that made all the prescriptions necessary in the first place. The battery of social and legal controls also indicate the exact areas of masculine anxiety; and there was no part of the female body that did not in some way give rise to panic, fear, anger, or deep dread.

For women were dangerous in every part of their anatomy, from top to toe. Luxuriant hair could excite lust; accordingly the Jewish Talmud from AD 600 onwards allowed a man to divorce a wife who appeared in public with her hair uncovered, while St. Paul went so far as to instruct Christians that a woman who came bareheaded to church had better have her head shaved.[4] The female face was another Venus flytrap for helpless males—in a bizarre piece of theology dating from the third century AD, the early Christian father Tertullian held that "the bloom of virgins" was responsible for the fall of the angels: "so perilous a face, then, ought to be kept shaded when it has cast stumbling stones even so far as heaven."[5]

Within the face woman concealed one of her most potent and treacherous weapons, her tongue. A proverb found in almost all languages nervously insists that "the only good wife is a silent one," and among the Greeks of Asia Minor, for instance, during many hundreds of years, for a women "to have a tongue" was held to hinder her chances of a husband. Among Mongolian tribes for over a thousand years, women were tabooed the utterance of a wide range of words that only men were allowed to speak.[6] Further west under Islam, the worst vice of a wife was "*shaddaka*," "talk-a-lot."

This Semitic obsession with the gagging of women had emerged as early as the Jewish law of Moses at the birth of Judaism: "Women are to remain silent." Unmodified, it resurfaced as a Christian commandment in the Pauline requirement of all women: "silence and all subjection." Tongue-tying women as a precondition of their subjection was not confined to the Near and Middle East. In the Japanese Shinto teaching, woman spoke first at the dawn of the world, and her offspring was a monster as a result. The first man, her mate, recognized this as a message from the gods that man should always do the talking, and thus it has been ever since.

By the early modern period in Europe, the persecution of women who denied the demand for silence had taken on a ferocious brutality with the use of the device known as the "scold's bridle." In the North of England, for example, from the seventh to the seventeenth centuries "chiding and scoulding women" suffered this torture: led around the street on a rope, "wearing an engine called 'the branks', which is like a crown, it being of iron, which was muzzled over the head and face, with a great gag or tongue of iron forced into the mouth which forced the blood out." Also provided for "scolds" was the ducking or cucking stool, a wooden chair fixed on the end of a long pole at the water's edge, in which women were repeatedly immersed in water, mud or slime until they not infrequently drowned.

The head was at least the seat of whatever reason a woman might have. From there down her body was nothing but "the devil's playground." "Whenever a woman enters the bath," Muhammad pronounced, "the devil is with her."[8] As this shows, by assuming control over women's bodies, men laid themselves open to the unforeseen but logical outcome: that women could not be trusted to show any control over themselves. For they had none; they were seen as empty vessels drifting at will, moved only by the muscles that throbbed between their legs, as in this violent medieval denunciation of Arab womanhood:

> Women are demons, and were born as such;
> No one can trust them, as is known to all . . .
> They do not recoil to use a slave in the master's absence,
> If once their passions are aroused and they play tricks
> Assuredly, if once their vulva is in rut,
> They only think of getting some member in erection.[9]

Arab literature is shot through with this paranoid fear of woman's "insatiable cunt"—the Arab word for the female genitals is *al-farj*, "slit, crevice, crack," an opening that may look small, but into which a man could disappear without trace. "I saw her vulva!" laments one terrorized lover in the fifteenth-century erotic masterwork, *The Perfumed Garden*: "It opened like that of a mare at the approach of a stallion." That was not the worst of what an Arab male had to fear, as the author warned his readers: "Certain vulvas, wild with desire and lust, throw themselves upon the approaching member." Raging for intercourse, a woman's sex organ, "resembles the head of a lion. Oh, vulva! How many men's deaths lie at her door?"[10]

This rabid dread of the voracious vagina reached epidemic proportions among the Arab nations, and can hardly have been allayed by the Islamic institution of polygamy—there is an inherent conflict between the notion of the insatiable woman, and the demand that she be satisfied with only a quarter of a husband. But other cultures, too, evolved their own version of the vampire-vagina, the *vagina dentata* which men penetrate only at the risk of losing all they hold dear. This

produced a riot of castration fantasies, in which every dangling manhood was seen as hopelessly vulnerable to the wickedness of woman.
A highly-colored but not untypical image of all the pitiful penises
inadvertently mislaid by their owners haunted the nightmare fantasies
of Jacob Sprenger, the fifteenth-century German monk, witch-finder,
and author of the seminal witch-hunter's manual *Malleus Maleficarum*
(1484):

> And what, then, is to be thought of those witches who in this way sometimes collect
> male organs in great numbers, as many as twenty or thirty members together, and
> put them in a bird's nest, or shut them up in a box, where they move themselves
> like living members and eat corn and oats as has been seen by many and is a matter
> of common report.[11]

Interestingly, it is not only within the highly organized framework of
Eastern patriarchal religions that this theme of the omni-sexual woman
threatening male dominance with her 'insatiable cunt' is to be found.
Among the Navajo people of New Mexico this story evolved to explain
why men had to rule over women:

> First Man taunted his wife with being interested in sex alone. His rebuke gave rise
> to a quarrel in which she said that women could get along without men. To prove
> the challenge, the men moved across the river and destroyed the rafts that carried
> them. As years went by the women grew weaker; they needed the men's strength
> to produce food, and they became maddened with desire. As a result of self-abuse
> they gave birth to monsters. . . . The men too practiced perversion, but from their
> excesses no evil survived. After many had died and great suffering had ensued, the
> women yielded and begged the men to take them back. They did so and all agreed
> that henceforth the man should be the leader since he belonged to the stronger
> sex.[12]

The stronger sex? These centuries of strenuous myth-making in fact
reveal the very opposite, the atavistic fear of the weakness that women
caused in men, but never had to share. The very power of this historical
propaganda, amounting at certain times in certain places to a campaign
of hate, evokes a world subject to the tyranny of female desire, where
man is fragile, woman unwearied in strength. For in sex, while women
bloom, men wilt. Man enters the vagina hard, erect, at the height of
his potency; he emerges drained, drooping, spent. Women by contrast
are the recipients of man's potency, his essence, his best self. The
vagina therefore is the source and center of incessantly renewed energy,
the penis fallible, inadequate, finite. Man, giving his all, was unmanned
by woman, and could not summon his manhood again at will. Small

wonder then that he should hate and fear the creature who robbed him of a power that none of his gods of power could restore.[13]

Nor was this all that a man risked in the arms of the rapacious "woman-crack." To penetrate the "place of devils," to "feed the animal between the woman's legs," was to jeopardize not merely body, but soul too. Hardening into certainty, then into religious orthodoxy during this time, was the hysterical preoccupation with women's bodies as sources of pollution, infecting and contaminating men. What were the historical roots of this damaging and enduring attack on women's citadels of self, their bodies? The answer to this conundrum brings us to the central issue: the issue of blood.

"A woman in her courses" . . . the female's body made her not simply less than human but worse than animal. Of all human substances, blood is the most highly charged with power and danger. Dietary prohibitions against eating blood have been in force for centuries among many cultures, from Jews to Sioux to Hindus. Menstruation is mysterious blood, dangerous, unclean and threatening:

> A menstruous woman is the work of Uhremaun, the Devil. A woman in her courses is not to gaze upon the sacred fire, sit in water, behold the sun, or hold conversation with a man.[14]

Menstruation taboos like those prescribed here by the Parsi sage Zoroaster meant that for a quarter of their adult lives, one week in every four, the women of earlier times were regularly stigmatized and set apart, disabled and debarred from the life of their society. The operation of this system of *apartheid* was at its most visible in primitive societies like the Kafe of Papua New Guinea; when a girl began to menstruate she was shut in a darkened hut for a week, deprived of food, and taught that she was dangerous to herself and to others if she failed to abide by the ritual restrictions: her body and blood would make a man vomit, turn his blood black, corrupt his flesh, addle his wits and waste him to death. These beliefs and taboos can be duplicated throughout all primitive societies, often in forms which clearly indicate the nature of the dominance-subordination struggle involved: the early native Americans of the Dakota territory believed that the *wakan* (sacredness or power) of a menstrual woman could weaken the *wakan* of all masculine objects of power, both of war and peace.[15]

Whatever the nature of the taboos, their strength demonstrates the high level of fear and danger associated with women's primitive blood-mystery and its uncontrollable nature: any woman breaking the taboos risked sudden violent death. In societies developing under more rigid patriarchal organizations, menstrual taboos were less visible, but no less severe. The gods of the Middle East, speaking through Judaism, Christianity and Islam, were especially harsh. In Judaism, rabbinical elaboration of the biblical texts like Leviticus branded a woman *niddah* (impure) for the twelve days during, before and after her period, and the ferocious penalties imposed on a *niddah* were restated in the sacred lawbook, the *Shulchan Aruch*, as late as 1565, where a *niddah* was forbidden to:

> sleep in the same bed as her husband
> eat with her family at mealtimes
> occupy the same room as anyone else
> light the Sabbath candles
> enter the synagogue
> touch her husband, or even pass him anything.

As a final stroke, in a grim foreshadowing of what the future held in store for the Jews, the *niddah* had to wear special clothing as a badge of her separate and despised status. Effectively, a woman became a nonperson, when all her human rights were so regularly and frequently withdrawn: as Chaim Bermant explains, "She was regarded as the ultimate in corruption, a walking, reeking, suppurating presence . . . one could not stop to inquire after her health, for her breath was poisonous, her glance was harmful, and she polluted the very air about her."[16]

Both Christianity and Islam borrowed heavily from Judaism in laws of their own which instituted the primitive tribal taboos of Palestine as religious fact. All three strictly forbade any access of males to women "in their sickness," and from earliest days custom hardened along the lines laid down in the Koran: "They will ask thee also concerning the courses of women; answer, they are a pollution; therefore, separate yourselves from women in their courses and go not near them till they be cleansed." It is worth noting that Muhammad as an individual sought to reverse this attack on women at the very source and site of their womanhood—he would make a point of honoring his wife in front of his disciples during her period, receiving even his prayer mat from her hand, and drinking from the same cup, saying "Your menstruation is not in your hand, it is not in your cup." But this honorable effort to teach his followers that women were not more dangerous nor infectious at this time, any more than they were themselves when they ate, slept or evacuated, was a historical failure.

In terms of understanding the patriarchal struggle for control of women's bodies, the issue of blood is a major preoccupation. For not only did women bleed every month, from girlhood for all of their adult lives; every stage of their journey as women, every passage from one state to the next (menarche, defloration, childbirth) was also marked by the flow of blood with its frighteningly ambivalent signal of both life and death. The greater the danger, the stronger the taboo. All these "courses" of women's lives have triggered an intricate and often savage set of myths, beliefs and customs in which the containment of cultural fears overrode any personal concern for the female who was ostensibly the cause and center of it all.

So from the introduction of the One God religions down to the twentieth century, the handling of a virgin's first sex experience, for example, focused only on the vagina as "a place of devils," never on the owner of it. This organ was seen as most dangerous when first penetrated; the task accordingly was to protect the man, who in rupturing a woman's hymen plunged his most vulnerable part into what Leviticus called "the fountain of her blood." For many centuries it was thought prudent to devolve this risk:

> From ancient Egypt to surviving cults in modern India and Persia . . . every virgin before wedlock was made to sit up on the golden phallus of the sun-god so that ruptured and bled her. Hymeneal blood, otherwise deemed foul, was thereby hallowed; and no decent youth would marry a girl who was not thus consecrated.[17]

Alternatively, a human instrument could be used, and "the taking of maidenhead was regarded as porter's work in many parts of the East," high-caste males in particular would "sooner penetrate the bride with an iron rod, or command a black slave to deflower her, then defile themselves in the act."[18] In other countries, particularly those of Northern Europe, the risk was taken for the bridegroom by an older man whose superior strength and status, taken with his personal lack of interest in the virgin concerned, was held to be his protection against her evil. The surrogate male could be the groom's father, uncle, older brother or feudal lord. If the young man was a member of a military organization, the *droit de seigneur* naturally went to his superior officer. Comradely generosity was known to override husbandly consideration on these occasions—in one episode of the ceremony known to the Turkish army as "opening the cabinet," a virgin bride underwent intercourse with 100 men of the groom's regiment in one night. Not surprisingly, a number of the Arab countries of Asia minor have a version of the Arabic word *seyyib*, which denotes a woman who suffered such brutality during defloration that she fled from her groom in a state of shock. After experiences like these of a husband's freedom with or overestimation of the *jus primae noctis*, most *seyyib* were never seen alive again.[19]

In the nature of things, historical accounts of these events from a female point of view are few and far between. For most women, reared in ignorance of what to expect, unacquainted with the man in question, and scarcely out of childhood, the induction to sexual experience must have been traumatic. One worm's-eye view of the process was recorded by the Japanese aristocrat Lady Nijō, who in 1271 at the age of fourteen was given by her father to the Emperor GoFukasaka. The first Nijō knew of this was awakening to find the aged GoFukasaka in her bedchamber, where "he treated me so mercilessly," she wrote in her diary, that "I had nothing more to lose, I despised my own existence."[20]

Sexual violence, not least within the supposed safe stronghold of marriage, has been a commonplace of women's experience throughout history. Exalted for motherhood, they were despised for the process that made them mothers; defined and confined by their sex, they were punished through their sexuality by a range of techniques devised to control all use and disposal of female bodies by males.

First, throughout the known world both legislation and social custom enshrined the power of a father to marry his daughter where he chose, and to take any steps necessary to ensure that his choice was obeyed. When the young Elizabeth Paston refused an elderly, deformed, but rich suitor as a husband, her father "mewed her up" in a dark room without food or any human contact to make her change her mind. She was beaten once or twice a week, "and some tyme twyes on one day, and hir hed broken in to or thre places." Elizabeth held out, and went on to make not one but two happy marriages which made her one of the richest women in medieval England. Others were not so lucky. Across the water in Ireland in the same period it took three men to drag one poor girl, Isabella Heron, half a mile to the church door, after which her father beat her and forced her inside. Nor were fathers the only offenders. At the betrothal of Catherine McKesky in the same church her mother beat her with "a bed-oak" so grievously that she broke it—"after which her father beat her to the ground."[21]

An Indian father, however, never ran these risks of recalcitrant daughters, since his system ensured that every woman was safely married before she knew she was one. Since, throughout Europe, the age of sexual consent for a girl was twelve, this might seem young enough for marriage, sexual intercourse and all its consequences. But an Indian girl right up to and including the period of the British Empire commonly looked for motherhood nine months after reaching puberty (in the subcontinent, any time after eight or nine years old), and she would have been married well in advance of that; the prudent husband had his child-wife well broken in to regular intercourse before she began to menstruate, in order to take advantage of her "first fruits."

Inevitably enough, he very often failed of his harvest. Child marriage all too readily reveals itself as a sophisticated form of female infanticide, for millions of these girls died from gynecological damage, or in child-birth, every year. As late as 1921, the British Government Official Census of India recorded that 3,200,000 child-brides had died during the previous 12 months, under circumstances recorded by British Army doctors: "A. Aged 9. Day after marriage. Left femur dislocated, pelvis crushed out of shape. Flesh hanging in shreds. B. Aged 10. Unable to stand, bleeding profusely, flesh much lacerated. C. Aged 9. So completely ravished as to be almost beyond surgical repair. Her husband had two other living wives, and spoke very fine English. I. Aged 7. Living with husband. Died in great agony after three days. M. Aged about 10. Crawled to hospital on her hands and knees. Has never been able to stand erect since her marriage." All the more reason, then, the sages insisted, to catch them young before they succumbed to the weakness of women. "Early to marry and early to die is the motto of Indian women," ran the proverb. "The life of a wife is two monsoons."[22]

Under these circumstances, fortune may have favored the little wife whose experience of marriage was so nasty, brutish and short. A curious footnote to the history of enforced marriage is provided by the "bride-sales" of early modern Europe, in which a rich young heiress would be bartered to the highest bidder in a transaction of naked commercialism. For although under much contemporary legislation a woman could hold land, inherit, sell it or give it away, in practice her life was spent under the guardianship of a man, not simply her father or husband, but also the feudal lord of her father or husband. An heiress was simply part of his patrimony: in 1185 King Henry II of England had all his heiresses inventoried like cattle, no matter how small their holdings were:

One Alice de Beaufow, widow of Thomas, is in the gift of the lord king. She is twenty and has one son as heir, who is two. Her land is worth £5 6s 8d, with this stock, namely two ploughs, a hundred sheep, two draught animals, five sows, one boar and four cows.[23]

Alice of course was "a ploughed field," and encumbered with a living heir she would not have been a prime target for a fortune hunter. For a virgin, vacuum-sealed and factory-fresh, the price was higher in a rising market—one three-month old girl sold for £100 was rated at £333 as she outlived her babyhood and became a marriageable proposition. What this meant for the women involved may be inferred from one example, when in 1225 King John gave the young Lady Margaret, widow of the Earl of Devon's heir, as a prize to his leading captain of mercenaries Falkes de Breauté. This union of an English lady with French thug struck the scandalized chronicler Matthew de Paris at the time as "nobility united to meanness, piety to impiety, beauty to dishonour." Margaret endured this marriage for nine years before her husband's fall from royal favor enabled her to win an annulment. At this, de Breauté went instantly to Rome to lodge a claim to possession of his ex-wife's patrimony. In a clear sign from Heaven, so it was said by contemporaries, he died there before the Holy Father could pronounce on his case.

Among the indignities that de Breauté might well have visited upon his wife was the barbarous device known as the "chastity belt." These vile contraptions made their way into Europe from the Semitic East in the wake of the Crusades against the Holy Land from the eleventh century onwards. Like other instruments and techniques of genital control, the "chastity belt" was a far more substantial and horrific thing than its euphemistic title would suggest. It consisted in fact of an iron or silver corset welded tightly to the woman's flesh, with a metal bar passing between her legs; equally close fitting, this had two narrow slits edged with sharp teeth for bodily evacuation. Wearing one of these, a woman could not wash genitals condemned to be perpetually befouled, as the iron between the legs impeded and retained her urine, menstrual discharge, and bowel movements. As they also made normal locomotion extremely difficult, their use was not general. But the widespread interest in the mechanics of genital control may be gauged from the instant fame won by the Provost of Padua in the Middle Ages, who invented an iron version encasing the whole of the lower part of a woman's body. As late as the sixteenth century, the Abbé de Brantôme recorded ironmongers at a fair selling "a dozen contraptions for bridling up women's parts," while subsequent excavations, particularly in Germany, have shown that it was not unknown for women to be buried in them.[24]

Genital control in this form was a latecomer to the West; in the East it had been a fact of life time out of mind, with the first action of any slaveowner being the insertion of one or more rings through the *labia majora* of all female slaves to prevent unwanted pregnancy or despoliation. Slave women, already suffering a double subjection to their masters, were particularly vulnerable to forms of genital control almost amounting to rape and torture, as this account makes clear: "In Sudanese harems, following defloration by the master, women . . . were protected from lustful eunuchs by a thick, 12-inch bamboo staff thrust a third of the way into the vagina and strapped about the waist and thighs, with a woven straw shield in front to cover the vulva."[25] What was new in the wake of the establishing of the patriarchal religions was the extension of the severest forms of control to *all* women via a technique which betrays a conscious determination to deal with the "problem" of women's sexuality by destroying it wholesale.

As with the "chastity belt," the true nature of this practice has been obscured by its more familiar name of "female circumcision." In reality this mutilation of women, which involves the amputation of all the external female sex organs, bears no relation to the removal of the male foreskin. The operation on women's genitals that spread so widely through the Middle East in the wake of Islam and on down through Africa, where it continues to this day, is so appalling that its survival can only be explained by a general, total ignorance.[26]

The facts are these. In a private ceremony of women, the traditional female practitioner or "circumcisor," chanting "Allah is great and Muhammad is his prophet: may Allah keep away all evils," operates on a girl child anywhere between the ages of five and eight, with a sharpened stone, iron blade or piece of glass. In the first stage, the whole of the clitoris and its sheath are cut away, then the *labia minora* are scraped off, followed by most of the inside flesh of the *labia majora*. The flaps of skin that remain are then pulled together and pinned with thorns, thus obliterating the vaginal opening except for a very small aperture kept open with a minute splint of wood or a reed, to allow for the passage of urine and menstrual blood. As the work proceeds the mother and the other female guests "verify" the work, putting their fingers into the wound, along with the earth and ashes used to staunch the bleeding. When it is over, the girls' legs are tied together from hip to ankle for 40 days, to ensure that the stitched skin heals together and will not reopen. Throughout all this, the child is held down by her female relatives and is fully conscious.

The consequences of this procedure, usually undertaken by an aged woman with defective vision and unsteady hands on the floor of a poorly lit tent or mud hut, can readily be imagined: hemorrhaging, infection, slashing of the urethra, bladder and anus, vulval abcessing and incontinence. Medical practitioners were only engaged if the scar formation on the vulva was so severe as to prevent walking. In later life girls could suffer retention of menstrual blood (one French military doctor operated on a 16-year-old Djibouti girl to release 3.4 litres of black and decayed menstruum), sterility, and intense pain during intercourse and childbirth.

Neither intercourse nor childbirth could in any case be undertaken without severe pain in the first instance, since the original stitching up (painlessly dismissed as "infibulation" by those who have never experienced it) is deliberately designed to render a woman quite unable to accept a penis. One authority described the ritual of the wedding night in Somalia, when the husband, having beaten his wife with a leather whip, used his knife to "open" her. He then has "prolonged and repeated intercourse with her for the next three days."

> This "work" is in order to "make an opening" by preventing the scar from closing again. . . . The morning after the wedding night, the husband puts his bloody dagger on his shoulder and makes the rounds in order to obtain general admiration, while the wife stays in bed and moves as little as possible in order to keep the wound open.[27]

If intercourse results in pregnancy, the woman may have to have further surgery of this primitive nature to open her further, since the first wound is only large enough to admit the penis. Ideally she labors until delivery and is not opened further, regardless of any rupturing of the perineum. If she has to be opened in order to release her baby, she will be re-sewn immediately after delivery, which with high childbirth and child mortality rates, could be as many as 12 times or more.

Genital amputation was and remains a serious but localized practice. Not confined to any one place or period has been the use of the ultimate sexual violence against women: murder. Under patriarchy, being female was a life sentence, but many women never lived to serve it; in these raw times it was often a death sentence too. For female infanticide was pandemic. From the earliest existence of historical records down to the present day, to be born female in India, China or the Arab states, indeed anywhere between Morocco and Shanghai, was extremely dangerous. In pre-revolutionary China, childbirth preparations for thousands of years included the provision of a box of ashes next to the birthing bed, to suffocate a girl child as soon as she was born. Throughout India, methods of killing little girls took ingenious new forms in each different place; they were strangled, poisoned, thrown into the sea, exposed in the jungle, fed to sharks as a sacrifice to the gods, or drowned in milk with a prayer that they would come again as sons. As late as 1808 a British political commission found only half a dozen houses in the whole of Cutch where the fathers had not had all daughters born to them killed at birth.[28]

In each case the victim died by order of her father because she had no future outside marriage and motherhood: he therefore faced ruinous expense if he succeeded in marrying her, or public dishonor if he failed. But high dowry expenses alone do not explain the pandemic of female infant slaughter, when reproducing their own kind was for women in the cruelest sense labor in vain. The daughters were killed in a planned and sustained campaign to reduce the number of females in the world; in the face of their systematic program of gynocide the patriarchs' bleating about dowry expenses and too many mouths looks like transparent motive-hunting. It was attacked as such even in its own time, as the Koran made clear:

> When the sun shall be folded up
> And when the female child that has been buried alive shall be asked
> For what crime she was put to death . . .
> Then every soul will know what it did.[29]

As the patriarchs stood by to block a woman's right of entry to this world, so they invoked the power to precipitate her out of it; and since in almost every country of the world a man was lord, guardian and sole custodian of his womenfolk, for the woman there was no appeal, and no escape. History holds only the scantest record of the millions of nameless women who died under the fists, boots, belts and cudgels of their men. But social position did not necessarily afford any more protection; even her royal blood was not enough to save the Princess Dolguruky of Russia when her husband Ivan IV ("the Terrible") ordered her to be drowned because she failed to give satisfaction.

Ivan had learned this particular technique of wife-disposal from a near neighbor, the Sultan of the Ottoman Empire, where unwanted females were traditionally sewn into weighted sacks and cast off Seraglio Point into the Bosphorus.[30] For women were disposable, and even in the West, which prided itself on its Christian morality and superiority to "the lustful Turk," their value throughout the whole of the early modern period was low. In addition, if a woman had in any way compromised her one true function of childbearing, her life was worthless, while a man's, whatever his transgression, was *inherently* more valuable. This story of a French woman of the early Middle Ages

and her lover, the priest of Le Mans, as related by the chronicler
Geoffrey of Tours, illustrates this point with brutal clarity:

[The priest] often debauching himself with a woman of free status and good family,
he cropped her hair, dressed her up as a man, and led her off to another town,
hoping to dispel the suspicion of adultery [fornication] by going to live among
strangers. When some time afterwards her relatives discovered what had happened,
they rushed to revenge the family's disgrace . . . the woman they burned alive, but
being driven by the greed for gold they decided to ransom the priest. . . . Hearing
of the case, Bishop Aetharius took pity on the man and snatched him from certain
death by paying 20 solidi of gold for him.[31]

Presumably a priest could be recycled; but this woman's sexual sin
annihilated her as a human being. Yet sinfulness is not the real issue
here. The key to the destruction of her body lies in the fact that she
could no longer fulfill her ordained role of wife and mother, once she
had been contaminated by illicit sex; and without function, she was
as disposable as any odalisque of the sultan's seraglio. And certainly
she could not be allowed to survive as a living proof that women could
manage as free individuals, outside the framework of the patriarchal
society. Again, function is the key—a woman who is not locked into
that chain of command between her husband and his children is a
dangerous threat to the stability of the society, and to herself. Worse,
like the Frenchwoman whose sinfulness put her beyond the pale, she
was no use to anybody any more. In these harsh times, it was only a
short step to the belief that she was better off dead.

Something of this sort seems to underlie the Indian custom of wife-
destruction called *sati* or *suttee*. By Hindu custom enshrined in law
from early days, when a husband died his wife had no further need
of life on her own account; as the law book of the Hindus makes clear,
"No other effectual duty is known for virtuous women after the deaths
of their lords, except casting themselves into the same fire."[32] The
simple difference was that the dead husband was unlikely to feel the
flames of his funeral pyre while the living wife had to be terrorized,
drugged and finally pinned down to undergo the dreadful death of
being burned alive because she had outlived her use and purpose, as
this eyewitness report of one eighteenth-century *sati* in Bengal makes
clear:

The relation whose office it was to set fire to the pile led her six times around it
. . . she lay down by the corpse and put one arm under its neck and the other over
it, when a quantity of dry cocoa leaves and other substances were heaped over them
to a considerable height, and then ghee, or melted preserved butter, poured on the

top. Two bamboos were then put over them and held fast down, and the fire put to the pile, which immediately blazed very fiercely. . . . No sooner was the fire kindled than all the people set up a great shout. . . . It was impossible to have heard the woman had she groaned or even cried aloud on account of the mad noise of the people, and it was impossible for her to stir or struggle on account of the bamboos which were holding her down like the levers of a press. We made much objection to their way of using these bamboos, and insisted it was using force to prevent the woman from getting up when the fire burned her. But they declared it was only done to keep the pile from falling down. We could not bear to see any more, but left them, exclaiming loudly against the murder, and full of horror at what we had seen.[33]

This sense of outrage, transparently genuine and doubtless the only comfort to be derived in a situation of such overwhelming powerlessness, consistently marks European responses to Eastern social practices. Yet it is noteworthy that the witness records the victim as being serene and acquiescent in her own death. This effect, of supreme importance to the sanctity of the proceedings, was achieved by a combination of techniques combining brutal bullying and drugging on the day with lifelong ideological manipulation—victims were taught from infancy that a *sati* (faithful) widow earned herself and her husband 35 million years of heavenly bliss, while a refuser plunged to the lowest depths of the reincarnation spiral, to be returned to earth again in the most disgusting and despised form. In addition, the Indian custom of child marriage meant that many of these widows were in no position to decide for themselves; there are countless recorded incidents of the burning of child widows of ten, nine, eight and younger.

European moral outrage at this custom, however, sits uneasily with Europe's own record of female disposal—this eyewitness account was made in 1798, only a decade or two after the last European "witch" was burned alive. Witches, like *sati* women, were unwanted, anomalous, often widows, or in some way threatening outsiders to the patriarchal rule of order. For as the historical record shows, *in no country at no period of time, were women safe from the supreme sexual violence, the insistence that their bodies existed only in relation to man, for his pleasure and progeny.* Once beyond that framework of justification for their existence, whatever the reason, they were at best surplus to establishment, at worst lepers, pariahs, criminals too—and either way, the fathers of church and society knew how to handle them.

"Look well then unto the sins of the daughters . . ." Perhaps the ultimate example of the disposable woman is the one who is, in every sense of the word, fair game for men—the prostitute. Called into being by man's lust, then punished for pandering to it, the prostitute expressed through her body the eternal sexual tension between pleasure and danger, while her trade was the battleground where male desire and contempt for women met head on. First one won, then the other, in an unchanging pattern of use and abuse from the earliest days. Even the briefest historical survey, however, shows the situation of prostitutes worsening during the 1000 years that separated the rise of the father gods from the birth of the modern state; paradoxically, as wives, mothers and "virtuous" women became more restricted, more subject to oppressive controls, and more heavily punished for any deviance, so too did their illicit sisters, the daughters of the game.

This is abundantly clear from the general increase in the severity of the penalties for "harlots and whores" over the centuries that elsewhere saw the emergence from barbarism, and the mitigation of the worst of the judicial inflictions for other crimes. One of the earliest-known of sexual laws, that of the Visigoths around 450, provided that whores should be publicly scourged, and their noses slit as a mark of their shame.[34] By the twelfth century in England, a whore was defined by the statutes of King Henry II as a creature so vile and unwomanly, that in addition to the penalties above, she was forbidden to have a lover on pain of a fine, three weeks in prison, once on the cucking-stool, and banishment from the city. Two hundred years later, in the reign of King Edward III, like the *niddah* of Jewry, the prostitute had to wear a special badge or hood, "to set a deformed mark on foulness, to make it appear more odious." Finally, as puritanism tightened its grip throughout Europe, the women's punishments reached an unprecedented peak of sadism and savagery, and the public executioner was stretched to the fullest extent of his repertoire, as this record shows:

> Mary Kürssnerin, a young prostitute . . . Mary's ears were cut off, and she was hanged.
> Anna Peyelstainin of Nuremberg, because she had intercourse with a father and son . . . and similarly with 21 men and youths, her husband conniving, was beheaded here with the sword, standing.
> Ursala Grimin, landlady . . . a prostitute, bawd and procuress . . . was stood in the pillory, flogged as far as the stocks, there branded on both cheeks, and afterwards whipped out of town.
> Magdalen Fisherin . . . an unmarried servant . . . had a child by father and son . . . beheaded with the sword here as a favor.[35]

The "favor" referred to here in his private diary by Franz Schmidt, the public executioner of Nuremberg from 1573 to 1617, was the substitution of the relatively milder death by decapitation for the horror of slow strangulation at the end of a rope. Doubtless the victim or some belated benefactor would have paid handsomely for this "favor," but at the end, with a baying mob of respectable citizens come to make a holiday of her doom, it was all the mercy she would get. This poor young woman, of whom nothing is known except her name and her "offence," stands for all the magdalens of the world who, finding themselves outside the prescribed role of wife and motherhood, were cast away—in the classic formula of pornography, dying for sex.

Under these harsh laws, men suffered too. Their own sexuality was inevitably tainted by association with that of the female "animal." To play by their own rules meant denying themselves any possibility of sex for fun; while as wives, mothers, daughters, lovers, women commandeered the affections of men constantly under standing orders to hate, fear and subordinate them. Other men paid in other ways for failing to live up to the rules. The witch-hunting of homosexuals has been documented elsewhere. But the severe punishment of males who transgressed the restriction of sex to heterosexual coupling links them with women who similarly defied patriarchal definitions. When a woman was to be burned as a witch at the height of that terror in Europe, men accused of homosexuality were bound and mixed with the faggots of brushwood and kindling round her feet, "to kindle a flame foul enough for a witch to burn in."[36] A male, however, did not have to finish up as a faggot; women had almost no chance of escaping the odium that attached to her whole sex, and with it the underlying rage to degrade and destroy.

For there is no mistaking the sexual and sadistic nature of these punishments imposed on women. The infamous Judge Jeffreys, a pillar of the state in seventeenth-century England, summed it up, when sentencing a prostitute to be whipped: "Hangman, I charge you to pay particular attention to this lady. Scourge her soundly, man—scourge her till the blood runs down. It is Christmas, a cold time for madam to strip. See that you warm her shoulders thoroughly."[37]

Sex, sin, suffering—the prominence of these themes in the story of prostitution is to be found in the lives of their married sisters, too. For whores and wives were not, as patriarchal propaganda had it, "devils and angels," opposing species, but two sides of the same coin. As women, both groups were subjected to the same punitively narrow definition of their sexuality and the same restrictions of the deployment of it. Despite a relentless ideological and physical battery, some women chose the preferred mode of winning respectability through submission, others most decisively did not. How did women find the strength and knowledge to resist their own downgrading, to discover their power to make their own definitions and by so doing transcend those of men?

6

A LITTLE LEARNING

By God, if women had written stories
As clerks have written their oratories,
They would have written of men more wickedness,
Than all the race of Adam may redress.
CHAUCER, The Wife of Bath's Tale

Women should not learn to read and write unless
they are going to be nuns, as much harm as come
from such knowledge.
PHILIPPE OF NAVARRE

Gather what little drops of learning you can, and
consider them a great treasure.
CHRISTINE DE PISAN

For countless generations of women, the tyranny of the father gods and gynophobes had seemed absolute, unassailable. But as the first thousand years of Christianity drew to a close, the impetus for change emerged where it was least expected, within the steel heart of the systems themselves. They were too harsh, too inflexible, and over the years, the men and women of these societies slowly declined to live by them. The barrage of bans forbidding intercourse, for instance, undoubtedly hoisted the patriarchal lawgivers with their own petard, punishing men as well as women. In the early Middle Ages, Christians were prohibited from sex on Sundays, Wednesdays, Fridays, Ember days, during Lent and Advent, or before communion. Sex was also forbidden when a woman was menstruating, pregnant or lactating, a severe restriction considering the frequency of pregnancy, for of course contraception was also forbidden. On the occasional free Tuesday, a couple had to observe the regulations governing the approved positions: "missionary" was in, "after the dog's fashion" definitely out. Even in the heyday of the Church's anti-sex hysteria, it is hard to believe that there were no backsliders, of both sexes.

For as long as women and men loved and desired one another, attacks on female sexuality could never have been totally successful.

Not all women consented to be made victims of their own biology; many showed a baffling inability to learn the lesson of their secondary status. This spirited rebuke to the early Christian fathers came from within the Church itself, in the teaching of the sixteenth-century leader of the Counter-Reformation, St. Teresa of Avila:

> When thou wert in the world, Lord, thou didst not despise women, but didst find more faith and no less love in them than in men . . . it is not right to repel minds which are virtuous and brave, even though they be the minds of women.[1]

But as this shows, to mount a successful challenge to the denigration of women, and to assert the value of their minds, meant meeting male authority on its own ground. Women had to gain entry to the processes of definition and the making of meaning. They too had to be able to read, study and debate. Ignorant, they were inferior; learned, they were armed. So learning became the next battleground as it assumed the crucial centrality it holds to this day, when without it there is no hope for women of penetrating men's space—mental space.

Of course women had always had their own kind of space. This most commonly derived from territory carved out as female through the rites and traditions shared with other women. From the range of historical records of the early modern period, there is abundant evidence of the existence of secret societies of women practicing rituals of a fertility or sexual nature in many parts of Eastern Europe, and particularly Africa. Often these spilled over into public demonstrations. In medieval Ukraine, for instance, village women at weddings united to overthrow all normal canons of modest wifely behavior: in a ceremony of female flashing known as "burning the bride's hair" they would hold their skirts waist high and jump over a roaring fire. Men who intruded on these activities did so at their own risk. In Schleswig at the same period any man who met the women of his village in their ceremonial procession to celebrate the birth of a child would have his hat filled with horse dung and rammed back on his head; while in the Trobriand Islands women had the right to attack a man who ventured onto their fields while they were working..[2]

All these customs, and there are many more worldwide, express a common theme of aggression against men, often coupled with erotic or obscene activities. Yet they were condoned by individual husbands and sanctioned by the society at large. It is hard to find any culture, in fact, where women *as a group* did not enjoy some form of the space or freedom that was denied to them as individuals. Throughout their history, Australian Aboriginal males have been notoriously harsh to

their womenfolk, sticking spears through their upper arms as a punishment, slicing off lumps of flesh from their buttocks, or cracking
their skulls. Yet alongside the often savage oppressions coexisted something not known elsewhere in the world, the *jilimi*, or "single women's
camp."

> Here live widows who have chosen not to remarry, estranged wives of violent
> husbands, women who are ill or visiting from another country, and all their de-
> pendent children. In fact any woman who wants to live free of the conflicts of
> heterosexual society may seek refuge in the *jilimi*. Married women living with their
> husbands congregate in the *jilimi* in the day to talk and plan visits, family affairs
> and ritual matters. The *jilimi* is taboo to all men, who must often travel long
> circuitous routes to avoid passing nearby . . .[3]

In other forms of resistance to men's control, women were known to
mount a flagrant challenge to their husbands, as in this custom of the
San bush people of South Africa:

> Only women played flutes. They would leave the camp when the spirit moved them
> to challenge another group in a fluting competition . . . for three or four days they
> gave themselves over to fluting, dancing, sex with their male hosts, and feasting
> till all the food was consumed. Then they walked back fluting to their camp . . .
> no man dared follow them . . .[4]

European and Asian women of the Middle Ages showed a lively interest
in what they knew of their African counterparts, generally sympa-
thizing with them for their "primitive" and "barbaric" condition. Yet
in many ways African women like these were more fortunate than
their sisters in the more "advanced" part of the globe. Ibn Batuta, a
prudish Islamic merchant visiting Mali in the fourteenth century, was
horrified to see the bare breasts of the unmarried women as they met
freely in the marketplace, and the unregulated sociability of the wives.[5]

This was the golden age of Mali under the greatest of its emperors,
Mansa Musa. But throughout Africa the ancient tribal patterns, closer
to nature and to their own origins, respected women's rights and lent
them freedoms that in the rest of the world had vanished into mythology. Nowhere in Africa south of the Sahara were women veiled,
nowhere physically restrained or secluded. The slow pace of change
and the continuance of age-old traditions often favored them—one
major all-female ceremonial, the celebration of the "Feast of Salt,"
which lasted until the colonial invasions, was first recorded by Herodotus in the fifth century.

From their highly valued work as the managers of the all-important salt harvest, as well as their centrality in cultivating, marketing and trading, African women derived an enhanced status. Uduk males, for instance, had no truck with dowries or bride-sales, saying they would not sell their sister for a goat or two as if she were a goat herself. Ashanti customs gave women primacy over men on the grounds that the highest debt was owed to the mother, since she had formed each human body from her own body and blood. For the African delight at the birth of a daughter, for the African woman's freedom to come and go as she pleased, to meet her friends in the marketplace for the cheery gossip so frowned on by Ibn Batuta, and to play a leading role in the life of her family and group, the European or Asian woman denied all of these might well have questioned which of these societies was the more primitive.

Aristocratic women, especially in Europe, had more freedom, and some used it to the full. In the reign of Henry III of England (1207–72), Isabella Countess of Arundel shouted down the king in an angry challenge to his authority over the bride-sale of one of the royal wards, and then swept out without waiting or even asking for the customary leave to depart. Another Isabella, of Angoulême, widow of King John, and hence Henry's stepmother, wrote from France to her "dearest son" the king that she had "improved upon" his arrangements for the dynastic marriage of her ten-year-old daughter by marrying the man herself. King Henry was no match for forceful women, even those who according to the rules owed him unquestioning obedience. His sister Eleanor had been married at nine to the King's Earl Marshal in an important dynastic union. Widowed at sixteen, she deliberately compromised herself with the man she loved in order to forestall another unwelcome marriage by forcing the king to agree to this one. Despite threats and fulminations against her "defiler," the king had to repair the royal honor, and himself gave her away at the wedding ceremony in 1238.

Not all women, though, had the clout bestowed by high social class. And with the emergence from the Dark Ages, the concept of power itself was changing from the older power games of bash and grab. Now knowledge became the high road to control, and for women the pen had one major advantage over the sword; it fitted neatly into a female fist of any size, age, creed or country in the world. Following the imposition of monotheism, the principal escape for women into the wider world of learning lay paradoxically behind the locked doors of an enclosed community. Most familiar to us now are the well-documented nunneries of Western Europe, but it is noteworthy that

Buddhism, Hinduism and Islam all had their own religious sisterhoods in early modern times. One famous female Sufi mystic and religious teacher was Rabi-'ah al-'Adawiyyah (712–801), who after a girlhood in slavery fled to the desert, where she rejected all offers of marriage and devoted herself to prayer and scholarship. Although the most distinguished of women Sufis, Rabi'ah was not unique, since Sufism gave all women the chance to attain a holy dignity equal to that of a man.[6]

Rabi'ah's achievement built on a tradition of female literacy, scholarship and intellectual creativity reaching back to the dawn of thought. Countless ancient myths ascribe the birth of language to women or goddesses, in a ritual formulation of the primeval truth that the first words any human being hears are the mother's. In Indian mythology the Vedic goddess Vac means "language," she personifies the birth of speech, and is represented as a maternal mouth-cavity open to give birth to the living word. The Hindu prayer to Devaki, mother of Krishna, begins, "Goddess of the Logos, Mother of the Gods, One with Creation, thou art Intelligence, the Mother of Science, the Mother of Courage . . ." In other myths women invent not merely language, but the forms to write it down, as Elise Boulding explains: "Carmenta created a Latin language from the Greek, Medusa gave the alphabet to Hercules, Queen Isis to the Egyptians [while] the priestess-goddess Kali invented the Sanskrit alphabet."[7]

In many cultures, the early learned women and their work were much admired; Egypt had a caste of scribe-priestesses under Seshat, goddess of the alphabet and "mistress of the house of books," while the Indian Veda contains a prayer for a scholarly daughter. Ancient Vedic texts, indeed, contain many admiring references to female scholars, poets and seers, and these learned women were permitted to display their knowledge and skills of disquisition in public on occasions.[8] Later, in Greece, the genius of certain women scholars and philosophers was freely acknowledged by their contemporaries, though not at all by history; Pythagoras, for instance, whom every schoolboy knows, was taught by one woman (Aristoclea), married to another, Theano, a leading mathematician and teacher of philosophy when he met her, and influenced by a third, his daughter Dano, who also concerned herself with the question of women's education. A further woman in this circle, Diotima, also taught Socrates, whose principal teacher and that of Plato was the peerless Aspatia of Miletos, dubbed "the first lady of Athens." Like Dano she championed the education of women, and fearlessly used her position as a non-Greek to flout legislation restricting women to their houses, visiting other women in their homes and educating them herself.

As this shows, the severest restriction could not ultimately prevent private study, and may well have even encouraged it. A classic example of the way patriarchal rules could sometimes work to the advantage of women, not against them, is provided by the fine tradition of Japanese women's writing. At the Emperor's court only men were permitted to use the scholarly language of Chinese: women were restricted to their own Japanese vernacular, on pain of mockery, disgrace or punishment. The "beautiful irony" of this has not escaped later commentators. "Dozens of women wrote brilliant literature that is still read today, while the men, whose 'superior' Chinese produced a stilted and unnatural literature, are read only for historical information."[9] For it was in her own tongue that Lady Murasaki wrote the world's first novel and still one of its greatest, *The Tale of Genji*, at the beginning of the eleventh century, a golden age of female creativity in Japan, when education for women was a requirement, not a stigma.

Yet as the story of Lady Murasaki shows (she only became a writer after her husband died and her father placed her at court with orders to amuse the emperor), there were deep contradictions within the demands made on women in the interests of men, that could be turned to women's advantage. With the gruesome parodies of both the marriage and funerary rituals (the novices were initiated wearing wedding finery, as "brides of Christ" and were given the last rites, as dying to the world) the convents of Europe have been seen as naked manifestations of patriarchal tyranny. But for some women, they provided the only sanctioned avenue of *escape* from the tyranny of enforced marriage and its inescapable infliction of motherhood. As to dying, the virgin recluse living a life of quiet contemplation and scholarship had every chance of living for two, three or four times longer than her married sister; convent records show that nuns very often survived to the age of 80, 90, even 100, while the reality of contemporary childbirth is clearly indicated in the words of Psalm 116, directed for the use of women in labor: "The snares of death compassed me round: and the pains of hell gat hold on me. . . . O Lord I beseech thee, deliver my soul . . ."

Within a convent, however, a woman could preserve both her soul and her body, and it is a striking illustration of women's power to convert a disability into a source of strength that so many of them used their conventual retreat as a platform from which they could, in Mary Ritter Beard's words, "spring into freedom." The origin and base of the convent life may have been the harsh patriarchal disgust with women's bodies which dictated that they had best be covered, denied, shut away, and as such it is close to kindred restrictive practices in Islam like veiling and seclusion. But as a logical consequence, the women who rose above their filthy bodies with the transcendent act of "virgin sacrifice" won high esteem from contemporary males who naturally assumed that forswearing heterosexual activity was the greatest sacrifice in the world. By firmly demonstrating that sex was not on their agenda, religious women sloughed off the odium attaching to sexually active women, and gained an almost mystical power from their inviolate status—a card that was still being played with confidence and success by Elizabeth I centuries later.

In refusing marriage, nuns were also rejecting its associated roles of mother and housekeeper. This "sacrifice" has to be assessed in the light of one thirteenth-century vignette of the wife who "hears when she comes in her baby screaming, sees the cat at the flitch and the hound at the hide, her cake burning on the stone hearth and her calf suckling all the milk, the crock running into the fire and the churl [man of the house] chiding."[10] Freed from such cares, women were free to concentrate upon themselves, if only after a lifetime of the traditional work of concentrating on others (many married women retired to convents after rearing their families, in the early modern equivalent of mutual-consent divorce). Having taken the only permitted way out of marriage to be found this side of the grave, the sisters were thereby positioned in a sanctioned independence and poised to achieve not simply in the solitude of the study but in the world at large.

For running counter to the notion of the enclosed life of the religious was the importance of each "house of women" in its community. This conferred on the women who ran it a license to move in the public arena, to take charge, to initiate change. From the Brigid of the fifth century who founded the first women's community in Ireland, to her Swedish namesake who established a new order "the Brigetines" in 1370, there is an unbroken line of women of extraordinary drive and organizational ability, who used to the full the privilege of their position of being outside the control of any man. Some shrewd tacticians indeed sought the power base that only religion could provide, like Radegund, queen of the Franks, who, having founded the abbey of the Holy Cross at Poitiers in the sixth century, then bullied the archbishop to make her a deacon of the church on the strength of it.

As this shows, the leadership of a women's community gave access to a considerable degree of political power; the medieval abbess of Kildare in Ireland, it was gratefully recorded, "turned back the streams of war" by her skillful negotiation between warring kingdoms,[11] and Catherine of Siena was personally responsible for the return of the Papacy to Rome in 1375. Nuns were also, in the words of Mary Ritter Beard, more than political figures:

> [They] were remarkable businesswomen. They were outstanding doctors and surgeons. They were great educators. They were feudal lords operating self-sustaining estates, and directing the manifold activities involved in producing goods, settling controversies as lawyers and judges settle them today, governing and participating in all the arts of social living.[12]

Inevitably not all the nunneries and their inhabitants were as able, industrious and worthy as this wholesome evocation of feminine competence might suggest. The picture of European convent life during its thousand-year history is a complex one, and not without its dark and desperate moments. These lubricious and perfervid instructions from St. Jerome to a young novice give some idea of the fetid atmosphere of imperfectly sublimated sensuality endemic to the life: "Ever let the Bridegroom sport with you within your chamber. . . . When sleep overtakes you He will come behind and put His hand through the hole of the door . . . and you will rise up and say, 'I am sick of love'."[13] The consequence of such overstimulation may be seen in one of the better-documented of the sexual scandals that have always surrounded communities of women, the harrowing story of Sister Benedetta Carlini. This Renaissance abbess, convicted at 33 of forcing lesbian acts on one of the younger sisters through her impersonation of a male angel, "Splenditello," spent the last 40 years of her life in solitary confinement in a prison cell within the abbey, fed only on bread and water "several times a week," and only allowed out to hear Mass or to be whipped.[14]

The Carlini story is a necessary reminder that the much-prized serenity of the "bride of Christ" was not easily achieved; within the enclosed life, passions could build to murderous fury. After Radegund's death, one of her nuns was so enraged at not being elected abbess that she mounted an armed attack during which the new abbess was captured and some of her followers killed. The abbess had to be rescued by a force of men-at-arms dispatched by the local seigneur, after which the aggressor-nun continued to harry her supplanter with false changes of adultery, sorcery and murder until finally banished on pain of death.[15]

Yet despite such events, and the tabloid-style sensationalization of their activities by later Protestant propagandists, the communities of women were always more significant for their intellectual rather than their sexual activity. Not all were equally distinguished. But there was none which ever neglected the basis of private scholarship, so much so that, along with the male religious houses, they were often the sole glimmers of light in the wastes of the Dark Ages when the lamps of learning were going out all over Europe. The knowledge they kept alive included the elements of all known arts and sciences. The study of languages frequently rose to a high level: in the tragic aftermath of their doomed love Abelard poignantly congratulated the nuns of the convent of the Paraclete on gaining in Héloïse a sister who was familiar "not only with Latin, but also with Greek and Hebrew literature . . . the only woman now living who has attained that knowledge of the three languages which is extolled above all things by St. Jerome as a matchless grace."[16]

Exceptional though she was, "la Belle Heloise" was by no means the only woman to excel in her chosen field. Another twelfth-century abbess, Herrade of Landsburg, left 324 parchment sheets of unrivalled miniatures, while the amazing Hrotsvitha of Gandersheim two centuries earlier, during a quiet life of prolific endeavor made history as Germany's first poet, its first woman writer, and the first known European dramatist. Even more staggering was the achievement of Hildegard of Bingen—walled up in a convent cell with the last rites at the age of seven in 1105, Hildegard survived to become abbess, founder of a number of other religious houses, and political adviser to Henri II, Frederick Barbarossa and the Pope. A mystic and visionary, in her private work she distinguished herself in medicine, natural history, mineralogy, cosmology and theology. A gifted musician, she wrote hymns and the first European opera; her musical legacy alone consisted of seventy-four pieces. As a writer she produced poems, biography and mystery plays, and was still hard at work when she died in her eighties.

The achievement of women like Hildegard, however, did little to improve the intellectual prospects of the rest of their sex. For the cripplingly low opinion of women's intelligence entertained by even the dullest male of every culture showed little sign of abating with the passage of time. On the contrary, as the widespread sexual terror of women began to abate, it fed and fostered another damaging myth, that women's *brains* were as weak as their bodies were believed to be. This was no new idea, since it is the complement and logical corollary of the belief that women were created only as bodily vessels—an incubator is not equipped with any powers of thought.

This bilious notion of women's innate mental inferiority crops up in the patriarchs' earliest recorded pronouncements on the subject, like these ramblings of the dying Buddha to his faithful disciple:

> How are we to conduct ourselves, Lord, with regard to women?
> Women are full of passion, Ananda; women are envious, Ananda; women are stupid, Ananda. That is the reason, Ananda, that is the cause, why women have no place in public assemblies, do not carry on business, and do not earn their living by any profession.[17]

A prejudice of this antiquity is not lightly overthrown. By the birth of the early modern period, it had found new life in a flurry of fresh reasons and observations: women had "but little brains," their brains were "gruel" not "meat" like men's, education dried up their innards and thinking drove them mad. Some of this, in an uncomfortable foreshadowing of science's later attitude to the female, had its origins in the historical rebirth of interest in medicine, chemistry, surgery— women had wandering wombs, smaller skull capacity, weaker composition of "the elements." It was also generally supported by daily experience of women whose highest knowledge was hard or trivial labor (working the land or the embroidery frame depending on their culture and class), gossip and old wives' tales, and whose heads were literally empty of anything that could provide grist to the mills of the mind. The English lawyer who in the later sixteenth century wrote that "every *feme covert* [married woman] is a sort of infant"[18] was consequently speaking no more than the truth.

As this suggests, marriage itself was in general the enemy of any woman's intellectual development. It is no accident that the brilliant Hildegard had escaped from the iron maiden of enforced wedlock. The convent movement as a whole, especially in its early days, had provided one bright thread in the history of women's long imprisonment within systems that first denied them learning, then dismissed them as irredeemably ignorant. For denied they were, kept in ignorance of anything that might challenge the power of God the Father and man the husband, whose neatly dovetailing exactions were eloquently rendered by John Milton's Eve in her submission to Adam:

> My author and disposer, what thou bidst
> Unargued I obey; so God ordains;
> God is thy law; thou mine; to know no more

Is Woman's happiest knowledge, and her praise[19]

Once locked into this structure, and as daughters of Eve located at the bottom of it, the majority of women had no access to education of any kind. Not for them were the classic avenues of advancement open to men, rising through the ranks of the clergy from the priest's school for "ragged boys," or being taken up by the local landowner to train as a secretary or "factor." Nor is there, to this day, any general recognition of women's educational deprivation and suffering—no accounts of "Shakespeare's sister" or Jade the Obscure. Yet the women of these times paid heavily for their lack of learning. Their ignorance did not merely serve to confirm their inferiority; it put them at risk of harassment, torture and vile death. For in a fatal historical conjunction, fears of women's filthy, inexplicable bodies, of their weak, suggestible minds, and of the brute evil of their intractable stupidity combined to provoke one of the worst outbreaks of gynocide ever known, the witch hunts of Europe and early America.

From the very earliest stirrings of the first witches in the black lagoon of unconscious male fears, there was general unanimity that witches were female: a ninth-century decree of the Catholic Church identified "certain wicked women" who "reverting to Satan, and seduced by the illusions and phantasms of demons, believe and profess that they ride at night with Diana on certain beasts, with an innumerable multitude of women, passing over immense distances."[20] The reason why witches were women, and women became witches, was obvious to any thinking man:

> . . . this is not due to the frailty of the sex, for most of them are intractably obstinate.
> . . . Plato placed women between man and the brute beast. For one sees that the women's visceral parts are bigger than those of men, whose cupidity is less violent. Men on the other hand have larger heads and therefore have more brains and sense than women.[21]

There was no answer to that. Other *soi-disant* experts scrambled to support this pronouncement of the French jurist Jean Bodin, one of Europe's leading intellectuals and largest brains; women were "monthly filled full of superfluous humours" and "melancholic blood"[22]—note that resurfacing of the theme of women's "evil courses" and dangerous blood in a new and damning context. But the real issue was one of brain, not body as Europe's leading witch-finders, the German Dominican inquisitors, explained in their highly influential catalogue of sadism and perversion, the witch-finders' handbook *Malleus Malefi-*

carum "Women are more credulous . . . women are naturally more impressionable . . . through the first defect in their intelligence they are more likely to abjure the faith . . . for men, being by nature intellectually stronger than women, are more apt to abhor such practices."[23]

The man who believed that would believe anything. And the irony of using this as a basis for the final solution to the witch problem is that, whatever witches were, they were not all dull-witted or ignorant. The old images of the witch as a demented hag or malignant old bat have been undermined by more recent discoveries that they were very often self-possessed, highly purposive, and above all young. Hysterical or paranoid personalities maybe; yet the women punished for "the darkness of their ignorance" had in fact an extensive repertoire of their own form of knowledge, incorporating elements of religion, chemistry, alchemy, botany, astrology, natural science and pharmacology. Their knowledge of herbs and poisons, for instance, would be likely to exceed that of even the most highly qualified male medical practitioner.

For witchery was a craft, an ancient discipline. As such it had to be studied, and in the days before general literacy, or freely available writing materials, committed to memory. Some women undoubtedly became highly proficient in manipulating people and potions, procuring an abortion here, taking credit for a conception there, and the greater the degree of their skill, the greater would be the satisfaction of their customers and consequently, as with all successful rule-breakers, the less likely they would have been to get caught. In fact, to reverse the traditional historical formula, the truth seems to have been not that witches were ignorant, but that ignorant women were more in danger of being taken for witches. One prime candidate would have been the wretched female castaway who appeared one day at the door of Elizabeth Walker, a minister's wife and a noted philanthropist— she was "almost eat up with scabs and vermin, with scarce rags to cover her, and as ignorant of God and Christ as if she had been born and bred in Lapland or Japan."[24] To the witch-finder, that in itself would have been the mark of the beast. Elizabeth took her in, cured her of "the Itch," taught her to read, and finally found her a good home with a rich farmer.

But Elizabeth, though devout, was an open-minded woman—significantly, she also believed that "Blacks and Tawnys as well as Whites were descendants of the first Adam." Sadly, these centuries had too many women at risk, and too few Elizabeths; the indictment of 21-

year-old Ellinor Shaw, hanged for witchcraft in Northampton as late as 1705, explicitly states that her parents were "not willing, or at least not able to give their Daughter any manner of Education," so that she had been "left to shift for herself from the age of fourteen years."[25]

The persecution of the witch-hunts, arguably the first sustained use of terror as a political weapon, has been seen as the last convulsive throes of the dying Middle Ages, the final revenge of its grim, archaic form of patriarchy on anomalous or nonconformist women. Certainly the early design for the subjection of women to God and man, however pure in outline, was all too often less than perfect in execution, and the frenzy of the witch-burnings strongly suggests the convulsions of societies racked by an inexplicable dread of the aberrant female, together with a desperation to reassert the rightness and normality of patriarchal rule.

Can it be only historical accident that the witch-finders' campaign of gynocide coincided with the centuries which saw an astonishing upsurge of women's political power worldwide, as the following table makes clear?

962	Adelaide became queen of Italy and Holy Roman Empress
1010	The Saxon princess Aelgifu born, who, as mistress of Cnut of Denmark, regent of Norway, and mother of King Harold 'Harefoot' of England, ruled in three countries
1028	Zoe became empress of the Byzantine Empire in her own right
	Asma, the ruling queen of the Yemen, succeeded by Queen Arwa, her daughter-in-law, bypassing the Sultan, Al-Mukarram, with his consent.
1105	Melisande born from Melisande's girlhood to the death of Agnes in 1185 these two ruled as crusader queens of
1136	Agnes of Courtenay born Jerusalem governing its development for virtually the whole century
1226	Blanche of Castile, queen of France, became regent for her son, St. Louis, and dominated European politics for the next quarter of a century
1454	Caterina Corner born, later to rule as queen of Cyprus
1461	Anne of Beaujeu born, princess of France, later queen of the Bourbons and de facto ruler of France for her weak brother Charles VIII
1477	Anne of Brittany born, ruler of her own territories from the age of eleven, and later, through her marriage to two ineffectual kings, of France as well
1530	Grainne Mhaol (Grace O'Malley) born, Irish princess, war-leader and naval commander in the struggle against the English invasion
1560	Amina, Nigerian queen and war-leader born; as her father's heir she became a warrior, refused all husbands, and enormously extended her country by conquest

1571   The Persian Nur-Jahan born, later Mogul empress of India, ruling alone for her opium-addicted husband

1582   Nzinga born, ruling queen of Angola, Endongo and Matamba for over half a century of successful resistance to Portuguese invasion

All these were ruling women, not consorts. None of them was the only female monarch her country knew in the first half of the second millennium, for most of them came from countries where the tradition of women rulers was well established, indeed growing in political importance. Aelgifu, for instance, followed in a long line of Saxon queens like Bertha (d.616), Eadburgh and Cynethryth (fl. eighth century) and the pivotally significant Aethelflaed:

Daughter of King Alfred . . . the "Lady of the Mercians" as Aethelflaed was called, rebuilt the fortifications of Chester, [built] new fortified towns of which Warwick and Stafford were the most important, fought in Wales, led her own troops to the capture of Derby, and received the peaceful submission of Leicester. Before her death in June 918, even the people of York had promised to accept her governance.[26]

By uniting England and ruling it in her own right, Aethelflaed became one of the few English women who have permanently affected the course of history. Similarly the Empress Zoe of the Byzantines succeeded in a long line of women who showed no signs of believing themselves rightly subject to men. Her predecessor Irene had seized power in 780, retaining it by blinding and imprisoning her own son. The tenacity and longevity of these women was quite extraordinary— Queen Adelaide outlived five kings of Italy, two of them her husbands. It is not difficult to see how the continuity that such a woman provided could be a political advantage, indeed a necessity enabling her to tighten an already formidable grip.

Clearly the female monarchs won some advantages for women as a whole during the so-called "Age of Queens." Insistence on women's inferiority, or on doctrinal warrant for women's subjection to men, was inevitably undermined by the sight of women on all sides whom God had patently called to the highest earthly office. Their success as rulers, too, would have to be construed as further evidence of divine favor. As a final lesson, the ruling queens taught women and men that no patriarchal systems were monolithic and absolute, but contained cracks and openings through which a confident woman could move to master a decisive moment of personal or national history.

These women were always the exceptional few, each one an example but hardly a viable model to her less privileged sisters. But in the wider world, events had set in train a slow series of changes whose effect was to ensure that a woman did not have to be a queen to begin to enjoy status in the eyes of men. The cult of courtly love in early modern Europe had begun as a reaction against the patriarchal denigration of the second sex. In defiance of a hostile Church, it elevated women, affirmed the value of romantic, not religious, passion and glorified sexual relations in which women, not men had the upper hand:

> I should like to hold my knight
> Naked in my arms at eve,
> That he might be in ecstasy
> As I cushioned his head against my breast . . .
>
> Fair friend, charming and good,
> When shall I hold you in my power,
> And lie beside you for an hour,
> And amorous kisses give to you?
>
> Know that I would give almost anything
> To have you in my husband's place;
> But only if you swear
> To do everything I desire.[27]

Clearly women like Beatriz de Diaz, the twelfth-century Provençal lady who wrote this song of love and lust to her troubadour lover, declined to accept any definition of their bodies as disgusting, or any interference in their right to think for themselves. In a direct attack on the notion of women's worthless physicality, the queens of courtly love like Eleanor of Aquitaine succeeded in establishing women's higher value through their spiritual qualities of constancy and devotion. The fact that this was a real challenge to the power of men and not simply a courtly game is attested by the number of real-life incidents in which a husband, driven by rage against his wife's "court," and with no evidence of adultery or misconduct, killed her troubadour.[28] Safer under the circumstances were the "queens of love" who relied for their music and poetry on one of the numerous women troubadours known to have plied their trade throughout Europe, or on poets like Marie de France whose lyric and narrative genius influenced the whole course of European literature.

With the advent of the Renaissance, attitudes towards women softened yet further, the tenor of the new approaches quite at variance with the strident hysterical abuse of the old. For the first time in history a proto-feminist, Heinrich Cornelius Agrippa von Nettesheim, was prepared to argue against the doctrinal *diktat* of male supremacy;

his book, provocatively titled *Of the Nobility and Superiority of the Female Sex* (1505), roundly challenged the authority of the Bible on the inferiority of women:

> Adam means Earth; Eve stands for Life; ergo, Adam is the product of nature, and Eve the creation of God. Adam was admitted to the Paradise for the sole purpose that Eve might be created . . .[29]

Von Nettesheim was not preaching to deaf ears. Other men of influence were raising their voices in defense of woman and her right to share in the new bounty of humanist learning and thought. The Italian nobleman Castiglione, diplomat, cosmopolitan, and author of that bible of the age, *The Courtier,* summed up the new *zeitgeist* in one sentence: "The virtues of the mind are as necessary to a woman as to a man."[30]

As literacy spread like bushfire in comparison with the speed of its growth in previous centuries, numbers of women for the first time grasped the pen and with it its power to define. Small wonder, then, that there were many old scores to settle. As in these extracts from the leading women writers of sixteenth-century France, a principal grievance was the custom of enforced marriage, indeed husbands themselves:

> The old man kissed her, and it is as though a slug has dragged itself across her charming face . . .

> . . . He resembled not so much a man as some sort of monster, for he had a huge heavy head [and] a very short fat neck perched atop miserably hunched shoulders . . . from his belly there issued a fetid breath, through a putrid, black, sunken mouth . . .

> The moment they come home they bar the door [and] eat most untidily . . . in bed they wear great nightcaps two fingers thick, a nightshirt held together with rusty pins down past their navels, heavy wool stockings that come halfway up their thighs, and as they rest their heads on a warmed pillow that smells of melted grease, their sleep is accompanied by coughs and emissions of excrement that fill the bedcovers . . .[31]

The final vignette, for all its racy colloquialism, was written by a woman more famous for her lyric gift, the brilliant Louise Labé, poet, linguist, musician, horsewoman, and leader of the "Lyons School" of writers where she reigned supreme as France's greatest lyric poet of the age. As this shows, within an extraordinarily short time of obtaining access to the world of letters, women were displaying an often dazzling versatility and intellectual power. Foremost among these pioneer feminist intellectuals was Christine de Pisan, the fifteenth-century Italian scholar equally distinguished in history, philosophy, biography and poetry. Though lionized by kings and enormously successful in her own time, Christine never abandoned her loyalty to her sex, seeking to restore women's past achievements to the historical record and tirelessly defending women ancient and modern against the woman-haters who attacked her in person and the sex in general indiscriminately. Christine's most passionately held belief was in women's right to education, which she argued with the clarity that made her quoted and translated for generations to follow:

> If it were customary to send little girls to school and to teach them the same subjects as are taught to boys, they would learn just as fully and would understand the subtleties of all arts and sciences. Indeed, maybe they would understand them better, for just as women's bodies are softer than men's, so their understanding is more sharp. . . . There is nothing that teaches a reasonable creature so much as experience of many different things . . .[32]

Christine's cool lucidity was in marked contrast with the angry heat of her opponents. The intensity of the struggle in which she became embroiled indicates the deeper importance of the issue of learning for women. For this was no academic squabble; it was the redrawing of the battle lines. Where previously the division between the knowledgeable and the uninformed had been between rulers and ruled, it now reformulated along the sexual divide. With the emergence of the modern world, learning unfolded as the high road to freedom and the future. Study therefore took on a new, post-medieval significance—with the rebirth of learning it was seen less as a passive act of contemplation, more as the deployment of an intellectual tool-kit for dismantling the *deus ex machina* to see how it worked. The new humanists, flushed with the joy of self-discovery, could spend many a happy hour on the great question of "what a piece of work is man." They did not, however, view with the same unalloyed enthusiasm the prospect of a woman approaching them with her wrench in her hand.

For women still denied the right to public space, one obvious solution was to resort to private work—and for a sex so constantly berated for being stupid, it would have been only logical to look to education as the remedy. But this would be feminine logic, and as such held no power to persuade the masculine mind. Much genuine thought and effort, in contrast, went into confirming and maintaining the pristine condition of women's ignorance, which also had the beneficial side-effect of confirming the original diagnosis: "Books destroy women's brains, who have little enough of themselves."[33]

The Chinese, with the invention of writing, had created also the Mandarin class to administer it, rather than allow the powerful weapon of literacy to fall into unhallowed hands. In a hollow historical echo of this process, Western societies from the early centuries of the second millennium all found their own techniques for ensuring that the "new learning" did not penetrate the great underclass of the female sex. The Reformation therefore did not reform very much at all for the women: the Renaissance was no rebirth for those born already into the wrong bodies. The novel creed of hu*man*ism now reversed the original act of creation—where previously God had created man in his own image, now man was busy making a god of himself. This inevitably called for some refurbishment of woman to make her a fit companion for such a piece of work. Her task was not to fret after her own intellectual desires, but to study to become a perfect partner and consort. "Accomplishments" thus smoothly supersede any idea of personal achievements, and tailoring herself to the procrustean bed of marriage became a woman's highest imperative. What price learning for women in the face of all this?

The continuing conviction that women had no place, function, future nor hope outside marriage accounts for the strength of the resistance of education for women, even after the "glorious dawn" of the Renaissance. For a woman could have no use for it, in the role to which God and nature had called her—there were no economic advantages in educating women, since they could never earn a living by their brains, and there was every chance of direct economic *disadvantage*, since an educated woman could so easily price herself out of the marriage market. Even if she succeeded in securing a husband, her marriage could be poisoned from the start: the French historian Agrippa d'Aubigné was not the only sixteenth-century father to sympathize warmly with his daughters' desire to study with their brothers, while fearing the "bad effects" of this, "contempt for housekeeping . . . and for a husband less clever than oneself" and as a result, "discord."[34]

The risk of learning, then, was that it promoted a woman beyond her "place," and the most violent of the responses to educated women were clearly designed to return them to that black hole. The Italian classicist Nogarola, hailed as "the Divine Isotta" for her intellectual brilliance at 18, had only two years to enjoy her work before she was subject to a brutal reminder of her sexuality; in 1438 she and her sister

Ginevra, also a famous scholar, were falsely accused of promiscuity and incest. Broken, Nogarola abandoned her studies, fled Verona, and lived thereafter in total seclusion in her mother's house, devoting herself to sacred texts. Other women like Mira Bai, the Indian poet of the sixteenth century, were persecuted for challenging social and legal regulations by moving into the public world; some were forcibly returned to the private sphere, like Ninon de l'Enclos, locked up in a convent in seventeenth-century France because her study of Epicurean philosophy showed "a lack of religious respect." The English nun Mary Ward, who attempted to found an institute for the education of women (one of the very earliest proposals for a women's college), fared even worse at the hands of the Catholic Church—she was imprisoned in a tiny, windowless cell from which the rotting body of a dead sister had only just been removed, and almost died herself as a result.

Before her imprisonment Mary had been a great traveller in pursuit of her mission, and this in itself was problematic in an era that viewed unchaperoned women with much the same horror as masterless men. When women attempted to bring the fruits of their private study into the public arena as teachers or preachers, defying the scriptural ban against any such thing, the punishment could be savage:

Cambridge, December 1653. Complaint was forthwith made to William Pickering, then Mayor, that two women were preaching. . . . He asked their names and their husbands' names. They told him: they had no husband but Jesus Christ, and he sent them. Upon this the Major grew angry, called them whores, and issued his warrant to the Constable to whip them at the Market Cross till the blood ran down their bodies. . . . The executioner . . . stripped them naked to the waist, put their arms into the whipping post and executed the Mayor's warrant . . . so that their flesh was miserably cut and torn.[35]

All these were of course individual cases. But the cumulative effect of the denial of women's right to learn, to study, to share their knowledge, even to think, was serious. The decline of the nunneries coincided with the growth of grammar schools and universities, from both of which women were barred, and which from the first jealously guarded their monopoly on knowledge: in one celebrated case of 1322, a woman healer, Jacoba Felicie, was brought to trial by the Faculty of Medicine of the University of Paris for "illegal practice." Six people testified that she had succeeded where university-trained physicians had failed, and this ensured her conviction.

At the entry of the human race into the modern age, then, educational chances for women in the brave new world were strangled at birth. With the simultaneous demise of the convent movement, there remained no place of women's learning for studious young girls to join, no pool of older, educated women as teachers, and no escape route from men, children, diapers and domestic servitude. The new knowledge stirring was not for women. It is one of the ironies of the emergence from the Dark Ages and the world renaissance of learning that, while it freed women from some of the darker fears born of men's ignorance, it merely served to confirm others. Woman might no longer be stigmatized as a vagabond vulva or captious, capricious, capacious cunt; but she still came forth with all the dignity of one of the favorite freak shows of the Middle Ages, the acephalous monster exposed to public scorn at a fair. "Women do not grow worse by being educated," pleaded Christine de Pisan. But until this was generally recognized, all that women could do was to tend their husbands, houses and babies—and wait.

When one reads of a witch being ducked, or a woman possessed by devils, of a wise woman selling herbs, or even of a very remarkable man who had a mother, then I think we are on the track of a lost novelist, a suppressed poet, of some mute and inglorious Jane Austen, some Emily Brontë who dashed her brains out on the moor or mopped and mowed about the highways crazed with the torture her gift had put her to. Indeed I would venture that Anon, who wrote so many poems without signing them, was a woman.

                                                        VIRGINIA WOOLF

III
DOMINION AND DOMINATION

'O come and be my mate!' said the Eagle to the
Hen;
        'I love to soar, but then
        I want my mate to rest
        Forever in the nest!'
        Said the Hen, 'I cannot fly,
        I have no wish to try,
But I joy to see my mate, careering through the sky!'
They wed, and cried, 'Ah, this is Love, my own!'
    And the Hen sat, the Eagle soared, alone.
      CHARLOTTE PERKINS GILMAN, 'Wedded Bliss'

7

WOMAN'S WORK

Real solemn history I cannot be interested in . . .
the quarrels of popes and kings, with wars or pes-
tilences, in every page; the men all so good for
nothing and hardly any women at all.

JANE AUSTEN, *Northanger Abbey*

Women have worked, constantly, continuously, always and everywhere, in every type of society in
every part of the world since the beginning of human time.

HEATHER GORDON CREMONESI

An African woman, asked why her husband walked
unburdened while she carried the load, replied
'What would I do if we met a lion and he was
carrying the load?' We asked, how often does he
meet a lion? How often does she carry the load?
What does she do if she meets a lion—while carrying her load?

DIARY OF AN ENGLISH MISSIONARY

In 1431, convicted only of wearing men's clothes, Joan of Arc was
burned to death in France. In the next decade, the Chinese were
decisively thrust out of what then became the time bomb of Viet Nam
and African architects and masons began work on the great wall of
Zimbabwe. By the mid-century, the English had been driven out of
France, Gutenberg was presenting Europe with the first printed book
and international scholars were hastening to the pride of the Songhay
empire, the University of Timbuktu. But the Portuguese were already
casting eyes of greed and envy on African splendor, and elsewhere,
too, imperialist expansion was the order of the day; in South America
the Incas gobbled up lesser kingdoms to feed their hungry altars, while
the Ottoman Turks casually terminated the Byzantine empire with
the founding of their own, and Ivan III threw off the Mongol yoke
to make himself the first tsar of all the Russias.[1]

As the century turned, the world was registering Columbus's discovery of the New World; less than twenty years later, the first black slaves were en route to America. Other voyages of discovery (Vasco da Gama, Magellan) were echoed on land by explorations of the interior frontiers (the Renaissance, the revolt of Protestantism). Together these produced the first permanent colonial settlement of Jamestown, Virginia, one point of stability in a world turned upside down: elsewhere, the Portuguese swept through Africa like brush fire, destroying every civilization in their path, while England fell to Puritans and levellers, and killed its king. In India another great empire, the Mughal (Mogul) dynasty, crumbled like its African counterparts with the Death of Aurungzebe in 1707 while further East the might of the Manchu succeeded in establishing the last great dynasty of China's history.

Throughout all this women everywhere tended their children, milked their cattle, tilled their fields, washed, baked, cleaned and sewed, healed the sick, sat by the dying and laid out the dead—just as at this moment some women, somewhere are doing to this day. The extraordinary continuity of women's work, from country to country and age to age, is one of the reasons for its invisibility; the sight of a woman nursing a baby, stirring a cook-pot or cleaning a floor is as natural as the air we breathe, and like the air it attracted no scientific analysis before the modern period. While there was work to be done, women did it, and behind the vivid foreground activities of popes and kings, wars and discoveries, tyranny and defeat, working women wove the real fabric of the kind of history that has yet to receive its due.

For the unremarked, taken-for-granted status of women's work applied equally to their lives, and both combined to ensure that what women did went largely absent from the historical record. Official documents might carefully note the annual output of a farmer, for example, his total of meat, milk, eggs or grain, without ever questioning how much of that was produced by his wife's labor. The question itself would not apply—since the wife belonged to her husband by every law of the land and by her own consent too, then her labor and the fruits of it were also his. Consequently the idea of a separate reckoning would have been laughable. By definition, then, the only women whose activities were so recorded were not typical of the working majority—widows, for instance, seeking legal permission to carry on the trade of their late husbands, or deserted or runaway wives forced to fend for themselves. A women's history must seize with delight on the rare moments when a survey of property held in a bishop's name throws up a thriving bawdy-house keeper like Parnell Portjoie, with her neatly named pimp Nicholas Pluckrose in 1290, or the equally enterprising Eva Giffard of Waterford—this fourteenth-century Irishwoman entered a sheepfold by night and tore the wool off 20 sheep with her bare hands, to sell or spin as her own—but these women were exceptional.[2]

Exceptional only in making their way on to official lists, however—not at all in their energy, nor even in their unconventional occupations. For even the most cursory survey of women's work reveals that *its range, quantity and significance has been massively underestimated, not least by women themselves.* For in every era, they have simply got on with the job, whatever it was. Women have never questioned, for instance, the fact that, already burdened with an unequal share of the work of re-creating the race, they have had to work in fields and factories *as well*—nor that their role as wives, mothers and homemakers entails a disproportionate amount and variety of other kinds of work—domestic, social, medical, educational, emotional and sexual. The harder the conditions, the harder women had to work to maintain their families and create the best environment they could for them: the women of the American colonies, for instance, had to manage a far greater range of demands on their skills and flexibility than did their husbands. The men's work would be tough and unremitting, with land to clear, trees to fell and roots like boulders to be prized out of the reluctant ground. But most men would consider the resulting exhaustion a fair price to pay for being spared the washing, spinning, weaving, sewing and cob-baking (Indian-fashion, on the embers of a dying fire), then, having to salt the fish, scour the floor, plant the herb garden with all the old herbs from England to see which of them would take, try some onions and yarrow to flavor the stringy turkeys the men brought back from the woods, warn the children about those poisonous weeds, hear the maid's catechism, teach the boy to read . . . and write home to England to mother, to tell her "how well we do here . . . ," as so many of the colonists' letters stoutly sign off.

In the touching attempts of the women pioneers to make English gardens filled with all the familiar herbs and flowers, we see the continuity that also linked the endless work in the New World with that of the old, as far back in time as there are any traces of human activity. Historians and anthropologists have recently discovered something that has hardly been a secret to the women concerned:

The labors of early women were exacting, incessant, varied and hard. If a catalogue of primitive forms of labor were made, women would be found doing five things where men did one.[3]

Overseeing the women, perhaps?

In the light of this, the persistence of the myth that "working women" are a problem peculiar to the twentieth century is very hard to account for. The very earliest records, grave inscriptions for instance, tell of laundresses, female librarians and doctors, midwives, dressmakers, hairdressers throughout the Roman world. Their Greek sisters were more closely restricted, married women in particular being virtually imprisoned in the *gynaeceum* (women's quarters) of their husband's houses; the dismal bridal ceremony, when the axle of the chariot bearing the new wife from her father's to her husband's house was broken and burned, was designed to reinforce this. But even there, women worked as nurses, herb-sellers, garland-makers, and so on. By the first century AD, the writer Athenaeus recorded that 3000 women were working as *hetairai* musicians, while by the fourth century in Athens, the shortage of women oboists and singers resulted in their male patrons fighting in the streets to secure their services.[4]

Whatever its pressures, this was privileged work. Elsewhere the classic picture showed women worldwide saddled with the most degraded and disgusting occupations of their society. In the Arctic, for instance, women chewed the raw pelts of dead birds to soften them for wearing next to the skin. They also cured larger hides by rotting them till the putrid blubber and hair could be scraped off easily, sousing them in urine to clean them, then massaging them with animal brains as dressing. To observers, this seemed "the filthiest work in creation." It was equally seen to be "work which only women did."[5]

Yet this work was vital to the tribe's survival. Without hides, there would be no boots, parkas, trousers, containers for food and water, kayaks or tents. It also demanded creativity, precision, and a wide range of skills. None of these, however, have necessarily won status and respect for work performed by women. Nor did it ever exempt them from heavy work—the post-romantic fantasy of "the weaker sex" is another myth instantly exploded by the legion of women who were Egyptian pyramid-builders, temple masons of Lydia as noticed by Herodotus, Burmese canal-navvies and earth-movers in China. Portering, even of quite extraordinary weights (an Eskimo woman was observed to carry a boulder on her back weighing 300 pounds), was in fact regarded as women's work on the Russian edge of Europe and throughout the East. One astonished missionary to the Kurds observed a woman at an impasse with a loaded donkey; she simply shouldered the donkey's load herself and led the animal through; but she was already carrying a load of 100 pounds at the time, as well as spinning as she went with her spindle in her free (?) hand:

> I often saw the women looking like loaded beasts coming down the precipitous mountain path, one after the other, singing and spinning as they came . . . women with great panniers on their backs and babies on these or in their arms, go four days over that fearful Ishtazin pass, carrying grapes for sale and bringing back grain.[6]

This extract highlights another constant and universal feature of women's work, encapsulated in the old English couplet:

> For man's work ends at setting sun,
> Yet woman's work is never done.

The outdoor work of men, even begun at dawn, necessarily ended with the dark. For women, though, the first fire in the first cave also created an artificial light which would indefinitely extend their working day, so that leisure, a genuine respite at the end of labor, became what it largely remains today, a masculine prerogative. Spinning in particular, in the days before the spinning jenny, was never done, and became a byword for the endless, repetitive, unremitting and unrewarding labor generally understood as "women's work." Certainly a man would have recoiled in horror from the idea that he should have any contact with spinning, as the contemporary equivalent of an enforced sex-change, and even the enlightened Erasmus held firmly to the view that "the distaff and spindle are in truth the tools of all women, and suitable for avoiding idleness."[7] But some women were not sufficiently grateful for this thoughtful provision for their leisure hours (correction, "idleness"). And when the elastic hours put in at home were exacted under the factory conditions of early industrialized Europe, the wretches were even heard to complain, as in this bitter little work-song of the silk-spinners of medieval France:

> Always we reel the silk,
> Although we'll never be well dressed;
> We'll always be poor and naked,
> Always hungry and thirsty.
> They give us little bread
> Little in the morning and still less at night.[8]

Town girls may have had more learning than the million million women who were born, worked, and died after lives not far above those of their cattle in the depths of the country; or perhaps there was no one to record their feelings. Descriptions like this of the peasant woman's lot were obviously made at a safe distance from the alarming creature that the life produced:

> In this beautiful region we are obliged to say that the female sex is treated barbarously. Women are obliged to work the land and toil as farm laborers. Their appearance suffers from this, and the majority are unattractive. Sunburn, sweat and work ruin their figures and features. Before they are eighteen the girls have leathery faces, drooping breasts, calloused hands and a stoop.[9]

In every society, the lives of the landless peasants were cruelly hard, and men too did not escape being ground down to an animal level of daily existence. When the philosopher La Bruyère travelled through pre-Revolutionary France, he was horrified to see "throughout the country-side . . . wild male and female animals, black, livid and all burned by the sun . . . attached to the ground, in which they burrow and dig." These creatures made "a noise like speech," he went on ironically, but at night they withdrew "into lairs, where they live on black bread, water and roots."[10]

These observations of La Bruyère also help to lay to rest another profound misconception of the twentieth century: that there has always been "men's work" and "women's work" with a sex-segregated work-force such as we know today. In reality, although there was always work like spinning which men would never undertake, there was very little about which the same could be said of their wives and daughters. As a modern economic analysis stresses:

> Before the agricultural and industrial revolution there was hardly any job that was not also performed by women. No work was too hard, no labor too strenuous, to exclude them. In fields and mines, manufactories and shops, on markets and roads as well as in workshops and in their homes, women were busy assisting their men, replacing them in their absence or after their death, or contributing by their labor to the family income.[11]

What this meant in practice was an unquestioned and ingrained habit of cooperation, with men, women and children all working together in ways subsequently lost or mislaid as societies became more "advanced." An early traveller to Finistère has left this dramatic account of a community unselfconsciously absorbed in the work that all needed to do, if all were to survive:

> In storms, in deepest darkness, when the sea is high . . . all the inhabitants of the

region, men and women, girls and children, are especially busy . . . naked, unshod on the spikes of slippery rocks, armed with poles and long rakes, stretched over the abysses they hold back the gift which the sea brings them and would take away again if they did not haul it in.[12]

In certain ways these earlier societies could have taught the twentieth century something about genuinely egalitarian working practices. But the equality enjoyed here by the women seaweed harvesters extended only to capering naked at the midnight work-party on the dangerous rocks—they may have had the fun, but they failed to get the more substantial reward of money. For wherever records have survived of the pay of working people, women are shown either to receive less than men, or to get nothing at all, so entrenched was the notion of the paterfamilias as provider. So in seventeenth-century England, male laborers were paid 8d, "without meat and drink," and females only three-quarters of that, 6d, while male reapers earned 5d "with meat and drink" to the women's 3d—exactly the percentage of male to female earnings still obtaining worldwide today.[13]

This fundamental inequality was compounded by the fact that when a family lost the battle to survive on these starvation sums, it was almost always the women who were left with their children, to continue the desperate struggle without the one earner who was most likely to obtain employment. Parish registers throughout Europe, from the Middle Ages onwards, are full of poignant pleas from "poor disconsolate female creatures," "harbourless since Candlemas last," with their "impotent" children; for accommodation was very often tied to the man's labor, and if he vanished, so too did the roof over their heads. The homeless Eleanor Williams, of Worcester, England, was lucky that she only had one child, "her husband having left the soil where they lately dwelled and gone to some place to her unknown." Eleanor was as she declared willing and able "to relieve her child by her painful labour," if only she could obtain "house-room."[14] As a prototype "single parent family," Eleanor was already facing the struggle for accommodation, the sole burden of responsibility, above all the prospect of endless, over-exploited, underpaid work that is still the lot of the average deserted woman today.

Small wonder, then, that in countries where unmarried girls were allowed to have jobs outside the home, they used them to set themselves up for the marriage security that had eluded Eleanor. In a notary's agreement of a rural betrothal, a French contemporary of Eleanor's recorded her pride in the fruits of her working life, which, given the meager wages of a maid, were considerable: "Jeanne Valence, a farm laborer's daughter, provides for her own dowry the sum of £30 earned during the years she spent in service in the town of Brioude, plus a new woollen dress and a peasant-style wool tunic, a straw mattress, a white woollen blanket and a pinewood chest with a lock and key."[15] Domestic service was no featherbed for a girl, hardly even a straw mattress, as the shameful saga of the Pepys maidservants makes clear. In addition to the greasy mouth and groping hands so self-lovingly immortalized in the famous *Diary*, the master also had a brutal streak which found frequent play. Noticing that the maid Jane had left "some things laid up not as they should be," for instance, the Savior of the Navy "took a broom and basted her till she cried out extremely, which made me vext." On another occasion, when Pepys' brother had delayed the washing by distracting the maid, Pepys had his wife beat her till all the neighborhood was disturbed by her cries—"and then shut her in the cellar, where she lay all night."[16]

By his own account Pepys was a harsh and overbearing house-husband. The *Diary* records his merciless nagging as he perpetually found fault with his wife's "sluttish and dirty" housekeeping. He is angry with her when she burns her hand while dressing a turkey, buys a fowl too large for the oven, or sends the Sunday joint raw to the table when they have guests. Another row was raised when the sauce was too sweet for his leg of mutton, and Pepys candidly reports that he "takes occasion" to shout at his wife on any grounds that arise. But how would the hapless Elizabeth have learned housekeeping? A motherless child, she spent the short years of her childhood wandering around France with her father. Married at 15, she found the house-keeping money kept short while Pepys spent freely on his own plea-sures; for supper, she and the maid would share a glass of ale and a slice of brawn while Pepys and his cronies revelled at eight-course dinners, stuffing themselves to the point of nausea. When Elizabeth complained of being bored, confined as she was to the house and excluded from her husband's jaunts about fashionable London, Pepys deliberately set about making work for her: "keeping the house in dirt, and doing of this and everything else in the house but to find her employment." He was then angry to discover that Elizabeth was unhappy with his solution to her problem.

Still suffocating under the dead weight of the Judaeo-Christian com-pulsion to shut women up in their homes and carefully control their access to the public world, societies of the West created a very great deal of indoor or domestic work for women to do. Further afield from the urban centers women enjoyed a wider range of activities, many of which, if not fun already, became work-parties when their friends and their children joined in. On the islands around Hawaii, for instance, it was the task of Polynesian women to build the offshore dams that trapped the fish within the coral reef, thus ensuring a constant food supply. In the description of one observer, it perfectly conforms to D. H. Lawrence's pronouncement that "there is no point in work unless it absorbs you / Like an absorbing game":

[The] women would set out in their canoes through the heavy surf, before the sun was up. They shot the narrow entrances, beached their canoes, deposited their babies under the shade of palms on the soft sand and in the calm waters of these small lagoons, set to work. They cut lumps of coral rock and lifted them into the narrow entrances, trying not to scratch themselves, for some coral is poisonous. To cool themselves off they dived and swam, regaling themselves with fish and coconuts . . . [17]

Polynesian women were not the only ones whose climate favored outdoor living, in itself a greater basic freedom than many Western women have ever had. In Australia, Aboriginal women and girls would spend all day in the water at the height of summer, catching fish and gathering underwater roots, but relaxing and playing too. Similarly in Burma, although women had to work hard in their paddy fields, with or without their husbands, whose labor was not to be counted on, still there was some room to enjoy the warm and fertile world in which they lived, to spend time with other women, to feel that their work was valuable, to see its end product, and to dispose of the fruits of their efforts as they saw fit.

There could be no doubt, though, in the minds of women and men, that the real work of a woman's life was her husband and family. From earliest times this involved a wide range of different skills, plus the never-done labor and elastic working day already noticed, as this portrait of a good Jewish wife makes clear:

She seeketh wool and flax, and worketh willingly with her hands . . . She riseth also while it is yet night, and giveth meat to her household. . . . She considereth a field and buyeth it: with the fruit of her hands she planteth a vineyard . . . her candle goeth not out by night . . . Her husband is known in the gates, where he sitteth among the elders of the land. She maketh fine linen and selleth it; and delivereth girdles unto the merchant. . . . She looketh well to the ways of the household, and eateth not the bread of idleness. [18]

Spinning, weaving, agriculture, a little business on the side, running a household, supporting her husband in the demanding work of sitting

among the elders, successfully avoiding the bread of idleness and too
much sleep—this Canaanite housewife displays an astonishing continuity with her English counterpart of 3000 years later, whose duties
were set out by Sir Anthony Fitzherbert in a manual of 1555 detailing
"what works a wife should do," called, with the grave assurance of
unintentioned irony, *A Boke of Husbandrye:*

> First set all things in good order within thy house, milk the kine, suckle thy calves,
> strain up the milk . . . get corn and malt ready for the mill to bake and brew . . .
> make butter and cheese when thou may, serve thy swine both morning and evening
> . . . take heed how thy hens, ducks and geese do lay . . . and when they have
> brought forth their birds, see that they be well kept from crows and other vermin
> . . . [19]

This is merely the first round of tasks. Afterwards there are the
seasonal obligations: "March is time for a wife to make her garden.
. . . March is time to sow flax and hemp," which then had to be
"weeded, pulled, watered, washed, dried, beaten, braked, hatchelled,
spun, wound, wrapped and woven." From the woven result, the housewife then had to "make sheets, tablecloths, towels, shirts, smocks,
and other such necessaries"; if her husband had sheep, she had to
repeat the process with their wool. Even then, she was not through
with her chores—the author displays the standard patriarchal preoccupation with the danger of women's "idleness" in the stern injunction,
"meanwhile, do other work." It is a wife's responsibility, he continues:

> to winnow all manner of corns, to make malt, wash and wring, to make hay, to
> shear corn, and in time of need to help her husband to fill the muck wain or dung
> cart, drive the plough, to load hay, corn and such other. Also to go to the market,
> to sell butter, cheese, milk, eggs, chickens, capons, hens, pigs, geese, and all manner
> of corn. And also to buy all manner of necessary thing belonging to the household,
> and to make a true reckoning and account to her husband what she hath received
> and what she hath paid.

The wife who accomplished all this must have kept many candles
burning at night. Realistically, though, for every Tudor superwoman
there must have been weaker vessels who quailed at the very sight of
the job description, not to mention their cannier sisters who would
decide that life was too short to stuff a dung cart. Sir Anthony's paragon
obviously comes from the same region as bachelor's wives and old
maid's children, and may have been as little seen in real life as any of
those.

But these were the standards, however individual women might fall below them, and training for this demanding role began early. A "well-educated girl" could spin, weave, sew and make garments of all kinds before she was fifteen, and even those manuals which most stridently forbade teaching girls to read often argued that they should learn "the four rules of arithmetic" so that they could keep account of their husband's money. One Italian father of the Renaissance, while repeating the old idea that reading was wasted unless the daughter was destined to become a nun, left such a long list of prescribed study that she would never have had a moment to pick up a book: "teach her to do everything about the house, to make bread, to clean capons, sift, cook, launder, make beds, spin, weave French purses, embroider, cut wool and linen cloths, put new feet on to socks, and so forth, so that when you marry her off, she won't seem a fool freshly arrived from the wilds.[20] Paolo de Certaldo's "and so forth" here has an uneasy ring of Sir Anthony's "other works"—clearly the work to become women was never done, either—and since twelve was the legal age at which a girl could be married throughout Europe until the nineteenth century, these girls must have had a busy childhood.

They would however have needed all the training they could obtain to cope with what lay ahead. For every wife and mother in the pre-industrial period had to combine a number of skilled functions that have since become specialties (and often male mysteries too) in their own right. A housewife had to be able to kill her own pig, butchering the joints neatly for her salting tub. Her family only had bread if she knew every stage of the process from sowing through reaping, gleaning, winnowing, grinding, storing and baking, and performed them all correctly. In every country too, women were the brewers, of ale and cider in the northern world, of wine further south, while in Africa the Quissama women of Angola climbed the palm trees to tap off the highly prized palm beer.

Before the birth of shops, with markets often too remote or goods too costly, women had to be capable of making almost everything that they or their home needed: pots, curtains, bedrolls, hammocks, floor coverings, candles, containers. They made clothes, too, everything from an infant's belly-binder to a man's greatcoat—that end of the scale was later promoted to men's work as "tailoring," though men showed no such enthusiasm for taking over the tasks of mending, "turning," "rag-rugging," and putting new feet on socks.

When old and young lived together, and women were so often either pregnant, lactating or recovering from stillbirths and miscarriages, there was sure to be someone ill most of the time. And although each of these had its specialist practitioners from very early on, the expert was often either too expensive, engaged elsewhere, or not in time for the crisis. All women therefore developed some skills in these areas as a matter-of-fact, yet life-and-death, adjustment to their circumstances.

The way in which women made these tasks part of their everyday lives is evident from the career of Anne Hutchinson. Known to history as a religious radical who challenged the authority of the early American clergy, Anne only began her ministry in seventeenth-century Boston because she was grieved by the numbers of women whose workload prevented them from attending the Sunday services. Summarizing the sermons, she would "carry the voice of God" into homes where she was already known to the women colonists because of her skill in nursing and midwifery. The colony had its own official midwife, a veritable model of the doughty working woman, who came over with the 1630 convoy, where she could never know in advance on which of those eight ships her services would be needed. When a woman went into labor on the *Arbella*, therefore, a volley of cannon was the signal to the *Jewel*, far ahead with the midwife, to reef sails and delay. When the *Arbella* at last caught up, the intrepid midwife tied her skirts up between her legs, climbed down the side of one ship, and after a hair-raising transfer across the face of the Atlantic by long-boat, ascended the other to deliver the baby. This woman's skill was evidently equal to her courage, since mother and child survived. But in a colony where an unmarried female over 18 was unknown, and where "seldom any married woman but hath a child in her belly and one on her lap," as one observer reported, it would take more than one midwife to cope with all the "birthings."

The story of Anne, a woman of outstanding spiritual gifts yet deeply practical and effective, also illustrates the constant jumbling of high and low that characterizes women's work as homemakers from the very dawning of the notion of hearth and home. Many cultures like India charged women with the guardianship or maintenance of the sacred gods of their respective religious customs or practices; the Jewish mother was honored at the Sabbath feast, which she had prepared with all devout observance of the religious laws; and no Englishwoman, be she ever so humble, but was "Queen of the Feast" at her own harvest home. Yet those same women had previously presided over and taken part in activities considerably less elevated. The task of washing, for instance, was a grinding burden because of the sheer volume of clothes worn by men, women and children: shirts, caps, neckerchiefs, "bands" for men (still seen on British barristers), collars for women, bodices, kirtles, tuckers, shifts, petticoats, aprons, on top of sheets, towels, and "dishclouts." Nor was this work for the dainty-minded—the foul linen and "small clothes" that landed with the colonists in America had to be immediately plunged into the sea by the women while the men stood around with loaded muskets—though whether this was for defense against hostile attacks of native Americans or to dispose of anything that might crawl out of the months-old dirty linen has not been recorded.

Homemaking women, in any case, could not afford to be squeamish charged as they were with responsibility for the cleanliness and sanitation of their household. This would have had its pleasant side—women worldwide are known to have made all kinds of perfumed soaps and cleansing powders, and American women pioneered, among other things, a kind of toothbrush made of marshmallow roots, for use with a "toothpaste" of powdered orris root, chalk and bergamot of lavender oil. But overall, the disagreeables must have outweighed the pleasures. Everyone knows of the medieval custom of strewing floors with rushes mixed with fragrant rosemary, rue and sweet marjoram. What we forget is everything that was swept under the rush carpet, described by Erasmus as "an ancient collection of beer, grease, fragments, bones, spittle, excrement of dogs and cats and everything nasty."[21]

Worse than this must have been the unremitting task of dealing with the bodily waste of the household, which in the nature of things would be in continuous production. It may have been men who lugged around the wagons collecting the night-soil (in India, the so-called "untouchables"), but in every home, from hovel to palace, women emptied the chamber pots and closed stools, sluiced the privies and freshened the houses of easement for the next user. Women naturally dealt, too, with the results of their own physical functions; boiling the menstrual napkins or "rags" went on into the twentieth century, and in a household of women, most of whom would not live past 40, it would have been a recurrent and unavoidable chore.

All this would have been by way of valuable apprenticeship to a kind of labor not falling within the housework remit, but more properly categorized as pure *wife-work*. Wife-work comprised all the tasks that women had to do for their husbands, of a physical, sexual and often gorge-rising nature. At its highest, wife-work meant tasks that only fell upon women when they were married, because no matter how poorly off husbands were, they needed to have somebody below them, as in this description of a struggling peasant community in the primitive Auvergne:

> [The wives] go to bed later than the men, and rise before them. If snow has fallen it is up to one of them to clear a path to the fountain. Deep—sometimes up to her waist in snow, she will go back and forth until she has flattened out a passage for the other women. A man would think himself dishonored if he went for water himself; he would be the butt of the village. These mountain rustics have the deepest contempt for women and the despotic disdain of all wild, half-barbaric tribes. They look on them as slaves born to do all the chores which they consider base and beneath themselves.[22]

This wife-work fulfilled a group need—the women needed water for their children and for themselves, not just to keep the noses of their husbands clean. Lower down the scale, wife-work was low indeed. From Canaan to Abbeville, from Japan to Peru, the classic wife-task was the ritual performed, significantly enough, by Mary Magdalene for Jesus Christ and then by Christ in his turn as an act of abasement, washing the feet of the master. The French *Book of the Knight of the Tour Landry* (1371), widely influential throughout Europe for centuries, insists on foot-washing as a symbol of "cherishing a husband's person." On the other side of the globe, Japanese pillow-books similarly insist on foot-washing as a wife's proper greeting to her returning lord. A lady might delegate the job to a maidservant, but if she really wanted to be sure of her lord, she did it herself.

From toe to top: a dutiful wife was also expected to massage, comb and cleanse her husband's scalp. In the course of one such expedition, Elizabeth Pepys unearthed 16 lice, evidence at least that husband Samuel kept something other than wars and lechery under his fashionable hat. Shaving, washing, massaging and masturbating ("relief massage" in modern English, now in the hands of surrogate wives) were also part of the contract—but perhaps least to be envied were the women of the Indian state of Mysore, where:

> Women habitually attended their husbands, male children, relatives and sweethearts at the call of nature, cleansing their privy members when they were through. The individual merely said: "Meyn choonah hoon jow!" (I am going to leak) and one of the females of the house was obliged to attend him.[22]

Happily, not all the work of a wife was of this intimate and private nature. For many indeed, wifehood could bring a degree of freedom in the form of a license to trade in the public world—the woman who found that her hens had laid too many eggs one week was only being a good housewife if she took them to market and sold them to another woman who had lost hers to the crow, fox or thieving passerby. Some women, either through personal preference or force of circumstances, made trading their way of life, and worldwide, the ancient association of women with buying, selling and every aspect of merchandising is so marked as to make nonsense of another twentieth-century myth: that modern women are the first to work in any numbers outside the home.

> When [women] made most of the articles of trade, they were the best placed to exchange them. In some places like Nicaragua, women did not merely carry on trade, they absolutely controlled it. . . . In Tibet, trade was regulated by a council of women. . . . The North American fur trade until the nineteenth century was entirely in the hands of women. . . . In Melanesia, in New Britain and New Hanover . . . in Assam, in Manipur . . . in the Malay Peninsula . . . in the Luchu islands . . . in Burma, women carried on most of the retail trade and a good deal of the wholesaling even in the 1960s . . . [24]

Above all, the country where the market-woman ruled supreme was Africa: "In the Congo and Cameroons in Africa, women were in charge of the trading stations and markets. The markets of the Nigerian Ibo were run by a women's council presided over by a 'queen'." This verbal hangover from the days of the local matriarchy also indicates the importance of the markets as a reason for women to get together, to exchange news and gossip, and to renew old contacts; messages were passed hundreds of miles from market to market by virtue of the solemn undertaking, "I will speak it in the market."

In the less hospitable climate of the West, many women devoted their energies to indoor work, becoming proficient in a variety of highly skilled crafts, like the fine glover or the amorous spur-maker "Kate" hymned by the poet François Villon in the sixteenth century. The traditional way for women to gain entry to these generally restricted occupations was via their menfolk, as this list of sixteenth-century German women licensed to ply the following trades clearly indicates:

> Frau Nese Lantmennyn, blacksmith; Katherine, widow of Andreas Kremer, gardener; Katherine Rebestoeckyn, goldsmith; Agnes Broumattin, widow of Hans Hirtingheim, waggoner; Katherine, widow of Helle Hensel, grain dealer; Else von Ortemberg, Oberlin Rulin's daughter, tailor; Katherine, widow of Heinrich Husenbolz, cooper. [25]

Such licenses, however, were often not worth the parchment they were written on, for they constituted at best a grudging admission to the fringes of the mystery, and never the all-important full membership of a guild.[26] Without this, women could not hold any guild office, nor have any voice in the guild decisions regulating their trade. Given the busy woman's impatience with honorifics, they may have borne the first deprivation with equanimity, but the second was strongly resented, as a long history of legal actions and petitions by women demonstrates. Female traders suffered under other forms of discrimination, too—then as now, the working woman was frequently accused of taking work away from men, who really needed it. What must have hurt more, they were invariably paid less than their male counterparts for exactly the same work, on the grounds that as women they did not need a job as a man did; and that they worked more slowly, producing less, and also ate less, consequently needing less to live on.

Yet nothing could actually prevent women from harnessing their natural energies and resource into useful work, and the huge numbers of working women glimpsed everywhere in the historical records demonstrates once again that crucial gap between what a society *said* and what in practice it *did*, that women have been able to avail themselves of since time immemorial. For in truth the city fathers and guild legislators who struggled to restrict the activities of "wives, daughters, widows and maids" were straining against a force of which they knew nothing: the importance of women's work to the economy. Always treated as peripheral, in the lives of the individual women as well as of their society at large (the idea that women work for "pin money" is a long time dying), it is in fact central and indispensable, both in terms of women's direct production (weaving is a good example) and of their indirect labor of housework and wife-work which frees men for productive labor.

Women who as widows were relieved of that second burden of commitment often made a staggering success of their enterprise when they were able to move for and by themselves. The numbers of shrewd and energetic businesswomen, like their religious sisters of earlier centuries, argue another large body of women who either did not accept the oft-told tale of female inferiority, or by means known only to themselves, succeeded in reconciling it with being superior to most of the men around them. Alice Chester, for instance, an outstanding English entrepreneur at the end of the fifteenth century, trading wool, wine, iron and oil as far afield as Flanders and Spain, deferred to no one but God; and when she built Him a new high altar and rood loft in her favorite church, that too was in the nature of a prudent investment for the future. Not all women traders were as successful as

Alice. Margery Russell of Coventry in the heart of the English Midlands was robbed of eight hundred pounds' worth of goods by the men of Santander in Spain, a ruinous loss. Even worse was the fate that befell Agnes de Hagemon, a Shrewsbury brewer, who, as she was pouring a tub of liquor into the vat of hot mash, slipped and fell in, where she was so severely scalded that she died. Agnes's fate was recorded in the Coroner's Rolls of November 1296. As a gruesome footnote, although it must have contained some of Agnes's skin, flesh and hair, the beer was sold off, raising a profit of 2½d for the Crown.[27]

Both of these cases illustrate the element of danger that has always deterred a number of women from venturing out of their protected domestic enclaves into the public world. Yet many did, and not only into trade and commerce. These centuries saw, too, the birth of the first professional women. In the wake of the pioneering eleventh-century physician and gynecologist Trotula, there was a particular interest in medicine. With her colleagues, the "Ladies of Salerno," Trotula had established the first medieval center of scientific learning not under the control of the Church. Some of her theories were equally radical—she suggested that infertility could be as much due to the male as the female, for instance—but her definitive work, *The Diseases of Women*, was not superseded for generations. It was, however, generally attributed to a male authorship, either Trotula's husband, or another male practitioner. Medical women constantly faced such difficulties and impediments. By 1220, for instance, the University of Paris, one of the world's leading medical schools, had introduced statutes to debar women from admission, and also to disqualify any except their own bachelors from practicing. In 1485, Charles VIII of France issued a decree withdrawing the right of women to work as surgeons. Both these measures argue the existence of a number of women, both practicing and seeking training, great enough to have become a problem calling for legislation to resolve it.

Yet there were ways around this. Women could apply for individual licenses, they could learn from one another like Trotula's "Ladies of Salerno" or from the barber-surgeons who operated without university restriction, or they could move to a more hospitable locale. By a devious blend of these techniques, and with the stiffening of a fair dose of female grit and gumption, certain women succeeded even in the darkest times in ensuring that medicine was never wholly a male monopoly. Between 1389 and 1497 in Frankfurt alone, for instance, there were 15 licensed women doctors in practice, including three Jewish women who specialized in Arab ophthalmology. In the fifteenth century, German women were presenting medical theses for higher degrees at the universities, and in the sixteenth, a Swiss midwife-surgeon perfected new techniques of Caesarean section which in the hands of male surgeons had made virtually no progress since the days of the eponymous Julius.

This woman, Marie Colinet of Berne, was also the first to use a magnet to extract a piece of metal from a patient's eye, a breakthrough technique still in use today. (This successful innovation was subsequently attributed to Marie's husband, even though the only record of the operation was her husband's description of watching her perform it.) In Italy, too, while some universities had followed France's lead and barred women from attending, in the fourteenth century Bologna had appointed Dorotea Bocchi to succeed her father as professor of medicine and moral philosophy. Bologna also struck a famous blow for women by appointing 25-year-old Maria di Novella as professor and head of mathematics at the same time. The university's continuing tradition of medical women is demonstrated by the death there in 1526 of the first known woman pathologist. By tireless experimentation this pioneer had developed a revolutionary technique for withdrawing blood and replacing it with colored dye, thus allowing the circulatory system to be studied in great detail. "Consumed by her labors," as her grieving fiancé recorded, she died at only nineteen.[28]

Women's contribution to medicine remained however a flickering light, whose fitful gleam was always liable to hostile challenge. The only work to which women could lay a solid and inalienable claim, as the modern world took shape, was the work that could not be done by men, work that demanded the possession of a female body, breasts and vagina, for the fulfillment of the conditions of the contract. In practice, this meant acting and whoring, and it is no coincidence that throughout their history the two have so frequently been confused.

Of the two, acting initially represented no small triumph for women, since their employment in many countries broke down a rigid historic convention that the female parts in drama were always performed by males, a custom dating back to the very dawn of sacred drama among the Greeks. The transition to female participation had not been painless. The first women to appear on the London stage, a troupe of touring French actresses, brought the city to a standstill, and caused a national scandal. Frothing at the mouth, a leading Puritan, William Prynne, recorded the event:

Some French women, *or monsters rather*, in Michaelmas term 1629, attempted to act a French play at the playhouse in Blackfriars; an impudent, shameful, unwomanish, graceless, if not more than whorish attempt, to which there was great resort.[29]

Prynne was not alone in his view. The French actresses also failed to win the approbation of the international drama critics of the London mob, and they were "hissed, hooted and pippen-pelted from the stage."

More damaging than a few flying apples, however, was the immediate and lasting connection of this new profession for women with that traditionally hailed as the oldest: prostitution.[30] Women living independent lives, not married unless it suited them to be, earning and spending their own money, exhibiting their bodies to the gaze of any common stinkard who cared to put down his tuppence at the door—what could they be but whores? When the actress was also passionate, self-willed and autocratic, when she was known to the town as the Earl of Rochester's mistress but was clearly mistress of no one but herself, then the attribution was certain. The fact that Rochester's "mistress," the celebrated Elizabeth Barry, created more than a hundred leading roles during her stage career never distracted public attention for long from her equally vigorous and varied sex life; and when, in a performance of *The Rival Queens*, Mrs. Barry was so transported by emotion as to stab a real-life rival in the back, causing grievous bodily harm to Mrs. Boutel's stays, all that the public saw was a bawdy-house brawl, with two town trulls fighting over a customer.

Elizabeth Barry and the other first-generation actresses were women on a frontier every bit as much as their American sisters who had the courage to "go West" a couple of centuries later. Other women pushing back the artistic frontiers during the English Restoration, along with Barry, her rivals and colleagues, were those who for the first time succeeded in obtaining payment for something women had always previously done without charge: intellectual work. Among the millions of women who have ever written or wanted to write, the name of Aphra Behn rises supreme. Not the "first woman writer" of the modern period—the peerless American poet Anne Bradstreet who wrote under the considerably more difficult conditions of colonial settlement and eight children antedated Aphra, as did others—but the first woman known to have made a living as a professional writer, selling her work and supporting herself on the proceeds of it. During her creative career of almost twenty years, this bold and brilliant woman, ex-governess, former spy and world traveller, conquered the theatre, previously an all-male domain; she wrote ten plays in the 1680s alone, in addition to several long narrative poems, five translations from French, and five novels, thereby laying claim to another "first," the first novelist in English. Of course, they said she was a whore.

Since the term "whore" was so freely used against women who did not sell their bodies for money, it had very little power to insult the genuine "daughters of the game"—taunted as such by one of the other mistresses of Charles II, the Duchess of Portsmouth, Nell Gwynn sturdily replied, "As for me, it is my profession, I do not pretend to anything better."[31] Despite the howls of the moralists, many women worldwide have echoed Nell's view. Throughout history millions of women have been active in the prostitution services, not merely as the "poor bloody infantry" but as commanders too: of ten brothel-owners or "stewe-houlders" of the London Bankside fined by an ecclesiastical court in 1505, four were women, presiding at "le Hert," "le Hertys-horne" (hartshorn was a well-known aphrodisiac), "le Crosse Keyes," and "le fflower delyce."[32] For it was a living, and one whose advantages continued to outweigh the often punitive deterrents invoked against it. One of those advantages, without a doubt, was its freedom from the constraints that respectable married women labored under. No wives, however, saw it that way—both sides in fact scorned and pitied the other for their wretched, ground-down existence at the hands of exploitative men.

With the hindsight of an era struggling with the impact of demands for sexual equality and economic parity, it is easy to misjudge the experience of women's work in the pre-industrial period. Often hard, long, and demanding, it was not inherently and invariably oppressive, as the evidence of women's active and varied roles, their vigor, competence and enterprise, abundantly illustrates. Work could in fact provide women, legally without rights or even a separate identity, with ongoing outlets for their ability, and a strong measure of mobility, autonomy, equality and economic independence. While men controlled the land overall, their control did not deny women an important stake in the tilling, planting and growing that went on; and women for their part controlled the produce, both at a household micro-level, and at the macro-level of the disposal of surplus via trade or commerce. In a very real sense, therefore, man and wife working a smallholding were partners in a way quite unrecognized by the hollow letter of the law. Centered in her home, her family and her work, still at this stage a holy trinity, three in one, a woman could be proud, self-sufficient, strong and free. It all sounds too good to be true. It was. And with the coming of the machine age, it was to be swept away as if it had never been.

8
REVOLUTION THE GREAT ENGINE

Every revolution contains in it something of evil.
EDMUND BURKE

. . . at every house women and children making
cartridges, running bullets, making wallets, baking
biscuits, crying and bemoaning and at the same
time animating their husbands and sons to fight for
their liberties though not knowing whether they
should ever see them again . . .
EYEWITNESS ACCOUNT OF THE FIRST
ENGAGEMENT IN THE AMERICAN REVOLUTION
AT LEXINGTON IN 1774

For us, with heat and work, 'tis often known,
Not only sweat, but blood runs trickling down,
Our wrists and fingers: still our work demands
The constant action of our labouring hands.
MARY COLLIER, *The Woman's Labour* (1739)

Revolutions are not to be evaded.
BENJAMIN DISRAELI

Husband, home, family—for centuries, millennia even, the lives of
women have revolved around this holy trinity—immediate, eternal,
all-engrossing, in a safe and continuing pattern of almost changeless
domesticity. Some, however, were born to the trial of times when
patterns did not merely change, but collapsed into cataclysmic violence, when systems deemed perpetual melted into air, and with their
solemn temples and gorgeous palaces, left not a wrack behind. At such
times women faced a double burden, of bearing up to the shock of
the new, while still holding together the shreds and shards of the old;
while one upraised arm saluted the new dawn, the other still cradled
a baby or hoed a field; and even in the midst of a revolution, there
had to be food, love, warmth, shelter, light and life, or as much of
each as the female fighter on the home front could muster.

Domestic duties, though, generally proved no impediment to revolutionary activity when women's hearts and minds were enlisted in the cause. Thereafter, in war, as in work, it was remarkable how much women were able to do, and how little they were held back by notions either of bodily weakness or mental incapacity. From the first stirrings of revolutionary feeling in America, women were well to the fore, both in active engagement and in the courage of independent thought that fuelled it; in Bacon's 1676 rebellion, a female lieutenant was the first to gather his followers together, riding up and down the back country as his personal emissary, while a second, Sarah Grendon, was personally exempted by name from the subsequent free pardon because she had been such a "great encourager and assister in the late horrid Rebellion." Another Sarah, Mistress Drummond of Jamestown, Virginia, showed the spirit that animated all these women when she responded to the governor's threat of death for her part in the proceedings by breaking a stick under his nose with the scornful line: "I fear the power of England no more than a broken straw!"[1] After the defeat of the revolt, Sarah's pugnacious resolve continued to be her family's lifeline, when by the ferocity and persistence of her petitioning she finally succeeded in winning back the Drummond estates sequestered by the English Crown, just 100 years too early to witness the tables turned and the British swept into the sea.

When the American Revolution formally broke out, much was made of women's eagerness for the fray. Every nubile female colonist was supposed to be agog to see all the menfolk in arms, and scornful of shirkers: the *New-York Gazette* of October 2, 1775 ran the story of a group of young girls at a quilting frolic who stripped a young "Tory" loyalist to the waist and tarred and feathered him with molasses and weeds. Other apocryphal accounts told of women forming military-style companies, putting on uniform, or showing "masculine valor" at moments of crisis. Women themselves made the requisite heroic noises: Eliza Wilkinson spoke for many a valiant widow when she wrote to urge all wives to volunteer their husbands, for "if I had one who refused to enter the field for his country's cause, I believe I should despise him from my soul."[2]

Despite the evident propaganda value of these broadsides, they did not convince one and all. Sarah Hodkins was a 25-year-old mother of two, her second baby only newly born, when her husband enlisted in the militia besieging Boston in 1775. She could not reconcile herself to his absence, writing "I look for you almost every day, but I don't allow myself to depend on any thing for I find there is nothing . . .

but trouble and disappointments." Sending sarcastic regards to his commanding officer—"tell him I have wanted his bed fellow pretty much these cold nights"—she reproached him for leaving his wife and children: "I have got a Swete Babe almost six months old but have got no father for it."[3] Above all, Sarah exerted all the pressure she could muster to prevent her husband from enlisting for another three years, for reasons clearly apparent from this demand of the *Connecticut Courant* of September 8, 1777:

> How is it that the poor soldiers' wives in many of our towns do go from door to door, begging a supply of the necessaries of life . . . and are turned away, notwithstanding the solemn agreements of the towns to supply such?

For one loyal soldier, it was eventually too much. In 1779 Sergeant Samuel Glover, a veteran of engagements at Brandywine, Germantown and Stony Point and unpaid for fifteen months, led a mutiny of "his Brother Soldiers." He was shot. His widow petitioned the American Assembly for relief, demanding "to ask you, what must be the feeling of the Man . . . with Poverty staring him in the face and Injustice oppresses him and his family?"[4]

Wives like these knew that if they lost their husbands they lost not merely a partner, lover and friend, but their very prop and mainstay. For some, however, there would be a chance of marrying again, and colonial widowers were breathtakingly brisk at securing new wives before their beds had time to grow cold behind the dear departed. For a mother old enough to have sons of military age, though, there could be no replacing a darling boy, and conflict on this score ran high. In the famous Livingston family, when an aunt opined that "it was no wonder Mr. Washington was so weak, since Gentlemen did not order their Sons into the Army," and told her nephew in front of his mother that he should enlist "whether his Parents consented or not," "there arose," wrote an observer with masterly understatement, "a little Sharpness among the Ladies." What Mistress Livingston had to fear is all too evident from this army chaplain's record of the last words of "a youth, dying of his wounds" after the battle of September 13, 1776:

> Will you not send for my mother? If she were here to nurse me I could get well: O my mother, how I wish I could see her, she was opposed to my enlisting, I am now very sorry, do let her know I am sorry.[5]

This is not to underestimate the strength of American women's commitment to the "glorious cause," which depended upon their active support in a wide number of ways. Their agreement to the 1769 boycott of all English tea, luxury goods, silks, satins and broadcloth was crucial to the early resistance—at one level, it *was* the resistance—and their efforts alone supplied the consequent shortfall: the women of Middletown, Massachusetts, wove 20,522 yards of cloth in 1769, while Lancaster in Pennsylvania topped even that with 35,000 during the same period. The American men were well aware of the power of "the female artillery." During a later wave of boycott activity, when the "goodwives" of Edenton in North Carolina took "the earliest known political activity of American women in the American colonies" by organizing a formal resolution to implement the decision of Congress, their action was widely praised and publicized.[6]

Nor was the women's activity all of the distaff and tea-table sort. When hostilities began, so did the examples of female heroism on both sides. Among the British, Lady Harriet Acland, wife of the commander of grenadiers in Burgoyne's offensive in the summer of 1777, won undying renown when her husband was wounded and taken prisoner in the battle. Commandeering a small boat, she sailed down the Hudson by night under sniper fire, penetrated the enemy defenses, and at daybreak ventured into the mouth of the American guns to demand her husband. Even more astonishingly in view of his terrible injuries (John Dyke Acland had been shot through the stomach and both legs), Harriet not only kept him alive through the hazards of the return journey, but nursed him back to full health.

No less resolute was Baroness Riedesel, another British commander's wife. Arriving in America with three daughters under five, the Baroness nevertheless stuck by her husband's side despite all reversals; once she had to save her daughters' lives by hiding them beneath her own body under direct fire, and on another occasion she kept them and the rest of the British survivors alive for six days without food in a cellar awash with excrement until relief arrived. Women were involved, too, in the fighting itself. The Revolutionary heroine Mary Ludwig Hays had already won the nickname of "Pitcher Molly" for her courage in bringing water to the cannoneers at the height of the battle. When her husband, a barber-surgeon turned artillery sergeant, was struck down, Mary took his place at the cannon, where her coolness passed into legend. After a cannon ball passed between her legs, tearing away her petticoat, she merely looked down and "observed, with unconcern, that it was lucky it did not pass higher, for in that case it might have carried away something else; and so continued her occupation."[7]

The active participation at all levels in the American war by the women both of the threatened community and of its equally threatened masters contrasts interestingly with the part played by their forebears in the English Civil War of the previous century. From any point of comparison it is clear that the greater freedoms in the New World, the breakdown of certain systems and hierarchies, and the necessary solidarity of colonial life, all combined to create conditions in which women's contribution, both as individuals and as a sex, had a far greater chance to flourish. In the ragged and painful English conflict, however, nation turned in upon nation; a network of deep and often contradictory allegiances determined the decision "For the King" or "For Parliament," and the battlelines, when drawn, all too often severed parents from children, and friend from dearest friend.

In these circumstances, the community of female interest had little hope of being born. One quite exceptional example of women's joint action fared so poorly as to be a discouragement rather than example to others. This was the occasion when "the men durst no more petition," and "the women took it up"; the dangerous issue was the arrest of four parliamentary radicals in 1649. For three days in succession a crowd of women, hundreds strong, petitioned Parliament for their release, only to be repeatedly repulsed by armed soldiers counterattacking with pistols cocked, and dismissed at last with this contemptuous rebuke from the Mother of Parliaments:

> That the matter they petitioned about was of a higher concernment than they understood, that the House gave answer to their husbands [i.e., that Parliament was only accountable to men] and therefore desired them to go home, and look after their own business, and meddle with their husbandry.[8]

Well might the women, "assured of our creation in the image of God, and of an interest in Christ equal unto men . . . wonder and grieve that we should appear so despicable in your eyes," as they later wrote. But in the era of revolutions which the world was now entering, this was to be only one of many reminders to women that, though all were to be equal in each new revolutionary commonwealth, some were born with that special something that made them more equal than others.

Collective action by women may have been crushed; individually, however, they were indispensable, particularly to a banished Royalist.

"Indeed women were never so useful as now," wrote one harassed absentee to Sir Ralph Verney.[9] On behalf of their lords, aristocratic females turned "gallant She-Souldiers" to fight for their interests and to defend their property. Of numerous impressive examples, one of the most heroic was Lady Mary Banks who in 1643 held Corfe Castle against the Parliamentary forces, personally defending the whole of the upper ward with only her daughters, her waiting gentlewomen and five men—all of whom, however, hurled down stones, boiling water and red-hot embers so successfully that the besiegers "ran away crying."[10] Such heroism was not of course the monopoly of the upper classes, although aristocratic heroines are more likely to have come down to history by name. Many unsung "she-souldiers" also served in the Civil War, most notably at the siege of Lyme, a small port in Lady Bank's county of Dorset. There, women defenders assisted the fighting men by day, filling their bandoliers in the heat of the battle and hurling stones or any other projectiles in between, while at night they kept watch so that the men could get some sleep against the next day's assault. Their efforts were warmly commemorated by a local poet, who shows a lively sense that more than the house of Stuart had been overthrown "in this late Tempest":

> To most 'tis known
> The weaker vessels are the stronger grown . . .
> Alas! Who now keeps Lyme? Poor female cattell
> Who wake all night, labour all day in Battle
> And by their seasonable noise discover
> Our foes, when they the works [earthworks] are climbing over.[11]

Equality to fight alongside men also meant the same right to suffer as men had. Many women did so during the nine years of this bitterest of wars, though not all with the spirit of the maid maimed by a shell at the defense of Lyme, who refused all sympathy for the future loss of her livelihood with the firm pronouncement, "Truly, I am glad with all my heart that I had a hand to lose for Jesu Christ, for whose Cause I am as willing and ready to lose not only my other hand, but my life also."[12] What seventeenth-century Englishwomen never had was any influence on the course of events which promoted them to this spurious equality of suffering. High or low, they had no voice in councils, whether of Star Chamber or parish pump. Excluded from policy-making, condemned, however vigorous and able they were, to reactive roles and tactics, the women of the English Civil War with their huge losses of husbands, sons, homes and friends too often seem the victims of others' revolutionary zeal rather than victors in any cause of their own.

From the death of one king to the death of another: it was to take a further century and a half, another repetition of the earth-shattering assault on the divine right of kings, before women were admitted even as junior partners in the bloody business of revolution. The events in France, from the convulsion of the 1780s to the horrific ensuing *dégringolade*, throw into relief the flat black irony of Edward Bulwer Lytton: "Revolutions are not made with rose-water."[13] The women of the French Revolution were in fact far removed from the dainty femininity suggested here; and all the perfumes of Arabia would not sweeten hands steeped to the elbows in *ci-devant* blood. For in France, for the first time in history, women became a revolutionary force— and the impact of this was not the least shocking of the ceaseless shocks of that tortured time and place.

The prominence of women in the French Revolution owed something to the example of the successful American struggle in the New World. At bottom, though, the conditions of the people of France under the *ancien régime* were such as to have eroded many of the crucial distinctions between male and female long before those between *aristo* and *sans-culotte* came under scrutiny—there is no democracy to equal that of the starving. Maddened just as much as their men by hunger, frustration and despair, the women of Paris contributed a major part of the force which set in motion "the great engine of Revolution" and which subsequently powered its remorseless progress through the churning seas of blood.

For the women were there, as recording angels, avenging goddesses or raging fiends, depending on the perspective of the observer, from the very onset of the struggle. It was a woman, dressed as an Amazon, who led the attack in the storming of the Bastille. If this was a hollow victory, the empty fortress symbolic of the bankrupt regime it had both epitomized and propped up, then the action on the "Day of the Market-Women" certainly was not. Originating when angry women combed the markets of Paris in vain for bread, the riot drew to a head as it found a focus for its discontents in the king's absence from his city in crisis. So began the march to Versailles of October 5, 1789, whose outcome sealed the fate of Louis XVI, Marie Antoinette, the Dauphin, and all the rest of the doomed Capet dynasty.

Not all of the 8000 or so women on the famous march were ruthless revolutionaries daring all for the "glorious cause." A nurse, Jeanne

Marin, later deposed that she had been forced along by a gang of about 40 women, who thrust a cudgel into her hands, threatening to use it on her if she refused. All her protests and evasions (she had not had her breakfast, she had no money, not even a *sou*) were shouted down with the repeated cry, "March! March! You won't need anything!"[14] In this *ad hoc* battalion of Amazons, not all were even female—the ranks were swelled by an unknown number of men disguised as women, while some undisputed males had been press-ganged by the women as leaders or NCOs. Within the corps of women, there were divisions remarkable even to themselves—*poissardes* or fishwives, market-traders and those who traded in the lowest common denominator of all, human flesh, the Paris prostitutes, had found common cause with bevies of smartly dressed, well-spoken *bourgeoises*, who, however, proved themselves as vocal as their sisters of the marketplace and every bit as violent.

For, once unleashed, the fury of the female mob was terrifying. They swept down on Versailles, pausing only to pillage shops and taverns as they went, and stormed first the national assembly, where the deputies, even under the formidable Comte de Mirabeau, were helpless in the face of the onslaught. A deputation to the king, hastily arranged to placate the raging ringleaders, foundered when their spokeswoman, a flower-seller from the Palais Royal, only managed to utter, "Sire, we want bread" before fainting. Her comrades had to be prevented from stringing her up from the palace railings. The onset of night, with a steady downpour of rain, seemed to damp down the vengeance of the Furies. It was a delusion. Before dawn they had overrun the palace, tearing the guards to pieces, wrecking the royal apartments in search of the queen and howling for every last drop of her hated Austrian blood. Before the day was out Marie Antionette and all her family were returning to Paris on the last journey they would ever make, as prisoners of the people, the die cast by the anger of the women.

In retrospect this anger seems so overwhelming that political action alone was not enough to relieve it—every canon of female sanctity, of femininity itself, had to be violated, and as freely and publicly as possible. Contemporary commentators noted with wonder and horror that the respectable *bourgeoises* seemed to need no language lessons from the fishwives when they responded to a bishop's demand for "Order!" at the storming of the national assembly with "We don't give a fuck for your order!" and threatened to play *boules* with the head of the nearest *abbé*. Meanwhile the whores, who had no respectability to sacrifice for the glorious cause, were similarly driven to reach for their own expressions of excess, to find through new extremes of grossness that liberation from the controlling norms which all were frenziedly seeking in the anarchy of the moment. A curious and later famous incident secured the reputation of the Paris whores as the shock troops of the Revolution, in every sense of the term. In July of 1790, a band of prostitutes armed with pistols held up a detachment of the royal cavalry, ordering the soldiers to cry "Death to the king!" and boasting "We're all yours if you join the Revolution!" When the soldiers refused, a beautiful young girl, very fair and no more than sixteen, began dancing before the troopers in the street, as an eye-witness recounted:

> She had bared her breasts and was holding them in the palms of her hands, while she deliberately waggled her posterior like a duck. The other women immediately made a rush at her and lifted up her clothing, revealing to the blushing cavalrymen the prettiest figure imaginable, at the same time exclaiming, "If you'd like a taste of that, just shout 'Death to the King!' first!"[16]

This and other similar incidents read like recension of Edmund Burke's grave reflection on revolution, made in the light of the American experience 20 years before: "People crushed by laws have no hope but from power. If laws are their enemies, they will be enemies to laws; and those who have much to hope and nothing to lose will always be dangerous."[17]

For this brief, never-to-be-repeated period, revolutionary France abounded in such dangerous women. As a society out of control, it had shed the traditional governing principles and not yet restored or replaced them; riven from top to bottom it was, like a frontier society, wide open to the ambitious, the fearless and the tough. Among the earliest of the women who emerged without a trace and soared to heights previously unimaginable for a female was the complex figure of Théroigne de Méricourt. A gifted singer whose voice had been trained in London and Naples, a successful courtesan who had made a fortune in pre-Revolutionary Paris, she was the woman who led the storming of the Bastille dressed as an Amazon, and later in the same year, the women's march to Versailles; at the assault on the Tuileries three years later in 1792, she commanded a battalion of Amazons.

Yet de Méricourt was much more than a "she-souldier." An idol of the political clubs, she contributed vociferously to revolutionary discussions, and through her foundation of a number of women's political clubs, drew the previously disregarded female "citizens" into the debate. Eventually, though, she sacrificed her wealth and risked her life for a cause which eventually betrayed her; espousing the moderate faction at the height of the Terror, she lost her popularity and was attacked and severely beaten by the Parisian revolutionary women she had championed. The shock destroyed her reason, and she was confined to a lunatic asylum for the rest of her life.

De Méricourt's actions even at the height of her importance are not easy to assess. To contemporaries, even by the standards of the time, she often seemed free of all restraint of law, of custom, even of humanity: at the assault of the Tuileries, she used her influence over the mob to have a journalist who had lampooned her lynched before her eyes. Her reputation as a vampire pursued her to the end: "one of her last murders was that of a young Fleming, allegedly her first seducer. She . . . struck off his head with her own hand . . . then fell into a kind of maniacal ecstasy, singing a revolutionary ballad while she danced among the pools of blood."[18]

De Méricourt was not at all exceptional in her ferocious antipathy to the *ancien régime,* nor in the fervor with which she sought its destruction. "Peace will set us back," wrote Manon Roland passionately: "We can be regenerated through blood alone."[19] A gifted self-taught intellectual, Madame Roland bestrode the salons as de Méricourt did the streets, shaping and influencing revolutionary policy and democratic theory as much through the force of personal argument as through her writings. Although not operating on terms of complete equality with her male colleagues—her first radical writings came out under her husband's name, and her influence was at its height when he was minister for the interior in 1792—Roland was the acknowledged powerhouse of the Girondin moderate party. Her career thus represents one of the earliest points in history when a woman claimed and was granted, on merit and in her own right, a pivotal place at the nerve center of a major political enterprise.

Nor were these women, on the classic pattern of female endeavor, merely serving the cause of men. In keeping with an upheaval of such violence, the equally revolutionary ideas of feminism now took root and began to flourish. Previously these had been little more than the seeds of scattered impulses borne across the surface of human thought by random winds. In France alone, *"la question des femmes"* had been under discussion for many years, the terms of the argument laid down by women like the gifted Marie le Jars de Gournay. The adopted daughter of Montaigne, Marie was a staunch defender of women's right to education and a remorseless campaigner against any ideas of women's "natural" inferiority. Her independence and refusal to adopt "feminine" frills and furbelows or submissive, ingratiating manners also mark her out as a protofeminist, as do her *Egalité des Hommes et des Femmes* (1622) and *Grief des Dames* (1626). But now feminist challenges, protests and demands gathered together to find an articulate political form, as in the "Petition of the Women of the Third Estate to the King."

> . . . all women of the Third Estate are born poor. Their eduction is either neglected or misconceived. . . . At the age of fifteen or sixteen, girls can earn five or six sous a day. . . . They get married, without a dowry, to unfortunate artisans and drag out a gruelling existence . . . producing children whom they are unable to bring up. . . . If old age overtakes unmarried women, they spend it in tears and as objects of contempt for their nearest relatives. To counter such misfortunes, Sire, we ask that man be excluded from practising those crafts that are women's prerogative . . .[20]

Considering that the women were suffering a massive invasion of their traditional crafts by men who already earned an average daily wage of thirty sous, while women could expect only fourteen or fifteen, their protest seems very mild, an impression reinforced by the timid final disclaimer: "We ask, Sire, to be instructed and given jobs, not that we may usurp men's authority but so that we might have a means of livelihood." Male pamphleteers like the Marquis de Condorcet were less circumspect in drawing attention to the wrongs and grievances of the women, which had made the female sex into "the Third Estate of the Third Estate":

> Is there any stronger proof of the power of habit, even over enlightened men, than to see the principle of equal rights being invoked in favour of 300 or 400 men . . . while being forgotten in the case of 12,000 women?[21]

To a woman, however, goes the credit for unfurling the full flag of feminism in France with the rousing battle-cry, "Man, are you capable of justice? It is a woman putting the question . . . " At the onset of the Revolution, the constituent assembly of France had proclaimed the Rights of Man. In September 1791 Olympe de Gouges published a full-blown feminist riposte, her "Declaration of the Rights of Woman":

> Woman is born free and her rights are the same as those of a man. . . . The law must be an expression of the general will; all citizens, men and women alike, must participate in making it . . . it must be the same for all. . . . All citizens, be they men or women, being equal in its eyes, must be equally eligible for all public

offices, positions and jobs, according to their capacity and without any other criteria than those of their virtues and talents . . . [22]

Whatever the temper of the times, this was revolutionary stuff. There was more to come. With no more formal intellectual training than Manon Roland, de Gouges nevertheless succeeded in seeing beyond the French women's immediate economic grievances into the heart of their problem, exposing the way in which all their disabilities fed off and fed back into one another in an ever-more-vicious circle of deprivation. The low wages of women, she argued, and their lack of job prospects, arose out of women's lack of education, and forced them into early marriage or onto the streets; lack of education gave men a reason for refusing women political rights; and the lack of political rights made it impossible for women to legislate for any reforms, or to obtain the right to education, wage parity or equality before the law. The subsequent history of feminism has only confirmed the substantial accuracy of de Gouges's basic analysis.

Nor was this just a pale piece of theorizing. "Women, wake up!" called de Gouges, "Recognize your rights!" Scornfully, she exposed the blatant new oppressions brought in by the self-seeking revolutionary males: "Man, the slave, has multiplied his strength. . . . Once free, he became unjust to his companion. . . . What advantages have you [women] got from the Revolution? A more open contempt!" With sarcastic reflections upon "our wise legislators," de Gouges urged all women to "oppose the force of reason to man's empty pretence of superiority."

Reason, however, is a luxury revolution rarely affords. And however hollow, the superiority of man was no pretence. There was never any intention on the part of the revolutionaries to rectify the position of women, even to recognize their separate claims: "Now," declared Mirabeau in his famous salvo at the opening of hostilities, "we are beginning the history of man."[23] So it proved. Feminist issues had been raised only to be deliberately and systematically birth-strangled.

Who can tell what might have happened had any of these revolutionary feminists survived the apocalypse? But their sex, which disqualified them from full membership of their society, gave them no protection from being violently hurried out of it. Olympe de Gouges hastened her fate by courageously protesting at the death of Louis XVI, guillotined in January 1793. Manon Roland, victim of a show trial in which she was not allowed to speak in her own defense, faced her death with heroic strength and dignity: "You judge me worthy to share the fate of the great men you have assassinated," she told her judges, "I shall endeavour to carry to the scaffold the courage they displayed."

Fierce revolutionaries though they were, de Gouges founding the notorious Club des Tricoteuses and Roland a disciple of Voltaire and Rousseau and passionate enemy of Marie Antoinette, both women allied themselves with the moderate Girondins when irreconcilable tensions split the French Revolutionary Assembly apart. With a prophetic irony, de Gouges had claimed in her *Déclaration* that women should have the right to stand for parliament "if they have the right to go to the scaffold." This was the only true equality seen by the feminist pioneers of France in their foreshortened lives. For their opposition to Robespierre, the evil genius of the Jacobin extremists, both women mounted the guillotine in the same month of November 1793.

It is, however, a poignant fact of history that most of the women who fell victim to the Terror had taken part in no revolutionary activity. The life of the young Lucille Desmoulins was forfeit simply because she was the wife of a leading Girondin, despite her mother's frenzied petitioning of Robespierre, who was godfather to Lucille's baby son. More inexplicable still were the countless, nameless victims like the "twenty peasant girls from Poitou," all brought to Paris to be guillotined together, for what offense is now lost. One of them had a baby at her breast as she mounted the scaffold, a common enough occurrence in these times that respected the sanctity of no human life; royal, common, male, female, old and young, all heads kissed in the basket, in the words of Danton's last black joke.

The political women at least recognized the face of the enemy. The instinctive opposition to Robespierre that had brought de Gouges and Roland to their deaths was all too well founded. When universal manhood suffrage was introduced that year, women were specifically excluded. The most active of de Méricourt's women's clubs, the Revolutionary Republican Women, organized a petition to the convention to demand the enfranchisement of women, and found themselves disbanded. Robespierre and his Jacobins then set about driving women out of politics and back into their homes; the fateful November that ended the lives of de Gouges and Roland saw also the suppression of all the women's political clubs. From this point onwards, women's active participation in French political life was effectively guillotined too, and for many generations to come the freedom of that dawn when it was bliss to be alive and female was to be nothing but a fading memory. "O Liberty!" as Manon Roland cried on the scaffold, "what crimes are committed in thy name!" English-speakers miss the fine irony implicit in this invocation of the revolutionary slogan: for "Liberté," immortalized by Delacroix as Marianne, is of course female: but somehow, on the way to "Egalité," she lost out to the real boss of the trinity, the undying, unchanging "Fraternité" of man.

The reign of terror in France, like the armed conflict in the newly sovereign state of America, had a fixed historical term, and those fated to suffer under the juggernaut of such times could at least hope to survive the crisis and live on to witness the world of reparation and restoration. Far more terrible in its way was the cataclysm that almost without warning overwhelmed the old world, took no hostages and left no survivors—a genuine war of worlds, the Industrial Revolution.

To the inhabitants of rural communities, many peaceably settled since Roman times, it was a catastrophe whose effects were immediate, spectacular and permanent:

> England of the first part of the eighteenth century was virtually a medieval England, quiet, primeval and undisturbed by the roar of trade and commerce. Suddenly, almost like a thunderbolt from a clear sky, were ushered in the storm and stress of the Industrial Revolution.[24]

Twentieth-century historians, with the benefit of hindsight, have shown that the concatenation of forces uniting to produce the machine age had been stealthily building up for some time beforehand—the signs were there to be read. But for the unwitting conscripts in this conflict, there was little access to advance warning of contemporary social and economic trends, and no chance to take evasive action. Unlike other wars, this claimed as casualties not only the able-bodied male conscripts, but women and children too, the pitiful cannon fodder whose recruitment remains an everlasting disgrace.

Iron, coal, steam—the new sources of power developed in the Britain of the eighteenth century revolutionized more than manufacturing technology. In an astonishingly short time their effect was to shatter the traditional structure of women's lives by splitting apart what had previously been the one indivisible whole of husband, home and family. The work of the pre-industrial housewife combined all these elements without strain, and centered her strongly both in her own world and in the wider scheme of things as a person of some significance:

> In their role as agriculturalists, women produced the bulk of the country's food

supply. The entire management of the dairy, including the milking of cows and the making of butter and cheese, was in women's hands, and the women were also responsible for the growing of flax and hemp, for the milling of corn, for the care of the poultry, pigs, orchards and gardens.[25]

With the shift from an agricultural to an industrial economy, from country to town, from home to factory, women lost the previous flexibility, status and control of their work. In its place they were granted the privilege of low-grade, exploited occupations, the double burden of waged and domestic labor, and the sole responsibility for child care that has weighed them down ever since. Each of the changes of the Industrial Revolution proved to have an adverse impact upon women's lives; coming together, the result was devastating, in ways that could never have been foreseen.

At the simplest level, the shift from home to factory production had a number of damaging consequences for women workers. Among the first was the loss of any previous partnership status, when a wife was denied the opportunity to share her husband's work. Before industrialization, women frequently worked alongside their menfolk or in close harmony with them, reaping, gleaning, binding, threshing, digging; a central image of the Middle Ages, and a metaphor for the mutual interdependence of the well-balanced couple, was the husbandman ploughing the furrow while his wife follows behind sowing the seed. This primitive pastoral which had endured through so many thousands of years was one of the first casualties of the revolution in labor.

Another was the control women had enjoyed as the head of their own home units of production, along with the often considerable sums of money they could generate. The pre-industrial housewife made little or no distinction between domestic or commercial activities; she brewed, baked, wove, collected eggs or raised pigs, and whatever she had left over from her own household requirements she would sell. The harder she worked, and the more successful her sidelines, the more money she made. As with the shared outdoor work of the agricultural calendar, the division of labor was reciprocal, and there was no concept of the only or principal male breadwinner supporting his wife and children—all were productive, the wife doubly so. As a waged laborer, by contrast, a woman was on a fixed weekly sum, fixed moreover at a rate often lower than that of children, let alone that of men, for reasons which were crystal clear to the boss-persons:

The low price of female labour makes it the most profitable as well as the most agreeable occupation for a female to superintend her own domestic establishment, and her low wages do not tempt her to abandon the care of her own children [i.e., because she cannot be tempted to what she cannot afford, a nurse or mother-substitute] . . . Mr. E., a manufacturer, employs females exclusively . . . [with] a decided preference to married females, especially those who have families at home dependent on them for support; they are attentive, docile, more so than unmarried females, and are compelled to use their utmost exertions to produce the necessities of life.[26]

As this shows, the factory system both reduced and dehumanized its operatives, regarding them "in no other light than as tools let out to hire." It also from the first created a hierarchy even of the exploited, for women were universally worked harder than their male fellow sufferers and paid less, employers everywhere agreeing that women were "more easily induced to undergo severe bodily fatigue than men," hence a better investment for "the master," as "a more obedient servant to himself, and an equally efficient slave to his machinery"—"cruelty!" wrote one reformer passionately, "though it may be voluntary, for God help them, the hands dare not refuse."[27]

So women, previously autonomous, now economically crippled, were forced into dependence on men, which in turn reinforced and indeed recreated for the modern world fresh notions of women's natural inferiority. Female subordination to males also took a new turn with the relocation of women's work from home to factories; subjection to the power of males was one thing when the patriarch was your own husband or father, and quite another under industrial organization, when the authority of the absent owner was vested in and expressed through the daily tyranny of a brutal and bullying overseer, as in this report on the first factories in America, deploring the use of "the cowhide, or well-seasoned strap of American manufacture":

We could show *many* females who have had corporeal punishment inflicted on them; one girl, 11 years of age, who had her leg broken with a billet of wood; another who had a board split over her head by a heartless monster in the shape of an overseer of a cotton-mill . . . *foreign overseers* are frequently placed over American women and children, and we are sorry to add that sometimes *foreigners in this country* have employed American overseers to carry into effect their tyrannical rule in these mills.[28]

For the women catapulted out of their home-based working lives into a factory routine, the harsh discipline was only one of a number of shocks. First came the hours of unremitting labor: a working day of 5 AM to 8 PM was common, and at peak times work would begin at 3 AM continuing till 10 PM, without any extra pay. The hours themselves would not have been so different from the workload of a home-based woman. But the forced pace of the labor, with the inability to break off, to rest or to vary the work in any way, made it a mental as well as physical torment.

And even the humblest homes compared favorably with factories where the heat of the machines kept the temperature at a constant 80 to 84 degrees; where the workers were not allowed to break off to have a drink, even the rainwater being locked up to prevent any such temptation; and where all doors and windows were kept locked, on pain of a fine of one shilling for anyone trying to open them. (This, interestingly enough, was exactly the same as that imposed for any homosexual activity in the factory lavatory: "Any two spinners *found together* in the *necessary*, each man . . . 1s. [shilling].") A contemporary eye (or rather nose) witness reported the effect of these working conditions on the victims of them:

> . . . not a breath of sweet air . . . the abominable and pernicious stink of the *gas* to assist in the murderous effects of the heat . . . noxious effluvia, mixed with the steam . . . the dust, and what is called cotton-flyings, or fuz, which the unfortunate creatures have to inhale . . . [29]

Not surprisingly, all industrial workers were very prone to lung diseases, usually grouped together as "consumption." But the nature of the disease or damage related very specifically to the trade: cutlers and grinders suffered from "embarrassment of breathing," coughing, vomiting and dust and mucus, "night sweats, diarrhea, extreme emaciation, together with all the symptoms of pulmonary consumption." This last was always in wait to get a grip on an enfeebled frame; it was a particular enemy of lace-workers, who from infancy had to wear stout wooden billets inside their stays to prevent their backs from giving out during the long hours of stooping over their work. This deformed the sternum, ribs and chest cavity, rendering the young women especially vulnerable to all respiratory diseases, but above all the "wasting away" of consumption.

Long-term industrial damage like this, which rendered young women "old, decrepit, deformed, and past labor at forty," was only one of the hazards which factory women had to face. Injury was a frequent occurrence in the early factories, and women were more vulnerable than men by virtue of their flowing garments, skirts, petticoats, pinafores and long hair. Factory records abound in cases of female workers like "Mary Richards, made a cripple" through being "lapped up by the strap underneath the drawing frame" of a power loom.[30] With all this, however, factory work was still preferred to what was undoubtedly the most dangerous and degraded form of labor exacted from the women of the time: coal mining. To unprepared observers, the spectacle of the pit-women in action was like a scene from hell itself: "Chained, belted, harnessed, like dogs in a go-cart—black, saturated with wet, and more than half naked—crawling upon their hands and feet, and dragging heavy loads behind them—they present an appearance indescribably disgusting and unnatural!" reported one horrified gentleman.

Mining women, of course, had no time or occasion to worry about their appearance. The work was so cruelly hard that it was not unknown for a girl to fall into a dead faint from exhaustion as soon as she climbed into the basket to be drawn up to the surface at the end of her shift; when this happened, she usually pitched out of the shallow wicker container and down the shaft to her death. Other fatalities were caused by the weight of the trucks the women had to pull—at twelve and a half hundredweight, a runaway wagon easily crushed or mangled its "drawer." Even normal conditions of working were horrifyingly severe: the youngest girls had to crawl through passages as low as 16 to 18 inches, while grown women were expected to navigate tunnels no higher than 30 inches. In a 14-hour day, they would crawl for anything between 10 and 20 miles, with no opportunity at any point to stand up or straighten their limbs. In the winter, said Fanny Drake, a Yorkshire pit-woman, she worked for six months up to her calves in water; this took the skin off her feet "just as if they were scalded." Betty Harris of Little Bolton in the neighboring county of Lancashire found that her troubles came more from the girdle and chain by which she pulled her truck along, for it cut and blistered her sides "till I have had the skin off me"; but the only time it really bothered her was "when I was in the family way."[31]

Betty was thirty-seven when she made this statement. Work like this could only get harder as women grew older, especially if they had a number of pregnancies, for with "the great sore of labour," reported a Scots pit-woman Isabel Hogg, "false births [miscarriages] are frequent, and very dangerous." Isabel Wilson of the East Lothian colliery miscarried five times and delivered her last baby on the Saturday morning after she had just completed her Friday night shift. Another coal-wife, Betty Wardle, did not manage to follow Isabel's fine timing; her baby was born down the pit, and she had to bring it up the shaft wrapped in her skirt; she said the "belt and chain" brought her labor on.

And still these women labored. In mines without lifting gear, women carried the coal to the surface on their backs. "I make 40 or 50 journeys [to the surface] a day," said Scotswoman Mary Duncan, "and can carry 2 cwt as my burthen. Some females carry 2½ to 3 cwt, but it is overstraining." In this way, each individual woman would bring up between one and a half and two tons of coal in the course of a day's work, for which the wage was often no more than 8d. Small wonder then that the Scots civil engineer Robert Bald recorded seeing the women coming up from the pit "weep most bitterly" from the strain of their labor, and one "married woman . . . groaning under an excessive weight of coals, trembling in every nerve and almost unable to keep her knees from sinking under her" who spoke for all when she said, in a voice that haunted him thereafter, "O Sir, this is sore, sore work. I wish to God the first woman who tried to bear coals had broken her back, and none would have tried it again."[32]

Any consideration of the lives of the female laborers of the Industrial Revolution bears out to its fullest the savage attack of Margaret, Duchess of Newcastle in the seventeenth century: "Women live like *bats* or *owls*, labor like *beasts* and die like *worms*." Yet even the appalling work, snuffed-out hopes and truncated lives, these women had more to suffer still. Themselves often enough exploited child slaves—little girls began down the mines, opening doors for the coal wagons to pass, as young as five, "invariably set to work at an earlier age than boys . . . from a notion very generally entertained among the parents, that girls are more acute and capable of making themselves useful at an earlier age than boys"[33]—they had no alternative but to see their own children ruined in their turn. What this meant for both mother and child can be seen in this examination of a 17-year-old textile worker who had been laboring for ten years in a factory in the North of England:

> When I had worked about half a year, a weakness fell into my knees and ankles; it continued, and it got worse and worse. In the morning I could scarcely walk, and my brother and sister used out of kindness to take me under each arm, and run with me, a good mile, to the mill, and my legs dragged on the ground in consequence of the pain; I could not walk. If we were five minutes late, the overlooker would take a strap and beat us till we were black and blue. . . . I was as straight and healthful as any when I was seven years and a quarter old . . .
> Your mother being a widow . . . could not afford to take you away?—No.

> Was she made very unhappy by seeing that you were getting crooked and deformed?—I have seen her weep sometimes, and I have asked her why she was weeping, but she would not tell me then, but she has told me since . . . [34]

Condemned to work the same hours as their parents, and to shoulder as nearly as possible an adult workload (several cases were reported in which a full-grown male miner ruptured himself by lifting his child's load of coals on to its back) the "offspring of the laboring poor" were children only in name. If they faltered under these unreasonable demands, the punishments could be brutal and sadistic: a "bad" boy nail-maker would have his ear nailed to his workbench, a "disobedient" girl risked being dragged the length of the factory by her hair. Between fear of a repetition of the punishment, and fear of losing the "place" and with it the child's income, most families were powerless to challenge the abusers of their children. For one woman, however, when her young son was beaten with a "billy-roller" (a wooden loom-shaft between two and three yards long, and about five inches in diameter) till he vomited blood, it was too much. In the boy's own words:

> I entreated my mother not to make a complaint, lest I be further beaten. The next morning after I went to work, she followed me, and came to the slubber that had used me in that way, and gave him a sharp lecture . . . as soon as she was gone, he beat me again severely for telling, when one of the young men . . . went out and found my mother, and told her, and she came in again and enquired of me what instrument it was I was beaten with, but I durst not do it; some of the bystanders pointed out the instrument, the billy-roller, and she seized it immediately, and beat it about the fellow's head, and gave him one or two black eyes . . . [35]

Stories like this provide welcome evidence that the experience of the Industrial Revolution was not one of unrelieved female submission to the purgatory of cruelty, suffering and deprivation. Nor was pre-industrial life the rosy pastoral that it has often seemed; there was no sudden pantomimic scene-change from agrarian utopia to dark satanic mills, and the country women described by La Bruyère as living, working and dying in holes in the ground "like wild animals" would have been most surprised to learn that theirs was about to become a paradise lost. Nor can all the evils of this crowded century be blamed on factory organization. The soaring population, for instance, as more babies survived their birth and infancy and more women survived childbirth to complete their reproductive years, certainly contributed to the contemporary evils of urban overcrowding and desperate poverty; but it was itself a force of nature, attributable to the oldest source of power, not to any of the newfangled discoveries.

It has been argued, too, that the Industrial Revolution, despite the sufferings of those who went down in the struggle against the machine, was a convulsion unavoidably necessary for society to survive. "He that will not apply new remedies, must expect new evils," warned Francis Bacon, one of the earliest social philosophers of the modern age; and the alternative scenario, of the disaster averted rather than the cataclysm that occurred, is forcefully outlined by a leading historian on the period, T. S. Ashton:

> The central problem of the age was how to feed and clothe and employ generations of children outnumbering by far those of any earlier time. Ireland was faced with the same problem. Failing to solve it, she lost in the forties about a fifth of her people by emigration or starvation and disease. If England had remained a nation of cultivators and craftsmen, she could hardly have escaped the same fate. . . . There are today on the plains of India and China men and women, plague-ridden and hungry, living lives little better, to outward appearance, than those of the cattle that toil with them by day and share their places of sleep by night. Such Asiatic standards, and such unmechanized horrors, are the lot of those who increase their numbers without passing through an Industrial Revolution.[36]

As a counterbalance to the doomsday version of these historical events, this argument has much to commend it. The march of progress, however, is rarely welcomed by those it tramples underfoot. To the women faced with feeding the machines brought into being by man's resistless innovation, women condemned to serve the new gods of power for an insult of a pittance, invention was truly the mother of necessity. With this work, on these wages, women could not live. Married or marriageable women were therefore manacled to matrimony by the steel-strong fetter of the survival imperative, while single women paid for their anomalous state with all they had—or, brutally, did not have. Female vagrants took to the roads in unprecedented numbers; in the one month of June 1817, the parish of Rugby in the English Midlands relieved eighteen vagrant women, one of whom was "lying in," to eight males. London magistrates recorded a steady rise in female suicides. Other women simply lay down and died—the prospective purchaser of a house near St. Paul's was horrified to discover that it contained three dead women, terribly emaciated, and in the garret two more women and a girl of sixteen on the point of death from starvation.[37] And while women were thrown back into dependence as the price of life, men confirmed their mastery over nature and machines, in a wide-ranging and interlocking scheme of domination that has yet to be dismantled.

Every revolution is a revolution of ideas—yet to innovate is not to reform. The revolutions of the eighteenth century, so different from each other in some of their most profound particulars, yet had one simple truth in common—each was a revolution for some, and not for all. And only some ideas were overturned in the general *bouleversement*. Of those that survived, the most enduring proved to be that of the natural superiority of man. And when borne on the great wave of expansion, as adventurers and empire-builders struck out for foreign fields, this antique nostrum travelled with them like a plague virus. Unexamined and unchecked, it was the first of the items of the white man's burden to be distributed throughout his new dominions.

9

THE ROD OF EMPIRE

Whoever sees Virginia,
  This he shall surely find
A land for men . . .

MICHAEL DRAYTON, 'Ode
to the Virginian Voyage', 1605

Women therefore must go into the Colonies as well
as men, that the plantations may spread into generations, and not be forever pieced from without.

FRANCIS BACON, addressing the
English Royal Council for Virginia, 1609

No, no—surely not! My God— *not more of those
damned whores!*

LIEUTENANT CLARK OF THE FIRST FLEET ON
SIGHTING A FEMALE CONVICT TRANSPORT SHIP
COMING INTO SYDNEY HARBOUR, JUNE 1790

Women are women the world over,
whatever their color.

RIDER HAGGARD, *King Solomon's Mines (1886)*

If the Industrial Revolution brought the rape of nature, the imperial
thrust which stimulated its growth and provided its market meant the
rape of the world. Between 1796 and 1818, Britain seized Ceylon,
South Africa, India, Burma, and Assam. By the Opium War of 1842,
the body count had risen to include Hong Kong, the Punjab, Kashmir,
Afghanistan and Singapore. Nor was empire a purely British theme—
Dutch, Spanish, French and Portuguese all scrambled to the global
carve-up like boys to a brawl, while the American expansion westward
echoed the imperial theme of the country's first founders and gave it
an internal empire within its own shores greater than many beyond.
The sum of these moments has proved a decisive legacy in the shaping
of the modern world; in everything from apartheid in South Africa to
the firearms *folie* of the USA, the spoor of the great imperial male
stalking gun in hand across the sands of time may be detected to this
day.

In song, story, myth and memory, and above all in official history, empire has always been seen in this way as an heroic male endeavor. Since Alexander the Great broke through to the limits of the last known frontier, then wept because there were no more worlds to conquer, women have been absent from the annals. Of those who sailed in the historic *Mayflower* voyage of 1620, the names of the Pilgrim Fathers are memorialized in stone on the Plymouth quayside—of the eighteen women who sailed too, there is no mention. And as the bounds of empire spread wider still and wider, pushed onward by Kipling's cold-eyed adventurers "that smell of tobacco and blood," the classic fiction of men-against-the-odds is summed up by the boast of the hero of the Rider Haggard epic, *King Solomon's Mines:* "I can safely say that there is not a *petticoat* in the whole history."

Yet as the place names from Port Elizabeth to Maryland indicate, the female influence cannot be denied. For women were always there, active as colonizers from the days of the Greeks, essential to the survival of empire, as Bacon had insisted from the outset. In the North American venture, the first-ever imperial baby was a girl, the aptly named Virginia Dare, safely delivered on Roanoke Island on Ascension Day 1587. Similarly the first white Australian was the baby Rebekah Small, who arrived shortly after the First Fleet landed in 1788; although born to one of the "damned whores" who had so disgusted Lieutenant Ralph Clark, Rebekah lived this down to marry a missionary and to present her new country with no less than fourteen little Australians.

In the history of empire, women were always there because, quite simply, the men could not manage without them. Worldwide, secure, and long-term settlement was virtually impossible without female workers; the first governor of the Cape Colony, the Dutch Colonel Van Riebeck, was horrified at his men's inability to tend cattle, make butter and cheese, or to do anything for themselves. An immediate draft of girls from orphanages in Amsterdam and Rotterdam had to be ordered to supply the deficiency. England, alerted by Bacon, recognized the problem from the outset—the London Company responsible for the successful foundation of the Jamestown settlement in Virginia systematically despatched to the New World "young women to make wives," to be "planted" alongside the men. These had to be "handsome and honestly educated maids," and "specially recommended into the colony for their good bringing-up." But neither their looks, education nor upbringing were to save them from being treated like the merchandise they were, and on arrival in Virginia they were "sold" for 120 pounds of best tobacco, the equivalent of $500 dollars apiece, and thereafter committed to the colonists who took them, as servants or wives, for life.

Other young girls had even less say in what happened to them. Pauper and orphan girls were swept up off the streets of London and despatched with unbecoming alacrity to indentured apprenticeships under masters they had never seen, in a country they had hardly heard of. These reluctant conscripts were usually embarked to the accompaniment of loud harborside speculation about which five of every six would be dead before the ship made landfall, and how fast the survivors would succumb to the mosquitos, malaria and fever-bearing swamps of the badly sited Jamestown, where strong men died like flies of "the bloody flux," "calentures" and "agues," or "starved to death with cold."

The harsher the country, the greater the abuses that were needed to feed the female famine. In the prison colony of Australia women were from the first transported for far milder offenses than the men's. Male transports had to be guilty of capital offenses, or vicious and repeated acts of crime. Female criminals, then as now, were in a tiny minority, less than one in ten of all convicts. As a consequence, English judges, obsessed with the imperial imperative to keep up the numbers of women, would transport a female offender for the most trivial of transgressions, and the lady's maid who had "borrowed" her mistress's gloves or sidecombs found herself on a par with the most brutal footpad, "resurrectionist" or murderer.

Schemes to bring in "honest" women were easier to devise than to carry out. From the first, the situation was ripe for exploitation. One clerk of the London Company forged himself a personal "Commission to take up yeomen's daughters to serve his Majesty for breeders in Virginia," where the price of a woman had rocketed from 120 pounds of tobacco to 150 pounds within two years. Another would-be fleshmonger, appropriately named R. F. Breed, solicited from the British government 150 guineas a head for shipping "sixteen respectable young females under twenty-three" to Hobart. Charitable institutions under the direction of the London Emigration Committee selected "deserving cases" for assisted passage, and shipped them out under the care of the contractor John Marshall. On arrival, however, the eagerly awaited cargo proved to have a high quotient of the undeserving in its ranks ("prostitutes and paupers!" said the critics), whom Marshall had "swept off the streets of London" to make up his full complement of passengers. Once on board, the undeserving had wasted no time in bringing the deserving round to their own way of thinking:

Management on board had been lax, leading to riotous scenes of drunkenness [and] debauchery . . . the women creating disgusting scenes on arrival, augmenting the population of prostitutes in the colony and doing more to corrupt than to civilise Australia . . . [1]

Even when the Female Emigration Societies had cleaned up their act, the problem of the female famine was not solved. As late as 1879, Australian men were still feeling the pinch, as these advertisements in the *Matrimonial Chronicle*, a paper devoted wholly to those seeking marriage, will indicate:

–Wanted a wife by a young man in the country, with a house and £500 a year.
–Wanted a wife who can work; by a selector in the Manora district. He has a large amount of land and sheep.
–Wanted a wife by a young man in Queensland . . . the lady must be well able to read and write, so that she can assist him in his business. [2]

Essentially, though, women were required for much, much more than their working capacity. There is no doubt that the primary production of imperial women was reproduction, the more so as hostile climates, disease and danger maximized infant mortality everywhere. The wife of the Reverend Samuel Sewall of Massachusetts bore him 14 children in 40 years of marriage, yet within four months of her death the patriarch was looking out for a new bride, "one young enough to bear." Women were equally expected to keep up their less tangible sexual duties, of setting a tone, maintaining standards and civilizing the men. Dismayed by the number of colonial administrators who fell victim to the temptation of "going native," the British government exported "English roses" by the shipload. These soon sent native concubines packing with a double-barrelled blast of Christianity and carbolic, to the open admiration of traveller Baron von Hubner: "It is the Englishwoman, courageous, devoted, well-educated, well-trained—the Christian guardian of the domestic hearth—who by her magic wand has brought this wholesome transformation." [3]

As this shows, English women were consciously used as a weapon of empire, to keep the master-race pure and to avoid the contemporary bogey of "miscegenation." Even the presence of his sister, old imperialists felt, "saved many a young fellow from drink and *ruin*" [intercourse with native women]. Exquisitely pink and white, fresh and fragile, innocent and inviolable, the Englishwoman incarnated all the values of "England, home and beauty" for which so many men suffered and died. But the task of keeping the moral conscience of the race was not merely a preoccupation of multi-racial imperial outposts, nor merely of patriarchal males. In 1847 the philanthropist Caroline Chisholm, whose devotion to the welfare of women was beyond question, issued this directive to the British government as a recipe for "the formation of a good and great people" in Australia: "For all the clergy you can dispatch, all the schoolmasters you can appoint, all the churches you can build, and all the books you can export, you will never do much good without what a gentleman in that Colony very appropriately called 'God's police'—good and virtuous women."[4] Even women whose own mothers could not have called them good or virtuous had a key role to play in keeping the menfolk in line, according to a historian of the "old Wild West": "When one considers the crudity of what was predominantly a male society, it must be admitted that the scarlet representatives of the gentler sex played an important part in taming the West." As one old Montanan put it, "many's the miner who'd never wash his face or comb his hair if it wasn't for thinkin' of the sportin' girls he might meet in the saloons."[5]

From the first, then, women only entered the empire adventure on male terms, as instruments of the overriding imperative of the patriarch: dominion and domination. Once they were there, strong systems continually reminded them of their purpose, and reinforced their status as the perennial underclass. In America, early laws prohibited the grant of land to single women, who were expected to live under "family government." In Maryland, a law of 1634 required every woman to marry within seven years of inheriting land, on pain of losing it to her male next-of-kin. A Salem woman was sentenced to be flogged for "reproaching the magistrates," after which she "had a cleft stick put on her tongue for half an hour" for similarly "reproaching the elders." She at least survived—the "preaching woman" Mary Dyer, "of a very proud spirit and much addicted to revelations," was banished from Boston, but returned and was hanged.[6]

In the second wave of imperial expansion, the use and abuse of women reached epidemic proportions. This sprang in part from the nature of the Australian experience: set up from the first as a penal colony, the country was never designed as a haven from persecution, nor even as a mirror image of contemporary life back home in England. But these circumstances conspired to make transportation, severe enough in itself, a double punishment for women, who suffered in addition to their sentence because of their sex. For their status as convicts served to rob them of all human rights of personal autonomy, and from the moment of sentence they became fair game. The sexual abuse of female convicts began with the crews of the transport ships, as one distressed observer reported to the Select Parliamentary Committee on the State of the Gaols, in 1819:

> These women informed me . . . that they were subject to every manner of insult from the master of the ship and the sailors; that the master stripped several of them and publicly whipped them; that one young woman, from ill-treatment, threw herself into the sea and perished; that the master beat one of the women with a rope with his own hands, till she was much bruised in her arms, breasts, and other parts of her body . . . [7]

The same witness recorded that "the youngest and handsomest of the women were selected from the other convicts . . . by order of the master . . . for the vilest purposes." Even the professional men on board were not above this grotesque abuse of their female charges; one convict woman, Elizabeth Barber, denounced the assistant surgeon of the ship on which she was transported as "a poxy blood-letter, who seduced innocent girls while treating them for the fever, using his surgery as a floating whore-house."[8]

To be a convict woman, in the eyes of any right-thinking man, was to be abandoned, and to be abandoned was to be a whore. Pre-judged, the women were all tarred with the same brush. One of the colony's first magistrates, ironically a former convict himself, described them as "the most disgusting objects that ever disgraced the female form." Another commentator put it even more bluntly: the women were "the lowest possible . . . they all smoke and drink, and in fact to speak plain language, I consider them *all prostitutes*."[9]

Undoubtedly some of the convict women transported to Australia (192 in the First Fleet of 1788 as against 586 men) *were* prostitutes. But it made no difference whether they were or not, since on arrival they were all treated as such, being immediately disposed of to the first man who cared to step up and ask for them. This custom, to disinterested observers quite breathtaking in its unabashed brutality and simplicity, caused much comment. One free settler wrote home:

> It will perhaps scarcely be believed that, on the arrival of a female convict ship, the custom has been to suffer the inhabitants of the colony each to select one at his pleasure, not only as servants, but as avowed objects of intercourse . . . rendering the whole colony little better than an extensive brothel.[10]

Nor was there even a limit on the number of female prisoners a man could have for his own personal use. Convict women were in fact given out to the men along with the rest of their share of the incoming commodities. There was even a special army issue: in 1803, 40 female transports were brazenly accounted for as "women allowed to the New South Wales Corps."[11]

This giving of women into prostitution ensured that they were punished twice over for their original offense, once by transportation, then by enforced whoredom. The best hope for a woman in this situation was to attach herself strongly to one male protector; the norm, however, was for "last fleet's woman" to be thrown out on the streets as soon as the next ships made landfall with their cargo of "fresh meat."

Yet under the same rules by which women who were denied access to society's privileges were still subject to the fullest of its penalties, imperial women, however low their status, bore an equal share of all the burdens of empire shoulder to shoulder with their men. There was no sex exemption, for instance, from the tortures of an intemperate climate like the heat: "hot as hell!—like Dives we were 'in torments',," recorded one victim of India's "six-month heat-waves" when the temperature rose to 114 degrees fahrenheit in the shade, never falling below 95 even at dead of night, and round the clock the air felt "like hot iron on your face." Other trials included waking up to find the bed swarming with red ants—the infallible remedy, from Assam to Arizona, was to put tin cans full of water under each leg—or collecting a legful of leeches on a walk to a local beauty spot: "I cannot tell you how pretty the place was, the banks covered with the loveliest flowers and down at the bottom the clear water running among grey stones . . . quantities of leeches biting me, nasty fat black creatures . . . bitten in 25 places and these bled a great deal though they did not hurt at all . . . " recorded one *burra memsahib* calmly.[12]

At this shows, the highest rank was no protector of persons. Arriving at Simla exhausted from her duties and after a "ghastly nightmare of a journey" spent wrapped in towels to soak up her uncontrollable perspiration, the Vicereine of India counted 50 mammoth blood-sucking insects on her bed, and was awake all night dealing with them: "I killed up to 4 in the morning . . . delighted to be back," she wrote laconically to her daughter.[13] This kind of resolution became even more necessary when the hungry predators were wolves, as in the American West, or more dangerous still; Ann Moffat of the famous Scottish missionary family in Africa once saved herself from a lion's spring by a well-judged leap straight into her ox-waggon, where she lay all night listening to the great cat crunching on the bones of her ox, which had suffered in her place.

The most dangerous of all the great predators, however, was undoubtedly the two-legged animal, and pioneer women had to be ready
to defend themselves at all times. Missionary preacher Dr. Anna Shaw
described her reaction to a rape threatened by a man she had hired
to drive her through a remote frontier region:

> I slipped my hand into the satchel on my lap, and it touched my revolver. No
> touch of human fingers ever brought such comfort. With a deep breath of thanks-
> giving I drew it out and cocked it . . . he recognised the sudden click. "By God!"
> he cried. "You wouldn't dare" . . . I felt my hair rise on my scalp with the horror
> of the moment, which seemed worse than any nightmare a woman could exper-
> ience . . . [14]

Anna's terrifying journey, with her revolver trained on her would-
be rapist as he drove all night through the depths of a black forest,
had a happy outcome. When she reached the isolated timber camp,
all the lumberjacks poured into town to see the lady preacher who
packed a gun as well as a Bible. The collection at the end of the service
was the largest ever taken in the history of the settlement, and Anna
herself was a great success, though not entirely for her preaching.
"Her sermon?" said one of the men afterwards. "I dunno what she
preached—but the little woman sure has got grit!"

Experiences like Anna's were a commonplace of empire, wherever
men were men and women had to reckon with it. Nor was the solitary
lustful male the only threat. Empire life was everywhere lived on the
edge of danger, and women learned all manner of new skills as naturally
as they had picked up needlework or domestic management in the
Old World. They learned to ride long distances, on anything with four
legs, ox, mule, camel or elephant, and to navigate when the guide
slipped off like a thief in the night, leaving them on their own devices.
They learned to cope with all kinds of crisis, like the philosophical
Margaret Carrington of America's northern plains, who rattled off her
everyday calamities with no sense of grievance: "The snapping of a
tent pole at midnight under three feet of snow; the blaze of the canvas
as it touched a red-hot stovepipe; the snowdrifts that slip through the
closely drawn entrance and sprinkle the bed; frozen water buckets
. . . the plains winds . . . whipping sheets and table-cloths into ribbons
or blowing them across the prairie . . . "[15]

Margaret's washing days must have been an ordeal of the first water.
But the housewifely concern here with niceties like tablecloths obscures
the fact that in addition to their inescapable burden of "women's
work," these females had to master the traditionally male tasks as well.

"I learned to handle a musket very well," declared Susie King Taylor, a black woman and former slave. "I could shoot straight, and often hit the target." Susie also knew how to load and re-load for firing, how to clean a gun, and how to dismantle and reassemble it. She had learned her skill with firearms while serving with a Unionist regiment for four years during the Civil War, "without receiving a dollar . . . glad to be allowed to go with the regiment."[16] Susie's duties included nursing as well as fighting, so the Army had double value from what it was getting for nothing in the first place.

Often the confidence and competence of these women seriously unnerved the men around them. Annie Blanche Sokalski was an army widow and real-life Calamity Jane, a famous sure-shot and trick rider. She dressed always in the skins of wolves she had killed herself, and went everywhere attended by her thirteen dogs, "the exact number of stripes in the American flag," she would say. When this vision in wolf-tails galloped past General Sherman at the head of his troops, the astonished commander was heard to gasp, "What the devil of a creature is that? Wild woman, Pawnee, Sioux or what?"[17]

For the women fortunate enough to enjoy the freedom of the empire along with high rank and social position, the rewards were great indeed. At its height the imperial life, "under the shadow of a dream," in Kipling's phrase, was an enchanted existence. The Vicereine of India describes here the guest quarters on a visit to a maharajah's palace:

> . . . pale blue silk hangings with lovely dressings and bathrooms with every known bath salt and perfume from the Rue de Paix. Next day we visited the fort, carried up in red velvet and gold chairs. . . . I wish you could have seen the Purdah Courtyard, all carved in white marble, like alabaster . . . [18]

And these were only the daytime amusements. By night there were "moonlight revels," parties of 500 or 1000 people in fancy dress dancing the night away on carpets of white waxed canvas surrounded by massed hydrangeas under trees festooned with red, white and blue lights. Even the old hands fell under the spell of India's magic again at times like these: "a full moon, the entire garden surrounded by walls of Dorothy Perkins in full bloom—*fairyland!*" pronounced the Vicereine with deep satisfaction. India above all called them, high-born or low: "I can never express how happy I am and how thoroughly I enjoy this delightful unconventional life here," recorded a young subaltern's mother on her first and only visit to him: "and the beauty of the people, such lovely saris and jewels, such lovely faces . . . "[19]

For empire women in general, however, life was no party, and nostalgia for its vanished glory denies the reality of the often appalling trials women had to face. The missionary wife Mary Edwards had not found Dr. Livingstone an easy guest when he inflicted himself on the couple for many months; but when he rashly provoked a lion to attack him, and Mrs. Edwards had to tend the suppurating wound crawling with maggots, nursing the gruff, arrogant, messianic Livingstone must have been the last straw.[20] The good doctor at least recovered. A far worse grief befell those who had to nurse their own dearly beloved and lost the struggle, like the wife of Sir Thomas Metcalfe. This British resident of Delhi had the evil fortune to be the instrument of an administrative decision to terminate the title and privilege of its king. The queen invoked an ancient Mogul revenge, and had him poisoned. The empire claimed many less famous lives, too, like that of 17-year-old Jeanie Goldie who married into the Indian Service, bore and lost a baby, and died of puerperal infection, all within eighteen months. "I felt," wrote her desolate husband, "like a murderer."[21]

These individual tragedies are merely representative of thousands upon thousands more. Indeed, from the first imperial settlements in America, when entire colonies were wiped out in hideous storms of terror of attack from the enemy without and disease within, and corn had to be sown across the graves so that none could number the dead, the saga of empire has included a running threnody of loss, defeat and death. Often this was of a most painful kind; the matron of the mission hospital at Peshawar had to see her husband, the doctor there, shot down by a man whose son he had failed to cure. Undeterred, Mrs. Starr returned to the hospital where he was murdered to work among his enemies and devoted her life to the people who had taken his. Later she was to perform another supremely courageous act when tribesmen of the same tribe as her husband's killer murdered the wife of a British army officer and abducted his daughter. Mrs. Starr, a fluent Pushtu speaker, volunteered to go alone into the enemy territory to try to secure the life of the girl. She succeeded in bringing the hostage back unharmed, without making any concessions in return.

For many women, though, there was no happy ending. Some went down in a last red cloud of blood, fighting to the death like Mrs. Beresford, only one of the heroine-victims of the terrible massacres of the Indian Mutiny in 1857. When the Bank of Delhi was attacked, of which her husband was the manager, an eyewitness recorded her unshrinking stand in defense of all she held dear:

Mr. Beresford . . . took refuge with his wife and family on the roof of one of the outbuildings. And there, for some time they stood at bay, he with a sword in his hand, while his courageous helpmate was armed with a spear. Thus with resolute bravery they defended the gorge of the staircase [and] made a gallant resistance . . . one man fell dead beneath the lady's spear . . . [22]

But the defenders were hopelessly outnumbered, and "to resist was but to protract the pains of death." Overpowered and hacked to pieces, Mrs. Beresford became just another example of the highest imperial type, "the love that never falters, the love that pays the price, / The love that makes undaunted the final sacrifice."[23]

"The final sacrifice," *pro patria mori* at the hands of the enemy in the heat of battle, was of course far more commonly the lot of men. But the risks faced by the soldiers in the front lines were scarcely greater than the routine hazard of the empire wife, the inevitability of childbirth under almost any circumstances. Even as the Beresfords were fighting for their lives, one officer's wife, Harriet Tytler, was giving birth alone and unaided in the back of a munitions wagon rattling her out of Delhi to safety. Against this, Mary Livingstone, dragged around Africa by the restless David, was lucky to be "confined in a field." Her mother, however, did not see it that way, as her powerful but unavailing reproach to Livingstone makes clear:

> Was it not enough that you lost one lovely babe and scarcely saved the others? . . . a pregnant woman with three little children trailing about . . . through the wilds of Africa, among savage men and beasts! Had you found a place to which you wished to go and commence missionary operations, the case would be altered. Not one word would I say, were it to the mountains of the moon. But to go with an exploring party; the thing is ridiculous . . . [24]

Ridiculous or not, it happened. Mary gave birth on the banks of the River Zouga with no shelter but a thorn tree. "Never had an easier or better time of it," was Livingstone's verdict on his fifth experience of fatherhood.

At least Mary Livingstone knew what to expect. When girls were married young and shipped off to imperial outposts with no mother or female relative to guide them through the mysteries of married life, the result could be staggering. One young bride, Emily Bayley, married at Delhi in March, had not completed her extended honeymoon trip to Simla when in October she felt "so very ill" that the doctor ordered her to return to England. All her luggage and possessions had been packed and sent on ahead when on the night before sailing, as she recalled, "we were startled by the birth of our first child."[25] To the mother and baby, the doctor soon added another patient, for the new

father fainted dead away when informed of the event. When he recovered he rushed out to buy some clothes for the unexpected arrival,
coming back in triumph with "an exquisitely embroidered French
cambric robe and a pink plush cloak"—not exactly the regulation wear
for a newborn child. But clearly a man who did not know that intercourse makes babies, and that his wife was advancing in pregnancy,
could not be expected to realize that babies need nappies.

But even with experience, the life of an empire wife was not easy.
One of its greatest distresses was the enforced separation from those
very children they had borne with such resolution in huts and on
highways, under gun-carriages and beside unknown waters. It was
holy writ throughout the British Empire that children must not, could
not be brought up in a hot climate. Yet a wife's duty was always to
remain at her husband's side. As a result, recalled the Anglo-Indian
novelist M. M. Kaye, "year after year weeping mothers took their
children down to the great trading ports . . . and handed them over
to the care of friends or nurses to be taken 'Home' and brought up
by relatives, or in many cases (Rudyard Kipling and his sister Trix
are among them) by strangers." The *memsahib* who had been so non-
chalant about leech bites permitted herself this lament for her absent
children: "I felt like Mahomet's coffin, suspended between my broken
family." But if they did not lose their children one way, Kaye recorded,
they lost them in another: "India was littered with the graves of dead
children [and] every mother expected to lose at least three out of every
five she bore."[26]

With these physical and emotional burdens on married women, it
is hardly surprising that those poised to take advantage of the moment
of empire were usually single. For the chances were there, openings
and possibilities almost unprecedented in the previous history of wom-
en's restricted lives. It took the factory-girl Mary Slessor a decade or
more of saving and studying to realize her ambition of going out to
Africa as a missionary. But when she arrived, she tackled tribal abuses
like human sacrifice and twin-murder with such vigor and success that
the government made her a ruling magistrate. Though single, she also
became the mother of no less than 12 pairs of the twins she had saved
from ritual sacrifice. Back in Scotland, she would have been still at
her loom in the mill.

Mary Slessor was a true daughter of a long line of women travellers
and explorers, from the phenomenal Jane Digby, who at the age of
46 enslaved a Syrian sheikh and became queen of his tribe, to Lady
Anne Blunt, the first woman to penetrate the Arabian peninsula. It

is almost impossible to exaggerate the extent to which travel offered some fortunate women the chance to escape from the excruciating boredom of their lives at home; Isabella Bird was so "delicate" that "the quietest life in London" reduced her to "nervous prostration," but anywhere else she could ride thirty miles a day, sleep rough in a blizzard, and outface grizzly bears and howling Chinese mobs.

Adventuring women could escape, too, from the rigors of Victorian sexual repression. The redoubtable Bird, having investigated the menfolk of Australia, the Pacific, China, Iraq and Tibet, and by now the first woman Fellow of the British Geographical Society, lost her heart in the American West to a "dear desperado," "Rocky Mountain Jim." The famous lepidopterist Margaret Fountaine briskly collected more than butterflies in her travels, and when she startled a toothsome young dragoman in Syria, she made this particularly fine specimen her common-law husband. Louisa Jebb, who with only another woman for company had ridden through Turkey and Iraq narrowly escaping death at the hands of Islamic fanatics, described coming upon a "screaming circle of dancing, stamping men." Although vividly remembering "I once did crochet-work in drawing-rooms!" Louisa did not hesitate:

> A feeling of wild rebellion took hold of me: I sprang into the circle.
> "Make me mad!" I cried out. "I want to be mad too!"
> The men seized me and on we went, on and on with the hopping and turning and stamping. And soon I too was a savage, a glorious free savage under the white moon.[27]

Whist in Winchester, checkers in Cheltenham and Mah Jong in Marlborough would all pale as a form of entertainment in comparison with this: and could the minuet or the waltz ever be the same again?

No less adventurous were the women who travelled to make their fortune, like the Jamaican businesswoman, traveller, gold prospector, writer and "doctress" Mary Seacole, a Creole of slave ancestry crossed with Scots, who left a thriving business in Kingston to follow the British army to the Crimea, where she became nationally famous for her dedication in provisioning the troops. As a widow, Mrs. Seacole was keen to stress that this was her choice and not something forced upon her: "it was from a confidence in my own powers, and not at all from necessity, that I remained an unprotected female."[28] Like Seacole, Mary Reibey had every reason to feel "confidence in her own powers": transported to Australia in 1790 at the age of thirteen for stealing a horse, this Mary became in time a hotelier, grain trader, importer, shipping magnate and property developer, Australia's most successful businesswoman in the history of the island.

Most of the Empire's businesswomen traded, however, in a more immediate commodity: flesh. Of these, the saloon-bar girls of the Wild West have passed into mythology, though their real-life stories needed no embellishment. As the laconic tribute on a played-out silver mine in Johannesburg, California, "dedicated to Hattie, Little Eva and the Girls of the Line," ruefully records, "While The Men Dug For Silver, They Dug For Gold."[29] One terrified traveller described the experience of seeing "about seventy-five" dance-hall girls descending on him:

> All of them had nicknames such as the Virgin, Cheekako Lil, Buntie, the Oregon Mare, the Utah Filly, Punch Grass, the Black Bear and her sister the Cub, another called "Wiggles," and so on down the line. You could pay your money and take your choice. If you didn't watch out they would help themselves to your money! . . . Do you wonder that we were anxious to leave that place where everything cost dollars [and] painted-cheeked ladies tempted us on every street corner?[30]

Certainly there was gold to be dug out of the pockets of the men who had spent long, harsh, deprived months and years extracting it from the far less accessible sources underground. Honora Ornstein, known as Diamond-Tooth Lil, the last surviving "dance-hall sweetheart" of Dawson, Texas, found her first fortune so easy to come by that she made a second, just like that. Among the ruling queens of the daughters of the game, Julia Bulette, who arrived in Virginia City just after the discovery of the fabulous Comstock lodes in 1859, charged the prospectors $1000 an hour for her services and amassed a collection of precious stones and jewels that would not have disgraced a tsarina or ranee. What is usually overlooked, however, in the romanticization of these women (the quintessential fantasy is Marilyn Monroe in *River of No Return*) is the risk they ran. Ornstein lost all her money and with it her mind, spending the last forty years of her life in mental institutions in the state of Washington, while Bulette was strangled by an unknown murderer in the gorgeous bedroom of her private palace, which was then denuded of all her jewels and valuables. The empire had a way with "unprotected females" of reminding them why females needed protection. Essentially this was a male preserve, a masculine adventure—and when women adventured, they did so at the risk of incurring a supreme reminder of men's dominion and domination, their own destruction.

Gold-diggers, "business girls," female travellers, traders and simple opportunists, these women colonizers had had at least some element of choice in their own lives. Most hapless and unprepared of all the women of the empire were those who were colonized; who simply by being born into a particular country fell victim to the domination of white males in addition to their own. For as the "gaming girls" remind us, one of the invisible exports of colonization was the age-old patriarchal division of women into madonna and whore, imposing on the women of the new worlds all the values and oppressions of the old. Nor were these "virgin lands," in the preferred imperial imagery, supinely awaiting the thrust of the great white male to rouse them from their primeval slumber. All had their own existing social and political systems, in most of which women were subordinate to men. With colonization, then, in a grim and unavoidable concatenation of interests, white male supremacy meshed with preexisting male domination to ensure that native women, when all the permutations of sexism and racism were completed, found themselves at the very bottom of the pile, the lowest of the low.

For even among their own people, the status of indigenous women could be horrifyingly degraded. One missionary to the New Hebrides, a Dr. Codrington, recorded the case of a woman who accidentally witnessed a newly initiated youth undergoing his purificatory washing. She fled immediately to the mission school for forgiveness for her "sin"—but when the men of her tribe came after her she gave herself up to them and submitted without a murmur to being buried alive.

A similar disregard of the value of female life could be demonstrated in almost every imperial territory, and was undoubtedly a major block to any hope of the white "masters" understanding the "subject races," when their own denial of the reality of women as people took the opposite form of exalting the female mystique. To hardened imperial adventurers and fresh-faced puppies of colonial administrators alike, episodes like this 1838 sacrifice of a Madagasca girl in her early teens merely confirmed their assessment of the native males as hopeless, irredeemable savages:

> . . . she was painted half red and half black, tied to a sort of ladder, slowly roasted over a slow fire, and then shot with arrows. The chief sacrificer tore out her heart and devoured it while the rest of her body was cut into small pieces and placed in baskets to be taken to a neighboring cornfield. There the blood was squeezed on the new grains of corn to vitalize them. The flesh was made into a sort of paste which was rubbed on the potatoes, beans and seeds to fertilize them . . . [31]

Anglo-Saxon males may have shrunk from roasting girls to death,

especially if they were attractive enough to be put to their practical uses; but in all other respects, the behavior of empire men to native women ensured that these women, already subject to their own men, were in effect colonized twice over. By a natural extension of the central metaphor of empire, the rape of the virgin land, so all the women of that land were also the conqueror's, to do with as he pleased. Each country was therefore a limitless pool of potential concubines for the rest and recreation of the troops, and such was the assumption of supremacy that the women so treated were expected to feel themselves highly favored into the bargain.

Yet the women so honored often found themselves with the worst of both worlds. The prototype experience was that of la Malinche, "the Mexican Eve," an Aztec noblewoman who was presented to Cortés in an effort to placate the *conquistador* when he invaded Mexico in 1519. She acted as his translator and adviser as well as his mistress, and is credited with consistently moderating his policies towards her country and its people. Yet to her contemporaries she was known as *La Vendida*, "she who sells out," or *La Chinçada*, "she who gets fucked."[32]

For some women, this situation could be the stepping-stone to advancement and influence. When Sir William Johnson, the British commander of the Northern Colonies of America and appropriately enough Superintendent of Indian Affairs, took a young Mohawk woman as his mistress, he may not have intended to change the course of local history. But "Molly Brant," as he called her, made herself invaluable in Johnson's relations with the local tribes, negotiating boundaries and other decisions that survive to this day. Johnson respected Molly enough to make her his official hostess, and she bore him nine children from 1759 onwards, living with him at the official residence as his wife until his death, when she was granted a pension for her services by a grateful British government.

To some men, these women were no less than wives. Many treated their native women with affection and respect, like this officer of the Hudson Bay Company in Canada writing home to describe the Ojibwa tribeswoman whom he firmly declines to describe as his mistress:

> I have said nothing yet about my wife, whence you will probably infer that I am rather ashamed of her. In this, however, you would be wrong. She is not exactly fitted to shine at the head of a nobleman's table, but she suits the sphere she has to move in better than any such toy. . . . As to beauty, she is quite as comely as her husband . . . [33]

The "country wives" of empire men the world over were, however, more accustomed to hear themselves described as a "bit of brown," a "squaw" or "brown jug," so-and-so's "piece of circulating copper," and much, much worse. Predictably too, love relationships of many years, even with a family of children, almost always failed to withstand the recall or transfer of the man back into "white society" once again.

Not infrequently the sexploitation of native women assumed proportions of horrifying cruelty. Nowhere were matters worse than in Australia, where the white men treated the Aboriginals not merely as a lower form of human being, but as a lower form of animal and used them worse than their horses or dogs. Both the flogging of Aboriginal women and the removing of flesh from their buttocks when food was in short supply were practices so regular that the sealers fiercely resisted any attempts to restrict these "rights" over their "gins."

On the credit side of the balance, relations between conquerors and conquered were not always so unrelievedly black. Empire women in particular were often strongly motivated by religious or humanitarian principles, to help those who would certainly receive no other help on the earthly side of the grave. One public health instructor in turn-of-the-century Lahore was called to a difficult delivery in circumstances that were by no means out of the way:

> Three o'clock one cold winter's morning . . . the house of an outcaste, a little mud hut with an interior perhaps eight by twelve feet square. In the room were ten people, three generations of the family, all save the patient fast asleep. Also a sheep, two goats, some chickens and a cow, because the owner did not trust his neighbors. No light but a glim in an earthen pot. No heat but that from the bodies of man and beast. No aperture but the door, which was closed. In a small alcove at the back of the room four cot beds planted one upon another, all occupied by members of the family. In the cot third from the ground, a woman in advanced labor.[34]

The midwife-instructor was, however, too short to reach the patient, although there was not a moment to be lost. But, by good fortune, the cow lay wedged against the bottom of the cot-pile—so standing on the back of the uncomplaining animal, the midwife, after a prolonged struggle, successfully delivered "a pair of tiny Hindus—boy and girl!"

Nor was the exchange between the women of empire always confined to a one-way flow of benefits from the colonizers to the colonized. The Scots missionary Mary Moffat wrote endearingly of learning from her

African neighbors how to keep house in the Kuruman Valley of the
Kalahari desert, "You will perhaps think it curious that we smear all
our room floors with cow dung once a week at least." On her own
admission, Mary had tried very hard to manage without "that dirty
trick." But as she confessed:

> I had not been here long but I was glad to have it done and I had hardly patience
> to wait till Saturday. It lays the dust better than anything, kills the fleas which
> would otherwise breed abundantly, and is a fine, clear green . . . it is mixed with
> water and laid on as thinly as possible. I now look on my floor smeared with cow
> dung with as much complacency as I used to do upon our best rooms when well
> scoured.[35]

On the whole, though, the advancement of empire meant not cooperation with the indigenous peoples, but the establishment of mastery, an aim which hardened rather than diminished as time went on.
In South Africa, for instance, the white settlers bitterly resented any
progress towards equality made by the black people who had hitherto,
in true patriarchal style, been their "dependents," and who could, if
freed, compete for land with their own sons. This was one of the
principal spurs to the Great Trek of 1835–48, when the Cape was
abandoned by those who could not stomach black emancipation. In
the new republics of Natal, the Transvaal and the Orange Free State,
there was an avowed rededication to the color bar just as it was beginning to fade away in the parent colony. This policy was pursued
with such success that after the union of the new territories with the
Cape in 1910, their descendants were strong enough to destroy any
vestige of liberalism in its own homeland, and to impose the tyranny
which subsequently proved so destructive and so durable.

As races, so individuals went under the heel, all suffering in different
ways the imposition of the alien values of the white male. It is one of
the graver ironies of imperial rule that colonial administrators, while
powerless or disinclined to terminate traditions often brutally oppressive of women, had no compunction in striking at established
customs that gave women some authority or economic control. In West
Africa, for instance, women have always dominated the market economy, often rising to become major entrepreneurs. White colonialists,
disapproving of this structure and determined to bring it in line with
Western patterns, systematically set about suppressing the market
women, and despite the women's agitation and demonstration finally
succeeded in vesting this power in the hands of the males. Omu Okwei

therefore became the last "Market Queen" when she was elected chairwoman of the ancient Council of Mothers, a survival of the matriarchy which was finally destroyed when the British transferred supervision of all retailing from the women's council to the local city authorities after Okwei's death in 1943.[36]

This then was the paradox of empire: that while some women discovered new and unknown worlds, "Britannia's daughters" in particular seizing the hope of escaping the stifling narrowness of home to become doctors, teachers, leaders, fighters or farmers in the field, others were condemned to the spiral of the old degradation from which women are still struggling to be free. Stories of the early pioneers show women adapting with great skill, courage and resourcefulness to the mixed message of their inherently inferior status, and yet at the same time of the vital necessity of their input to their infant communities. But as time went on, the toils of empire, itself only the parent country and society writ large, grew tighter, working to strangle women's newborn independence and initiative before it had a chance to thrive and take root.

In harsh contradiction to the jingoistic self-glorification in which the tales of empire have been couched, it is hard to look back on the entire historical episode as anything other than a massive bungled opportunity. For what the world has finally inherited in every instance is simply another version of the white male patriarchy that the imperialists had nominally left behind, and a restatement in the usurped name of the "mother" country of everything father wanted, needed, and stood to gain from since time began. The pattern was established at the very dawn of democracy in America, when the Founding Fathers chose to reproduce the two-tier system, in the teeth of the forceful plea of Abigail Adams to her husband John: "I desire you would remember the ladies, and be more favourable to them than your ancestors . . . put not such power in the hands of husbands. Remember all men would be tyrants if they could."[37]

They could, and they did. The machine of the patriarchs ground on, crushing women, children and native races as it went, consigning the flower of its youth to dusty death miles from home, making those same women, children, youths and natives the excuse for all its own self-serving, self-deluding obsessions. And when sexism combined with racism in the vicious circle of supremacy, women were victimized from both sides as in the worst atrocity of the Indian Mutiny when the rebel sepoy troops imprisoned the British women after the fall of

Cawnpore in the very *bibighar* (women's house) where the white officers had previously kept their Indian concubines. When the soldiers refused to pollute themselves with the women's blood, butchers were sent in.

The British army recaptured Cawnpore only to find the *bibighar* running with blood. The house was littered with female underwear, hair, scattered limbs and naked, mutilated bodies. The soldiers shared out the tresses of one of the young girls and swore that, for every hair, a sepoy should die. The British commander, General Neil, decreed that the rebels' punishment should be "the heaviest, the most revolting to their feelings, and what they must ever remember." Accordingly the captives were forced to lick the *bibighar* clean of blood, dooming them in their religion to eternal torment in perdition, before being whipped and hanged in "a frenzy of retributive savagery which is one of the most shameful episodes of British history."[38]

In this horrifying massacre and its aftermath, the imperial theme swells up loudly and unmistakably beneath all the contemporary cant. The message was simple—*dominion and domination*. Empire movements, in defiance of all the new freedoms they purported to offer, merely served to confirm women as the world's underclass, the perpetual subject race. But beneath the gentle swell of that eternal golden calm, something was stirring. After thousands of years of the human struggle, it was the turning of the tide.

IV
TURNING THE TIDE

As I sat watching Everyman at the Charterhouse
I said to myself, why not Everywoman?

GEORGE BERNARD SHAW

10
THE RIGHTS OF WOMAN

In Sex, Acquirements, and in the quantity and
quality of natural endowments whether of Feeling
or Intellect, you are the Inferior.

THE POET COLERIDGE TO HIS WIFE SARA

Husband and wife are one, and that one is the
husband.

SIR WILLIAM BLACKSTONE, "GREATEST OF

ALL ENGLISH JURISTS"

The history of mankind is the history of repeated
injuries and usurpations on the part of man toward
woman, having in direct object the establishment
of an absolute tyranny over her.

"DECLARATION OF SENTIMENTS AND

RESOLUTIONS" OF THE FIRST WOMEN'S

RIGHTS CONVENTION IN AMERICA,

SENECA FALLS, 1848

The Queen is most anxious to enlist everyone [to]
join in checking this mad, wicked folly of "Wom-
en's Rights" . . .

QUEEN VICTORIA TO SIR THEODORE MARTIN,

1870

In 1848, an Englishwoman, a Mrs. Dawson, applied for a divorce.
Her husband had been openly adulterous, while his private pleasures
included flogging her with a horsewhip and brutalizing her with a
metal-spiked hairbrush. Her petition was refused. This decision followed a judgement of eight years earlier in the case of another unhappy
wife, Cecilia Maria Cochrane. Escaping from an unhappy marriage to
live with her mother in France, Cecilia had been tricked into returning
to England by her husband, who then locked her up to ensure that
she would never leave him again. When her mother brought a writ of
habeas corpus to try to secure Cecilia's release, the Court of the Queen's
Bench took occasion to restate the legal position. Women were born
to live in a state of perpetual wardship to father or husband, and by

entering into marriage they gave their consent to their ensuing state of civil death. Accordingly "there can be no doubt of the general dominion which the law of England attributes to the husband over the wife . . . [He] may keep her by force . . . he may beat her." Cochrane's freedom to keep his wife under lock and key was confirmed even at the price of her liberty, as the judge made plain:

> It is urged that by refusing to discharge [Cecilia Cochrane] I am sentencing her to perpetual imprisonment. But I cannot doubt that a greater amount of happiness is produced in the married state from the mutual concession and forbearance which a sense that the union is indissoluble tends to produce, than could be enjoyed if the tie was less firm.[1]

These were not isolated cases. A Mrs. Addison was denied a divorce at the same time, although she proved that her sadistic husband was also her sister's lover, and a Mrs. Teush was refused "on grounds of public morality," although the Lord Chancellor himself "never recollected to have heard a better case presented by any woman." For in truth the "tie" of holy matrimony had never been firmer, even when all else was breaking apart. Between 1700 and 1850 the hydra-headed monster of revolution had torn Europe and the Americas apart, bursting the chains that had held the human race in subjection for thousands of years. In Africa, India, Arabia and the East, imperial adventurers both male and female had broken the bounds of geographical knowledge, and re-mapped the globe. Meanwhile the stay-at-homes, not to be outdone, had favored the world with the pocket watch, the repeat-loading rifle, the cotton gin, wireless telegraphy, the electric generator and Pitman's shorthand. But while barriers of ignorance and distance crumbled as if they had never been, one great anomaly remained. Women everywhere were still trapped in a state of sexual slavery virtually unchanged since the dawn of man-made civilization.

For the human race had progressed as far as the twentieth century of the Christian world, and considerably farther by the calendar of any other culture, without making any real dent in the universal belief in male superiority. Every woman still learned at her mother's knee that men were more important. At the turn of the century in post-revolutionary France, for example, a visitor recorded that at mealtimes "the master of the house is first to serve himself; next come the men in order prescribed by age and station; the mistress of the house, her daughters and female friends do not approach till the last farmhand has had his share."[2] By the middle of the nineteenth century, this masculine prerogative had hardened into a set of privileges which were only maintained by denying women everything that men awarded themselves. This "Declaration" written by Elizabeth Cady Stanton for the 1848 Women's Rights Convention at Seneca Falls, USA, set out the injustices visited on woman by man:

> He has never permitted her to exercise her inalienable right to the elective franchise. . . .
> He has made her, if married, civilly dead.
> He has taken from her all right in property, even to the wage she earns . . . becoming to all intents and purposes, her master. . . .
> He has so framed the laws of divorce . . . as to be wholly regardless of the happiness of women. . . .
> He has monopolized nearly all the profitable employments. . . .
> He has denied her the facilities for obtaining a thorough education. . . .
> He has created a false public sentiment by giving to the world a different code of morals for men and women. . . .[3]

Not unnaturally, men did not see it in this light. And the beneficiaries of the arrangement were not alone in their satisfaction with the status quo—the majority of women devoutly supported it too. Caroline Norton felt for herself the tyranny of masculine supremacy when her barrister husband exerted no more than his legal rights to accuse her of adultery, deprive her of her children, deny her any means of support and then, when she made some money for herself by writing, to sequester her earnings and assume copyright in all her work. Yet even while leading the campaign for the reform of these laws, Caroline could still proclaim, "I, for one . . . believe in the natural superiority of man as I do in the existence of God. The natural position of woman is inferiority to man."[4] Caroline Norton was confident that she spoke for "millions more" beside herself: "the wild and stupid theories advanced by a few women of 'equal rights' and 'equal intelligence' are not the opinion of their sex."

This view commanded international support at every level. From Britain, Queen Victoria expressed the feeling of ruling bodies everywhere with her implacable opposition to "this mad, wicked folly of 'Women's Rights' with all the attendant horrors on which her poor sex seems bent . . . "[5] Victoria's fears, that "woman would become the most hateful, heartless—and *disgusting*—of human beings, were she allowed to unsex herself!" were shared by women worldwide of every age and class. In America, women were the only group in the history of the country actively to fight against their own enfranchisement. Elsewhere, too, wherever a handful of reformers succeeded in getting women's rights on the national agenda, they were attacked violently and often physically by opponents of both sexes equally determined to maintain the natural dominance of man.

In fact, so far from being "natural," male domination was now being hastily reinvented. Patriarchal sanctions from legal exclusion to social taboo were wheeled out in battalions to meet the threat posed by women ready to risk "unsexing" themselves for the chance of getting their hands on some of the advantages than men had enjoyed for centuries without any apparent harm to their organs of generation. The socialist reformer Beatrice Webb experienced the process at first hand when she visited a Professor Marshall of London University in March 1889 to discuss her new research project. Already an experienced researcher with a considerable body of work behind her, she found herself subjected to this advice from her self-styled superior:

> . . . that woman was a subordinate being, and that, if she ceased to be subordinate, there would be no object for a man to marry. That marriage was a sacrifice of masculine freedom and would only be tolerated by male creatures so long as it meant the devotion, body and soul, of the female to the male. Hence the woman must not develop her faculties in any way unpleasant to the man: that strength, courage, independence were not attractive in women; that rivalry in men's pursuits was positively unpleasant. . . . "If you compete with us, we shan't marry you," he summed up with a laugh.[6]

The re-statement of women's inferiority was not however occurring solely through individual initiative. Behind every panicking patriarch, historical factors were combining to create new conditions of women's oppression; new fetters, traps, whips and goads appeared even with the very structures purporting to bring in the brave new modern world. Broadly, these fell into three separate but related developments:

- industrial organization and the rise of capitalism
- the birth of modern science and the redefinition of "the nature of woman"
- the response of the legislators to social change.

Of the three, the damage caused by the creeping blight of industrialization was the easiest to identify. Factory production, as the South African feminist Olive Schreiner showed, "robbed woman of her ancient domain of productive and social labor":

> Our spinning wheels are all broken, and we dare no longer say proudly as of old, that we and we alone clothe our peoples . . . for a time we kept possession of the kneading trough and the brewing vat [but] today steam often shapes our bread and the loaves are set down by our very door.[7]

The loss of the old-style family economy toppled women from their place at the center of a structure that had given them status and fulfilment. In exchange they faced, for the first time, a rigid sex seg-regation of work which decreed that man was that heroic novelty, "the bread-winner." This was a move that automatically relegated women to a lower, less important level than they had known before. The new working conditions in fact contrived to separate women not only from their former productive labor like baking and brewing, but also from their men. Where previously both had been necessary and valued partners in the household unit, wives now had to see their husbands singled out for the special training to perform sophisticated industrial tasks, while they were increasingly condemned to lowgrade, casual and poorly paid labor, with the inferior status that derived from their now inferior contribution to the economy overall.

This new and structured sex-segregation affected all women, not merely those of the emerging "working classes." In pre-industrial times most women lived and worked in family units which were part do-mestic, part commercial, and shared with children, widowed or or-phaned kin, elderly relatives, maids, servants and apprentices. The separation of home and work separated women not just from their fruitful labor and their men, but from the brood of children, from other women, from control over their own lives, and from access to the outside world. Neither the downtrodden wives of the "laboring poor" nor the idle wives of rich men were able to exert any significant influence, or play any part in the management of events. Effectively, they were squeezed out of any say in the world of work, while being forced, in most cases, to go on working. The course of the nineteenth century saw the women of all advanced economies pushed to opposing ends of the spectrum, high and low, as they were driven out of the middle, where they had formerly ranged across the board, according to their ability and circumstances, just as men had done.

With the creation of women as a separate section of society, a new underclass, came a growing sense that they posed a problem of a unique and unprecedented complexity: so "the woman question" was born. New dilemmas call for new solutions, and of all the emerging intel-lectual disciplines of the nineteenth century, none was more service-able to its troubled opinion-makers than science. This new realm of knowl-edge offered the comfort of absolute certainty—the human brain could now be accurately measured to the nearest micro-milligram—and so the new science of "craniology" was born.[8] Craniology made the un-questioned assumption that intelligence related directly to brain size, then proceeded to "prove" that the brain of the white male was larger than that of blacks, orientals, native Americans, or any of the "subject races."

Craniology's contribution to the "woman question" was the indisputable proof that the brain of a male is almost always larger than that of a female. The comfort this gave to the cause of male supremacy was, however, short-lived. On sheer brain mass, women lost out to men; but in the ratio of brain size to body size, women invariably came out ahead. As the idea of the superior masculine intelligence has been vital to the justification of male supremacy, this caused a severe difficulty. Craniology rose to the occasion; intelligence was located in the frontal lobes, the parietal, the occipital, anywhere in fact where the male brain could be shown to be bigger than the female. In all this flurry of false scientism, the central question went unaddressed: if the possession of a penis and an outsize brain were the distinguishing marks of the lords of creation, why was the world not ruled by whales?

Whales, though, were not the issue when the rulers of the world were busy proving themselves to be little more than overgrown monkeys. Once evolution had come to the aid of craniology, the case against female intelligence was complete—Darwin dismissed the "less highly evolved female brain" as "characteristic of the lower races, and therefore a past and lower state of civilization."[9] As this shows, the arrogant scientism which was so marked a feature of the emerging modern world was routinely employed not in the objective search for new truths, but in the determined recycling of the old lies. In addition, science itself became a new instrument of power; the swift colonization by men of this huge and virgin realm of knowledge placed in their hands the right to define what was, and what should be, what was "normal" and what "natural." The triumph of science completed a process stretching back to the dawn of humankind; the ultimate source of power, significance and creative might, once the miraculous female womb, then the sacred phallus, was now the masculine brain. And by the ultimate perversion of the great mother's supreme function, the scientific mind of man now gave birth to the stunted, dwarfish version of woman which still cripples us today.

For, like industrialization, modern science conspired to offer woman a new dimension of her role and purpose which in fact confirmed her second-class status and left her worse off than she had been before. The doctors, physiologists, biologists, gynecologists, phrenologists and quacks who made their contribution to "the woman question" with countless "scientific rationalizations" of "woman's nature" simply dis-

covered what any man on the street could have told them in the first
place: that women were weak while men were strong and that male
domination was therefore not only right but necessary. The distinctive
contribution of the good doctors, which indeed they offered in abun-
dance, was "scientific proof" that women were lifelong martyrs to "the
tyranny of their organization." What this meant for a woman was
movingly outlined by Dr. George J. Engelmann, president of the
American Gynecology Society, speaking in what can only be described
as a hot flush:

> Many a young life is battered and forever crippled in the breakers of puberty; if
> it cross these unharmed and is not dashed to pieces on the rock of childbirth, it
> may still ground on the ever-recurring shallows of menstruation, and lastly, upon
> the final bar of the menopause ere protection is found in the unruffled waters of
> the harbor beyond reach of sexual storms.[10]

With woman's every natural function seen as a life-threatening crisis,
the rational scientific male could not repose much confidence in such
a frail vessel. Woman, it now emerged under the scrutiny of pseudo-
biology, was a creature hopelessly fragile not only in body, but above
all in what the craniologists had grudgingly conceded her by way of
mind. Nervous disorders and mental instability were her lot, but there
could be no hope of remedying her deficiency in the little grey cells
by education: any learning for young ladies risked "excessive stimu-
lation" to their feeble mental parts and was incalculably dangerous.
The philosopher Herbert Spencer, previously savaged by Carlyle as
"the greatest ass in Christendom" for his part in the evolution debate,
was foremost among those who took it upon themselves to trumpet
the ill-effects of "brain-forcing" upon young women: diathesis (ner-
vousness), chlorosis ("green-sickness" or anemia), hysteria, stunted
growth and excessive thinness were the least they should expect if they
so much as touched a copy of Catullus. Nor was this all. Overtaxing
the brain, Spencer warned, "produces . . . flat-chested girls": consequently those who "survive their high-pressure education" could
never bear "a well-developed infant."[11]

Spencer was not the only man of his time to fear that the price of
rescuing women from their "natural" ignorance would be "a puny,
enfeebled and sickly race." Yet the creature who was too weak-minded
even to be educated out of it, could hardly be deemed fit for anything
else. Women's imputed physical and mental frailty thus became the
grounds for refusing her any civil or legal rights, indeed any change
from the "state of nature" in which she dwelt. As late as 1907, an

English earl blocked a bill to allow women limited and local voting rights in these terms:

> I think they are too hysterical, they are too much disposed to be guided by feeling and not by cold reason, and . . . to refuse any kind of compromise. I do not think women are safe guides in government, they are very unsafe guides . . . [12]

The speaker was supported by another of the leading lights of the British aristocracy in the wider terms of naked masculine self-interest: "What is to be feared is that if we take away the position which woman has hitherto occupied, which has come to her from no artificial education but from nature, if we transfer her from domestic into political life . . . the homes and happiness of every member of the community will be worsened by the transference." Although plainly not overburdened himself with "artificial" or any other kind of education, his lordship was quite clear on the main point at issue: any attempt by women to escape from their enforced inferiority could only damage the fabric of society, and must therefore be resisted.

Yet for a state of nature, women's lowly status and civil death took a good deal of social and cultural force to maintain. Along with the revolution of industrialism and the victory of science over common sense and reason, the nineteenth-century law became the third and most openly oppressive of the enemies of female emancipation. Nowhere was this process more blatant than in France, where the *Code Napoléon* was hailed as the most advanced legal monument of its age; history does not record whether this enthusiasm was in ignorance or in recognition of the fact that this was the most comprehensively repressive package of legislation against women of all time. Under the *ancien régime*, married women had enjoyed wide freedoms, control over their own property, and an influential place in their community, rights that the Revolution had only widened, by facilitating divorce, for example. Now, in his determination to rebuild the laws of France on a Roman, or rather Corsican, moral base, Napoleon firmly legislated to ensure woman's total subordination to man, and her slavish obedience to all his wishes.

There can be no doubt of the personal edge on Napoleon's legislative blade. "Women should stick to knitting," he informed the son of Madame de Staël, who, whatever else, was not famous for her skill with the needles. Napoleon's attitude to women consistently betrayed such narrow, reactionary, crude and sexist views, along with the determination that just as he was to be sole authority in the state, so every male should have total control over his family. Pushing his "reforms" through the council of state, Napoleon pronounced "the husband must possess the absolute power and right to say to his wife, 'Madam, you shall not go to the theater, you shall not receive such and such a person; for the children you will bear shall be mine.' " Equally, every woman "must be made to realize that on leaving the tutelage of her family, she passes under that of her husband."[13]

To this end, the *Code Napoléon* equipped every husband with extraordinary, unprecedented, indeed despotic powers. He could compel his wife either to reside in or to move to any place he decreed; everything she ever owned or earned became his; in divorce, he kept the children, the house and all the goods, for she had no right in their common property; in adultery, she could be sent to prison for up to two years, while he escaped scot free. French women had been better off in the Dark Ages than they were after Napoleon's Civil Code became law in 1804. Their modern tragedy was to be repeated with a Greek inevitability in countless other corners of the globe as the new model code, along with the metric system, swept most of the civilized world.

Yet even as the forces of patriarchy were vigorously regrouping, within these very structures of oppression lay the seeds of their eventual defeat. The revolution of industrialization made women's search for a new identity and purpose both urgent and inescapable; it had also unwittingly put into her hands the means by which to achieve it. The very success of the Industrial Revolution in creating wealth, created also the idle wife as the badge of her husband's social success. The production of surplus goods and surplus money led inevitably to the production of surplus women. It created, too, a concept entirely new in historical terms, the idea that women should be entirely supported by men. Large numbers of the females of the rising bourgeoisie thus found themselves lodged in a limbo somewhere between china doll and household pet, relegated to the classic "little woman" role still recognizable today. Deprived of work and significance, the idle wife was offered instead the newfangled flummery of Mrs. Beeton's "domestic arts," Emily Post on etiquette, and *The Language of Flowers*.

As time went on, however, "this strange masculine aberration that required women to be useless," in the words of historian Amaury de Riencourt, "proved to be a mistake of the first order": "the historical record shows that women, one way or another, always have to be at the center of things and will not for long stand being made idle or put on the shelf."[14] This enforced inactivity gave the "lady of leisure" the time to question her enervating and demoralizing lifestyle, her dependence on her man for money, status and meaning. When this brutally stupid and unnatural way of life was also forced down women's throats as the highest form of existence any female could hope to attain, the conflict between what life was and what it was supposed to be eventually became unmanageable.

At the other end of the scale, the working woman had no leisure to question her lot. Wholly subject to her lord and master, she groaned under the newly emerging "double burden," of working full-time by day, and carrying out the full load of all the household chores in whatever time was left at night. But before marriage these women had had the experience, however brief, of being part of a new breed. The transition through industrial organization to capitalism created an entire range of jobs that had never existed before, in banking and finance, in business, and in retail trade, and in the new technologies like telegraphy and typewriting. As stenographers, telephonists, cashiers, secretaries and store assistants, young women in their millions swelled the new army of "working girls." These new experiences inevitably taught them that "school French and school music, dancing, flower-painting, needlework and a diligent use of the back-board, did not necessarily qualify them to undertake remunerative employment," as one concerned critic noted.[15] In addition, the notion that young women only worked until marriage was being exploded by the experience of social workers like the British reformer Miss Rye, who gave this assessment of the situation of "young working girls" in 1861:

> My office is besieged every day by applicants for work, and there is scarcely a county or city in the United Kingdom that has not sent some anxious enquiries to me. Unfortunately my experience on this point is not singular. . . . I may state that at an office similar to those already alluded to, 120 women applied in *one day* to find that there was literally *not one situation for any one of them.*[16]

In these circumstances, working women were forced to reject the myth of the all-providing "bread-winner," and just as much as the idle wives, to recognize the separation of their lives and interests from those of men. In addition, as single women they tasted the fruit of economic independence only to have it snatched away on marriage—an economic independence that, with women's wages on average only half those of men, was in itself a constant humiliating reminder of their relative worthlessness.

Other factors, too, made it less and less possible for women to take themselves at the prevailing masculine valuation. Women who had survived empire adventures of blood and death, fire and famine, could not swallow the scientists' new discovery of women's weakness. Florence Nightingale has come down to history as "the Lady with the Lamp." In the Crimea, following a ferocious attack on a locked store-room when she needed nursing supplies, she was known as "the Lady with the Hammer."[17] Amid all the other checks and insults she was subjected to, no one dared to tell her that she was just a martyr to her "inferior organisation." Similarly Harriet "General" Tubman, better known for her work on the "underground railway" smuggling black American slaves to freedom from the Deep South of America to the Northern states, commanded an action during the Civil War which liberated more than 750 blacks; this remains the only military campaign in the history of the USA to be planned and led by a woman.[18]

Women like these, and the women who thrilled to their exploits, could not live at ease within the shallow and insulting sketch of womanhood still fervently advocated by the men of their time. Their protest was nowhere better expressed than in this outburst from Tubman's sister-slave and abolitionist Sojourner Truth, speaking at a women's rights convention in 1851:

> That man over there says women need to be helped into carriages and lifted over ditches, and to have the best place everywhere. Nobody ever helps me into carriages or over puddles, or gives me the best place—and ain't I a woman?
>
> Look at this arm! I have ploughed and planted and gathered into barns, and no man could head me—and ain't I a woman?
>
> I could work as much and eat as much as a man—when I could get it—and bear the lash as well. And ain't I a woman?
>
> I have borne thirteen children, and seen most of 'em sold off to slavery, and when I cried out with my mother's grief, none but Jesus heard me—*and ain't I a woman?*[19]

In the end, though, it was not the scientists but the legislators whose brutal and bungled attempts to shore up the shifting foundations of patriarchal power triggered the onset of women's revolt. In its essence, the clamor for women's rights to justice, to personal freedom, to full human status, represented the last wave of the great political upheavals of "the century of revolution." In making their claims, women were only following in the steps of men, who had succeeded almost everywhere in the industrialized world in striking out for a new understanding of social participation. By the very nature of the ideal of democracy, what was granted to one could not legitimately be withheld from another citizen group. This did not mean that the power-holders would not try to do so. As governments were driven to redraft older legislation in line with democratic demands, the opportunity was taken, for the first time in history, of deliberately and categorically denying women each and every one of the rights newly won by men. On both sides of the Atlantic, women were forced to confront the fact that "the Rights of Man" would be interpreted to mean precisely and literally that.

What made this particularly insulting, to Englishwomen at least, was the knowledge that even as men were winning new rights, of "one man, one vote" for example, women were being subject to restrictions that had never existed before. Previously, there was no legal reason for discrimination against women. The law had never forbidden women to sit in parliament, and for centuries the abbesses of Shaftesbury, Barking, Wilton and St. Mary Winchester had certainly done so. As late as the reign of the Stuarts, aristocratic women had held the right to select parliamentary candidates and to decide elections. These women were not disposed to have their political privileges trifled with, as the Countess of Dorset forcibly reminded the court *apparatchik* who tried to foist upon her a royal nominee: "I have been bullied by a Usurper [Cromwell], I have been ill-treated by a Court [the Countess had taken offense at Charles II], but I won't be dictated to by a subject. *Your man shall not stand.*"[20] However limited in practice to women of the upper classes, these rights were important in principle as breaching the absolute dogma of the male-only right to rule. Now women were to be formally and legally disbarred by acts unprecedented in the history of the "Mother of Parliaments," by which all proposed reforms and benefits accrued only to the male citizen of the species. This it was that sparked at last the birth of the women's movement.

The sparks fell on ground that had been ready to take fire for some time. The movement that seemed to spring up out of nowhere in the mid-nineteenth century had in fact taken root before the close of the eighteenth, when women's voices were at last raised to break the silence of millennia—after endless ages of acquiescence with the idea of male supremacy, women were recognizing this hoary old phallacy for what it was, hunting down each of the verminous practices and customs it had fostered, and nailing them to the wall. Among the first to force the revolution in thought that had not yet learned to call itself feminism was Mary Wollstonecraft. In outline, Mary's story was no more than might have happened to any other poor and friendless girl: employment as the "companion to a lady," an unsuccessful attempt to start a school, travels in France, a love affair with a man who abandoned her with their illegitimate child. But out of this stuff of penny-dreadful romance, Mary Wollstonecraft forged in 1792 one of the most powerful and assured of feminist critiques, her *Vindication of the Rights of Woman*.

Mary's starting point was her uncontrollable anger at the "baneful lurking gangrene" of "the tyranny of man over woman."[21] From this she traced all the social evils she had suffered herself, the lack of education, the denial of fulfilling work, and the sexual double standard that rewarded a man for being "a luxurious monster or fastidious sensualist," while making a whore of a woman for one indiscretion. She saw existing relations between men and women as damaging and exploitive—"man taking her body, her mind is left to rust"—and scornfully rejected the conventional ideal of female behavior: "How grossly do they insult us who thus advise us only to render ourselves gentle, domestic brutes!" With its trenchant demands for education, for work and for equal companionship with males, the *Vindication* both articulated some of the enduring concerns of feminism, and threw down the gauntlet in a way that could not be ignored: for after its dramatic exposé of the vicious stupidity and perverted childishness in which women fretfully languished, few could continue with the fiction that the "members of the fair sex" were happy with the lot enjoined on them by God and man.

The unfair sex, of course, could not be expected to be happy with this wholesale attack upon its power and prerogative, not to mention its manners, morals and mental darkness. No man is a tyrant to himself, and when Mary Wollstonecraft lifted this stone, there was a violent, often hysterical reaction to what she found under there. To the women, there was a great deal of amusement to be had from "men who cry 'Scandal!' before even examining the question," in the dry summary of one of Wollstonecraft's French disciples, Flora Tristan. Tristan's own life reads like a handbook of feminist struggle: precipitated into childhood poverty when her father died, she made a brief, unhappy marriage whose consequences darkened the whole of her adult life. Under the *Code Napoléon* she was unable to obtain a divorce, or any access to her children. When she published her autobiography, *Pérégrinations d'un Paria*, her husband tried to murder her. Harassed by the police as an undesirable, she met a premature death in 1844 at only forty-one. As a socialist, Tristan wholeheartedly endorsed Wollstonecraft's demands for education and the right to work. Her additional contribution was her insistence upon "the right to juridical equality between men and women" as "the only means of achieving the unity of humanity."[22] To man, who had always seen himself as humanity and felt himself to be perfectly unified, this suggestion was incomprehensible.

Yet just as women were learning to separate their interests from those of men, so were some men beginning to distinguish themselves from the rest of their sex by their refusal to maintain privileges only enjoyed at women's expense. In 1825 the socialist philosopher William Thomson, inspired by the otherwise forgotten freethinker Mrs. Wheeler, published his *Appeal of one-half the human race, Women, against the pretentions of the other half, Men* . . . This extraordinary, almost prophetic document made an explicit connection between sexual and racial oppression—women were "involuntary breeding machines and household slaves," reduced by the tyranny of men to "the condition of negroes in the West Indies."

This theme of the slavery of married life is the book's insistent note. "Home is the prison house of the wife," Thomson wrote. "The husband paints it as the abode of calm bliss, but takes care to find out of doors for his own use a species of bliss not quite so calm. . . . The house is his house with everything in it, and of all fixtures the most abjectly his is his breeding machine, the wife." Only by the granting of political equality could women be set free. Thomson ended with a rallying cry for votes for women designed to find an echo in every female breast throughout the world:

> Women of England, awake! Women, in whatever country ye breathe degraded—Awake. Awake to the contemplation of the happiness that awaits you when all your faculties of mind and body shall be fully cultivated and developed. . . . As your bondage has chained down Man to the ignorance and vices of despotism, so will your liberation reward him with knowledge, with freedom and with happiness.[23]

Thomson paid for his support of the women's cause with the ridicule and ostracism of his society. Forty years later in 1869, John Stuart Mill tried again with a wide-ranging and coolly logical essay exposing for what it was *The Subjection of Women*. Yet, for all the support of sympathetic fellow travellers, the battle for freedom, for justice, for full human status, was one that women had to fight for themselves. In another epochal historical departure, the women's rights movement became the first in history to have been planned and executed by women. The strength, dignity and justice of their demands was echoed in these leaders, and their extraordinary personal qualities as much as their political activities were responsible for the success of the cause. It was an international saga of inspiration and tenacity. In England, as the Home Secretary was informed, women were ready to die for Mrs. Pankhurst; her apocryphal advice to a frightened young suffragette, "Pray to God, my dear—*She* will hear you!" sums up her unselfconscious messianic power. Others drew their strength from the sublime simplicity of the cause: "Men, their rights and nothing *more:* women their rights and *nothing less*," in Susan B. Anthony's familiar phrase.

Above all, they held on. The French founder of the first Society for Women's Rights in 1866, Maria Desraismes, was already a well-known feminist and anticlericalist by 1860; her last work, *Eve dans l'Humanité*, appeared in 1891. Elizabeth Cady Stanton retired from the presidency of the National American Woman Suffrage Association in 1892 at the age of seventy-seven; Susan B. Anthony took over for the next eight years, only stepping down when she reached the age of eighty. In state after state, country after country, women fighting for the rights due to their sex fought on until they had outlived, burned off, or converted the opposition.

When the moment came, though, it came in England. Women already had more power in America, through a combination of their country's democratic ideal and their own active role as co-pioneers with their men, especially in the West. The British government, riding high on the world's earliest and most successful Industrial Revolution and the glory of an Empire on which the sun never set, already presided over a system which excluded women entirely from these key national enterprises. In 1832, with the First Reform Bill, it proposed to make this exclusion legal and perpetual. This act, which granted the vote to huge numbers previously disenfranchised, restricted it solely to "male persons" for the first time in English legislation.

Protest was immediate. So too was the masculine support without which the women's struggle would have been far longer: on August 3, 1832, the famous radical, "Orator" Hunt, presented a petition to parliament demanding that women who met the same property qualifications as men should get the vote too. In an echo of arguments from earlier revolutions in America and France, he urged that there should be no taxation without representation, and that women who were liable to be executed in strict equality with men, should enjoy the same equality in life.

Hunt's petition was hooted down amid scenes of the fatuous ribaldry that to this day disfigure the Mother of Parliaments when women's issues are in question. But the battle was now officially joined, on all fronts. At the world anti-slavery congress in 1840, English abolitionists imparted their feminist vision to their American sisters; this resulted in the 1848 Seneca Falls Convention which formally engaged the fight for "woman suffrage" on the other side of the Atlantic. When in 1869 Elizabeth Cady Stanton and Susan B. Anthony launched their radical feminist newsletter, *Revolution*, there could be no more room for doubt as to the nature of the change that women sought.

The right to vote was always the cornerstone of every emancipation program, its denial the central and most visible symbol of women's subordination. But the struggle for women's rights involved striking out for other freedoms too. As the oldest of the tyrannies, religion came high on the feminist hit-list, but for once the women were not alone. From the 1840s onwards a host of scholars, most of them German, had been producing work that not only demolished the Bible's value as historical evidence, but brought about a profound change in the status of the scriptures. Equally damaging to traditional Christian faith were the discoveries of geological science, which from the publication of Charles Lyell's *Principles of Geology* in 1830 overwhelmed the world with unassailable evidence that the biblical account of the creation was simply a myth. The creation story took another mortal blow when the "Monkey Man" Charles Darwin showed that man had not been uniquely privileged to be God's handiwork, but had evolved over time just like any other animal. Under the combined onslaught of historians, linguists, geologists and Darwinians, no reasonable individual in 1850 could continue to believe, as had been possible only ten or twenty years before, that the Bible and its account of masculine supremacy were literally true. Scenting blood, feminist freethinkers closed in fiercely for the kill. How could it ever have come about, they asked, that men had built a theory of male supremacy upon a story that showed Adam as weakly knuckling under to Eve, then whining about it?

Assaults on Christianity for its degradation of women were coming in from all sides, like this onslaught of 1876 from the Roman Catholic heartland of Italy:

> Women must withdraw themselves from the influence of the church, and with a new culture . . . they will be able to stop believing and making their children believe—thereby stunting the development of their intellects—that rain is sent us by Jesus, that thunder is a sign of divine anger and menace, and that successful crops and a good or bad harvest are to be attributed to the will of Providence . . .[24]

But it was from America, where Elizabeth Cady Stanton and Susan B. Anthony were united in their belief that the Bible had for 2000 years been the greatest block in the way of women's progress, that the most radical attacks came. To Stanton, the Old Testament was "the mere history of an ignorant, undeveloped people," subsequently manipulated to lend "heavenly authority" to man's demands for women's subjection. Women would not even begin to grasp the nature and extent of this cosmic confidence trick until they had access to a true version, which, in a mammoth undertaking, *The Woman's Bible* (1895–8), she eventually provided. For thousands of years, God had given anti-feminism its cloak of respectability and divinity. Now the white-bearded old patriarch was shown to be an emperor with no clothes.

The feminist rejection of the low view of women that Christianity had imposed upon so many nations had an important consequence for another of the key issues of the women's rights campaign: the demands for education. The ignorance of women had been bound in with Christian dogma—Eve's sin consisted of reaching out for the tree of knowledge, so her punishment was to be for ever deprived of it. Unchallenged for centuries, this attitude produced generations of women doomed to be brought up in mental darkness and then condemned as stupid: "We are educated to the grossest ignorance, and no art omitted to stifle our natural reason," complained Lady Mary Wortley Montagu bitterly in the eighteenth century.[25]

By the end of this century, protests against what passed for women's education had become widespread: "most in this depraved age think a woman learned and wise enough if she can distinguish her husband's bed from another's," observed the pioneer educationalist Hannah Woolley with her characteristic tartness. Yet the precedents for educating girls were not encouraging. Despite a long Western tradition of "learned ladies," their success had been private and patchy—the brilliant d'Andrea sisters, both fourteenth-century Italian lawyers, were taught by their father, Caterina Corner, fifteenth-century queen of Cyprus, by her brothers, and the sixteenth-century poet and "priestess of humanism" Tullia d'Aragona, by her lovers. There was nothing here to build on. In addition, the careers of individual "bluestockings" like that of "the Saxon nymph" Elizabeth Elstob, who made unimagined advances in the study of Anglo-Saxon through her "incredible industry," yet who ended her days in desperate poverty, struggling unsuccessfully to keep a dame school, were not encouraging. Worst of all had been the fate of Mary Astell's proposal for what would have been the first college of higher education for women in the world; when first floated, around the turn of the seventeenth century, it had attracted a promise of £10,000 from Queen Anne, but bitter opposition ensured that nothing similar was even suggested for another 150 years.

Yet the ferment of revolutionary ideas around the vexed "woman question" ensured that education for girls could not for ever be left off the agenda. One Victorian father, Thomas Huxley, born in the

very year that Thomson published his *Appeal* on behalf of the be-
nighted female sex, showed how far opinion had moved in one generation:

> I don't see how we are to make any permanent advancement while one-half of the
> race is sunk, as nine-tenths of all women are, in mere ignorant parsonese super-
> stitions; and to show you that my ideas are practical I have fully made up my mind
> . . . to give my daughters the same training in physical science as their brothers
> will get. . . . They, at any rate, shall not be got up as man-traps for the matrimonial
> market.[26]

The impact of these men, whose enlightened views located them in a
fine line running back through Cotton Mather to Sir Thomas More
and Erasmus, was to be incalculable. Barbara Bodichon, for instance,
read the first British paper on votes for women in 1865, and was one
of the key figures of the European suffrage struggle; she also funded
feminist publications, and helped to found Girton College, Cambridge.
All this only became possible because she had been brought up by a
progressive educationalist who, like Huxley, saw to it that his daughter
received an education exactly on a par with that given to his son.

The real breakthrough, however, came when, just as with the management of the suffrage struggle, women took matters into their own
hands. From Emma H. Willard's bold opening in 1821 of the Troy
Female Seminary in the US, through to Miss Beale's foundation of
St. Hilda's College, Oxford, England, in 1892, the achievements crowd
the calendar. These successes were won in the teeth of frequent fierce
divisions between the reformers themselves. Some, like Catherine
Beecher of the USA, believed passionately in women's traditional role,
and demanded education in "domestic science" to fit girls for married
life. Against this, others, like Emily Davies, the founder of Girton,
fought her colleagues with unshakable determination to ensure that
her students had the same educational opportunities, and satisfied the
same requirements as men did. Yet the divisions were overcome. Nor
was this explosion of education for women purely an Anglo-American
business: from the 1860s onwards, Learmonth White Dalrymple in
New Zealand, Kalliopi Kehajia in Greece, Pandita Ramabai in India,
and Marya Trubnikova in Russia worked with countless other women
to further the schooling of girls at every level from kindergarten to
graduate school.

For with the extension to female students of higher education (and
the women reformers had proved that if men would not let them into
their universities, they would found their own) the right to enter the

professions could no longer be withheld. Male doctors might puzzle their heads as to why women should want to be doctors rather than nurses, but the female aspirants lost no time in setting them right— "I should naturally prefer £1000 to £20 a year," observed the first British woman doctor, Elizabeth Garrett Anderson.[27] This dry speech masked a strong feminist idealism. Garrett Anderson had been inspired to think of becoming a doctor after hearing a lecture from Elizabeth Blackwell, the first woman doctor of America; like Blackwell she used her influence to help women in every way, working for suffrage and opening up the medical profession, finally becoming the first woman mayor in England, of Aldeburgh, Suffolk, in 1908.

These women needed every ounce of the courage of their convictions to withstand the rearguard action mounted against them at every turn. The Australian doctor Harriet Clisby struggled for years in England and America before she finally qualified in 1865 at the age of thirty-five. America was not always as hospitable as this to women hoping for a medical education; when Harriot Hunt was personally admitted to Harvard in 1850 by the dean, Oliver Wendell Holmes, rioting students objecting to "the sacrifice of her modesty" forced her to withdraw, never to return.

Even after qualification, the humiliations and obstructions heaped on female medics did not cease. To become Hungary's first woman doctor, Vilma Hugonnai-Wartha had to matriculate in advanced Latin and mathematics; to work as a nursing assistant to the professor of the medical school; to publish two dissertations; and to undergo a special *viva voce* exam; all this in addition to the normal course of study completed by men. At the end of all this in 1879, it was announced that as a woman she would only be awarded a certificate of midwifery. Later still, even after she had also qualified at Zurich University, she was checkmated once again by new legislation allowing women to practice medicine only in partnership with a male doctor.

These struggles were duplicated for each and every one of the professions that women sought to enter. Every country held, too, peculiar challenges for feminism; the struggle worldwide consisted not of imposing a set of general principles from nation to nation, but of winning what could be won from the local conditions and national conventions. So in India, Sarojini Naidu, Abala Bose and others campaigned against both widow burning and the caste system, in which a woman is invariably lower caste, because female, than the men of her own caste, while in Japan, Fusaye Ichikawa led the fight against the regulated prostitution that held thousands of Japanese women in virtual slavery.

Undoubtedly though, of all the causes that fuelled the fight for the rights of women, most important was the parallel struggle against the slavery of the southern states of America. Their horror at the plight of the Negroes pitched many women headlong into the quest for freedom—the campaigner Sarah Grimke was only four when she saw a female slave savagely flogged, and she never forgot it. While still a child she fought against the law forbidding anyone to educate a slave by teaching her personal slave to read and write, for which she was flogged herself. In these circumstances, abolitionism became the cradle of feminism as the violent and uncompromising hostility of masculine society turned these women into active campaigners for women's rights: "I ask no favors for my sex," declared Sarah Grimke. "All I ask is that they take their feet from off our necks." In any conflict between the two causes, there could be only one choice. "I was a woman before I was an abolitionist," Lucy Stone told the Massachusetts Anti-Slavery Society. "*I must speak for the women.*"[28]

And speak they did, raising their voices everywhere, for education, for law reform, employment, civil rights and, above all, "Votes for Women!" The symbolic power of the last is evident from the fact that it was not granted until after all the others had been won; women were admitted to secondary schools, universities and the professions, granted property rights and divorce laws, before they were permitted the sacred token of full citizenship. America, predictably, led the way, when a western state, Wyoming, enfranchised women in 1869. The first country to give women the vote, to its eternal credit, was New Zealand in 1893; the contemptible delaying tactics of the British government against Mrs. Pankhurst, her shock troops, and their sedate sisters in the suffragist arm of the movement ensured that Australia, Denmark, Finland, Iceland, Norway and Russia all brought their women to the polls before the British victory in 1918. But at last, after all the speeches, the petitions, the ridicule, the resistance, it was all over. Women's wrongs were rights now. Women had won.

Or had they? In the shadow of the guillotine, Olympe de Gouges had cried that revolution never changes things for women. The rights that women had won through the long century and more of struggle were essentially rights of men. Women had had no option but to batter their way into that age-old fortress of male privilege, and storm the citadel where masculine supremacy still held out. But those who saw it as the final victory were deceived. Even in the moment of triumph, there were those who clearly saw what lay ahead:

No one who understands the feminist movement, or who knows the soul of a real new woman would make the mistake of supposing that the modern woman is fighting for the vote, for education, and for economic freedom, because she wants to be a man. That idea is the invention of masculine intelligence. Woman is fighting today, as she has all the way up through the ages, for the freedom to be a woman.[29]

To be a woman . . . what was that? In the discovery of the answer to this question was to lie another struggle, another battleground. Wearily but without complaint, the world army of women shouldered arms and marched forward once again.

11
THE BODY POLITIC

No woman can call herself free who does not own
and control her own body.

MARGARET SANGER

Under no plea or promise can it be permissible to
submit the individuality, either mental or physical,
of the wife, to the will and coercion of the husband.
The functions of wifehood and motherhood must
remain solely and entirely within the wife's own
option.

ELIZABETH WOLSTENHOLME ELMY

Whenever a comparison was made which seemed
to be unfavourable to their sex, the ladies were able
to express a suspicion that we, as male analysts,
had never overcome certain deep-rooted prejudices
against the feminine. . . . We had only to say, "This
does not apply to you. You are an exception, in
this respect you are more masculine than feminine."

SIGMUND FREUD

So the vote was won. The crown and central symbol of the struggle
for women's rights, it stood for all the other new rights and freedoms
too—education, citizenship, entry to the professions, ownership of
property. But what use was the chance of higher education to an
unmarried mother of fourteen? What was the freedom of the ballot
box to a middle-aged woman who, crippled with a prolapsed uterus
after the birth of her seventeenth child in twenty years, could not drag
herself to the polls?

Even as the struggle for women's rights was in full swing, many
realized that without physical emancipation for women, it would be
a hollow victory. In 1919, Victor Robinson of the American Voluntary
Parenthood League located the battle for contraception as the cornerstone and culmination of the fight for freedom, and warned of the
opposition it would encounter just as every stage of women's progress
had before it:

When women first claimed admission to the privileges of higher education, men pointed out that a female who studied in botany that plants had sex organs would be unfit to associate with her respectable sisters. When she knocked on the gates of medicine, men declared that a woman who could listen to a lecture in anatomy was unworthy of honorable wifehood. When she asked for chloroform to assuage the pangs of childbirth, men quickly informed her that if women bear their children without pain, they will be unable to love them. When the married woman demanded the right to own property, men swore that such a radical step would totally annihilate woman's influence, explode a volcano under the foundations of family union, and destroy the true felicity of wedded life, and they assured us they opposed the change not because they loved justice less, but because they loved woman more. During the many years that woman fought for citizenship, men gathered in gambling-dives and bar-rooms and sadly commiserated with each other on the fact that woman was breaking up the home. Now woman demands the control of her own body, and there are men who reply that if women learn how to prevent pregnancy, they will abolish maternity. It seems there are always some men who are haunted by the fear that women are planning the extinction of the race. To attempt to reason with such men is folly, and we can only hope that a general knowledge of contraceptive methods, judiciously applied, will eliminate this type.[1]

Contraception was the key issue, then, in the battle for the body, its central pivotal demand, as the vote had been in the campaign for women's rights. But far more was involved here than the mechanics of birth control. If woman could be free from "the tyranny of her organization," she stood a chance of becoming an autonomous individual. If she could rescue herself from the endless cycle of sexual activity, pregnancy, childbirth, lactation, pregnancy, then personal growth and social identity were possible. If sex ceased to carry the dire consequences of unwanted pregnancy, social catastrophe, even death in childbirth, then woman could no longer be seen as sinning, sinful and justly punished. If every woman got hold of these ideas, along with the control and disposal of her own body, what price the patriarch and his power?

It was to be, and remains, for it is far from over, a terrible struggle. The task was nothing less than a redefinition of women's sexuality, as women wrenched from men the right to be more than vessels for their seed. The new industrial cultures of the world had taken advantage of nineteenth-century "progress," in particular of "scientific" prognostications, to redefine woman as weak and frail, a position from which others had never departed. There was no doubt as to the source of that frailty—the unpredictable uterus, the "wandering womb sans wit or will." To the modern medical experts, as to generations of men before them, woman was no more than "an admirably constructed apparatus for the most mysterious and sublime of nature's mysteries—

the reproductive process."[2] We are back 350 years with Luther's contemptuous outburst—"that's what women are *for!*"

When women are seen as dominated by their wombs, the condition is a life sentence. Nineteenth-century gynecologists, in full Shakespearean flight, identified the Seven Ages of Woman: her birth as a female, her menstruation, defloration, pregnancy, childbirth, lactation and menopause. All these focus exclusively upon "the great crown and joy of the woman's life—MOTHERHOOD," carrying the repeated reminder that "the natural vocation of every woman is that of wife and mother." This function is so much part of woman's "natural destiny" that "she is an imperfect, undeveloped being until she has borne a child." Yet the process, as seen by the good doctors, does not sound very natural:

> No woman passes through life without being ill. She suffers from "the custom of women," or she does not. In either case she is normally or abnormally ill. . . . Nature disables the whole sex . . .[3]

The whole sex? Absolutely, without exception: one prominent gynecologist told his patients that "if a woman knew what danger she was in from her pelvic organs, she would not step from her carriage to the pavement."

This pelvic preoccupation with women's rampant innards had more than a comic effect, however. Since women were seen as reproductive beings, any and every disorder they experienced was treated by treatment of the reproductive organs. Anemia, "hysteria," insanity, "criminality" were treated by sexual surgery, the gynecologists often removing one ovary or fallopian tube at a time, thereby prolonging the patient's original condition, her suffering, and her dependence on the doctor. Performing a dilation and curettage (forcibly dilating the cervix and scraping out the lining of the womb) for "the moral effect" was commonplace. This surgical rape was particularly recommended for unladylike or boisterous girls. Cruellest of all, yet defended as "vivisection of the noblest kind," was genital mutilation, the so-called "female circumcision," the excision of the clitoris and external genitalia. Throughout the whole of the nineteenth century and into the twentieth, this operation was performed to cure masturbation, hallucinations, "vaginal catarrh," "spinal irritation" and "hysterical mania," and was particularly recommended for epilepsy.[4] Leading the "advanced" countries in this specialized field of surgery, Britain and America marched complacently backwards into the dark ages of the Near and Middle East, where female sexual mutilation continued to be found

equally efficacious as a cure for the female condition called womanhood.

Yet a picture of women as eternal victims of their sex would be far
from the truth. The historical overview of the whole business of sex,
menstruation and reproduction shows how consistently women sought,
and how frequently they achieved, a measure of control. This is particularly true of contraception; since childbirth was and remains the
most life-threatening physical activity that women naturally undertake,
there was always a strong incentive to minimize or avoid it. The
staggering range of devices and potions from prehistory to the present
day, with women worldwide straining every nerve for non-mother-
hood, also casts an ironic sidelight on the myth of the "maternal
instinct." Anything and everything, it seems, that could possibly have
conferred the blessing of infertility was pressed into service.

For many of the women's contraceptive preparations were so horrific
that only the unwanted pregnancy could have been worse than the
remedy. In Japan, pillow-books advised a mixture of mercury, a horse-
fly and a leech, "the whole boiled to a pulp, and taken as soon as it
has come to the boil."[5] For those without asbestos throats, the recommended infusion consisted of "turnips in large quantities" lightly
fricasseed with "monkey's brains in cold water" and the silvering from
mirrors. Other countries showed an inexplicable fascination with animal excrement: the first mention of contraception by the Egyptians,
in a papyrus of 1850 BC, suggests a vaginal plug made from honey
and crocodile dung. Elsewhere in Africa, fresh supplies doubtless
governed by local availability, the preferred dung was that of elephants.
By AD 900, the dung wheeze had made its way to England, where the
Boke of Saxon Leechdoms counselled a contraceptive so dreadful that
it clearly operated as an early kind of aversion therapy: "Take a fresh
horses turd, lay it in hot gledes [coals], make it reek strongly between
the thighs up under the raiment, that the woman may sweat much
. . ."[6]

Other precautions relied on the barrier theory. In an otherwise
unconvincing field, the clear winner was the Japanese forerunner of
the cervical cap, an oiled disc of bamboo tissue paper, which, however,
would have been more easily displaced or destroyed in action than the
cervical discs of melted beeswax used by the German-Hungarian women
of Banat. Countless other ingredients—yoke of egg, foam from a
camel's mouth, walnut leaves, saffron, onion, peppermint, dried roots,
seaweed, rags, opium and grass—were used in different parts of the
world to form plugs to block up the mouth of the womb and prevent

the entry of the sperm. Most extraordinary of all were Casanova's personal specifics—a "golden ball" (size unspecified) dipped in alkali, and a half-lemon squeezed into the vagina so that the lumpy end entered and blocked the cervix; the cut end, presenting to the penis, would let down its juices during intercourse. The unforgettable nature of the ensuing experience for both parties helps to show why Casanova has fornicated his way into history while many a journeyman bed-presser passed unsung into oblivion.

As this shows, the women of history could not simply take intercourse lying down. On the contrary, a busy program of actions and motions was widely recommended as an antidote to conception. The Greek gynecologist of the second century AD, Solanas of Ephesus, prescribed a little ritual which continued in use for many centuries: "at the critical moment of coitus, when the man is about to discharge the seed, the woman must hold her breath and draw herself away a little, so that the seed may not be hurled too deep into the cavity of the uterus." From Roman whores to Spanish contessas, women were instructed that vigorous activity throughout the sex act would dislodge the sperm—the author of that advice clearly hoping for more in a sexual partner than a woman simply lying there holding her breath.

Among women themselves, though, the same beliefs prevailed. From Iceland to Peru, the old wives' nostrums included coughing, sneezing, jumping about, or even rushing outside for a roll in the snow to expel or freeze out the semen. Commonest of all, "hearty pissing in a pot," was known to prostitutes worldwide (and to their respectable sisters as well) for thousands of years and is still in use today, with the addition of a good sluice-down with wine or vinegar. When circumstances precluded any post-pokery jiggery, passive techniques were invoked instead; amulets women wore round their necks to ward off insemination included the tooth of a dead child, a verse of the Koran, or the left testicle of a weasel taken alive before the moon went down.

Women, of course, were not entirely alone in their efforts to enjoy sex without the inevitable consequence, as the long history of the humble condom makes plain. Whether made of linen, gut, the caecum of a sheep, fish membrane, leather, tortoishell or horn, these could hardly be said to be aids to pleasurable love-making: in 1650 Madame de Sevigné complained that a sheath "made of gold-beater's skin" was "armour against full enjoyment and only a spider's web against the danger of infection."[8] As this reminds us, condoms were originally devised for male not female protection, as a prophylactic against the venereal diseases that had ravaged Europe ever since their invisible importation by Columbus and his crew from the New World. What makes clearer a genuine male desire to avoid impregnating a female is the tricky and unnerving practice known as *coitus obstructus*, "full intercourse with ejaculation suppressed by depressing the base of the urethra [where?] and so forcing the ejaculate into the bladder."[9] With this demanding maneuver to perform, it is hard to imagine that either partner to the sex act would know if they were coming or going.

If a good deal of this sounds more like an ordeal than a delight, it almost certainly was. Equally dismal must have been the other practices to avoid having children, like late marriage, a primitive but essential birth control device in use from the France of the Middle Ages up to the present day in Ireland. *Coitus interruptus*, the snare of the "safe period" or "Vatican roulette," marital abstinence or Thoreau's "moral restraint" must also have come between the participants and any hope of sensuous joy and abandon. There were worse consequences, too. Where not distasteful, many of the contraceptive practices employed by women up to the modern period were positively dangerous; eating the dirt from a dead mule's ears, or the mercury-based silvering from mirrors, drinking the water in which smiths doused their tools (for its lead content), introducing into the vagina lugs of sheep's wool, bark, roots, alum or corrosives, all too often prevented conception in the simplest way, by killing the woman.

Above all, these techniques did not work. While some of the ingredients used, such as honey or gum arabic, would have had a sperm-retardant or spermicidal effect, the machinery of reproduction was too powerful and complex to yield to anything except the full onslaught of twentieth-century scientific knowledge. And as any rehearsal of this confusing and frequently revolting field suggests, a woman would have to have a strong stomach, a steady hand, an iron nerve and an almost inconceivable run of luck during a reproductive life that could stretch from twelve to over fifty, if in all those years she only had the children she wanted, when she wanted them.

In reality, whatever most women conceived of in the thousands of ages before our own, it was not of having any choice in this matter. Children were sent by God: "the more babes, the more blessings," was a pious Elizabethan formula. Motherhood was also a prime role and occupation for women: indeed in the centuries before they had any other prospect of individual employment, it was their major source of power and significance. "Who is the greatest woman, alive or dead?" Madame de Staël asked Napoleon. "The one that has the most children," snapped back the little dictator unhesitatingly.[10] Nor was this merely the preoccupation of the coarse Corsican. In America, the Puritan ethic combined with the vastness of the New World to make the production of large broods an imperative, while those under the sway of the Roman church had never been allowed to sign off from the duty of Catholic-making.

Elsewhere, especially in poorer countries, the huge infant mortality dictated a policy of continuous replenishment; the intricate connection between poverty, over-breeding, parental ignorance and the death of children had yet to be made. Almost everywhere too, rich or poor, there was a deep, unargued feeling that to tamper with the birth process in any way was "against nature as well as against God," as the daughter of Queen Victoria's premier, William Gladstone, wrote to him.[11] In most societies, neither babies nor mothers were necessarily expected to survive childbirth—prayers for the purification of women after childbirth commonly offer thanks for a safe journey through "the Valley of the Shadow of Death"—and all societies provided for wife-replacement by permitting polygamy, in the East of the simultaneous, in the West of the serial variety.

What this meant for women may be illustrated from the diary of a Renaissance merchant, Gregorio Dati. Dati's first "beloved wife, Bandecca, went to paradise after a nine-month illness caused by a miscarriage." Dati briefly consoled himself with his "Tartar slave girl," who bore him a son, but then married in the hope of legitimate children. His second wife died in childbirth after bearing him eight children in nine years. His third wife produced 11 children, after which "it was God's will to recall to Himself the blessed soul of my wife Ginevra. She died in childbirth after lengthy suffering." Undeterred, Dati married again, and his fourth wife had had six children and one miscarriage when he stopped recording the body count after 28 pregnancies by five women within 30 years.[12]

Dati was not as unusual as he may appear in his unquenchable appetite for fatherhood, or at least for the process that led up to it. Nor were the risks of illness and death incurred by his women through childbearing at all out of the way, in his or many subsequent generations—we can only marvel at the confidence with which Thomas Jefferson in the nineteenth century wrote to his daughter that childbirth was "no more than a jog of the elbow," when his wife had died in childbed, as this daughter was to do two months later. Much more honest was the anxiety evinced by Madame de Sevigné, when her beloved only daughter suffered three pregnancies in the first two years of her marriage, including a severe miscarriage. In a furious letter she warned her son-in-law that "the beauty, the health, the gaiety and the life of the woman you love can all be destroyed by frequent occurrences of the pain you make her suffer," threatening him, "I shall take your wife from you! Do you imagine I gave her to you so that you might kill her?" Françoise survived this pregnancy, but her mother's fears were not at an end. Immediately after the delivery she dashed off a hasty warning not to rely on breast-feeding to prevent conception: "if, after your periods start again, you as much as think of making love with M. de Grignan, you may consider yourself already pregnant, and if one of your midwives tells you differently, then your husband has bribed her!"[3]

The position of the husband in this all-too-common situation, caught between the options of lethally selfish sensualist or reluctant celibate, was not a happy one. He would, however, survive his sex life: very many women did not. And as the modern age with its much vaunted progress and prosperity broke about the ears of women in the West, they had the disconcerting experience of discovering that childbirth became worse, not better; for in one of the decisive power struggles that were to touch all women's lives, men finally won their long fight to take over the management of women in labor. Male attacks on women healers were nothing new—one facet of the witch hunts had been the determination of university-trained male physicians to eliminate the female opposition. But with the advent of drugs, obstetrical forceps, anesthesia and formal medical training, male practitioners were finally able to usurp women's age-old role as birth attendant and present themselves as the chief *accoucheur*.

Armed with the authority of the expert, the new men had no difficulty putting down the old women, even when they were horribly in the wrong. On his own admission "the great William Smellie," the mould-breaking "Master of British midwifery," when learning his trade once slashed a baby's umbilical cord so clumsily that the child almost bled to death. Smellie informed the suspicious midwife, whom his arrival had displaced, that this was a revolutionary new technique designed to prevent convulsions in the newly born. Privately, though, as he later disclosed, he was never so terrified in all his life.[14]

With the advent of chloroform and disinfectant in the West, medical science began at last to make headway against its own darkest prejudices that the suffering and death of women in childbirth were no more than a "necessary evil," to be seen "even as a blessing of the Gospel," as one leading British gynecologist wrote in 1848.[15] Elsewhere, though, it seemed that nothing could dislodge the fatalistic attitude to the loss of female life, nor change the habits and customs that promoted those deaths. From India, a British woman surgeon, Dr. Vaughan, sent this despairing report in the last days of the Raj:

> On the floor is the woman. With her are one or two dirty old women, their hands begrimed with dirt, their heads alive with vermin . . . the patient has been in labour for three days, and they cannot get the child out. On inspection, we find the vulva swollen and torn. They tell us, yes, it is a bad case, and they have had to use both feet and hands in their efforts to deliver her. . . . Chloroform is given, and the child extracted with forceps. We are sure to find holly-hock roots which have been pushed up inside the mother, sometimes string and a dirty rag containing quince seeds in the uterus itself. . . . Do not think it is only the poor who suffer like this. I can show you the homes of many Indian men with university degrees whose wives are confined on filthy rags and attended by these bazaar *dhais* . . . [16]

With great clarity, Vaughan saw that the root cause of this suffering, infection and death lay not with the *dhais* who ministered to the women, but in the attitudes of the husbands. In the post-industrial countries the same analysis was beginning to be made as Western women, apparently living under so much more advanced conditions, still found themselves trapped and punished by the views and expectations of masculine society. With the courage that had seen them through the suffrage struggle, and as part of that sweeping program of demands for their human rights, women in the West set about assuming the final responsibility for their own sexual existence. To achieve this, they faced another mammoth task—no less than that of reforming the attitudes of men who had never questioned their right to use women in this way—the task of remaking sexuality, female and male.

For women could never be their own mistresses while men still considered themselves lords and owners of the bodies in question. During the nineteenth century a pageant of violent unrest, disorder and revolution had come and gone without disturbing in the majority of masculine minds notions of women as sexual chattels that stretched back to the Dark Ages and beyond. During his tour of the North of England in 1844, Friedrich Engels noted that in every mill and factory that he visited, it was "a matter of course" that "factory servitude, like any other, and to an even greater degree, confers the *jus primae noctis* upon the master." The consent of his "girls" was extracted in the time-dishonored manner: "the threat of discharge suffices to overcome resistance in nine cases out of ten." The master, in short, "made his mill his harem;" his power was such that he was "sovereign over the person and charms of his employees," their absolute ruler.[17]

Nor was this simply a matter of a few "unfortunate" mill girls. As feminists began to look around, their senses sharpened to oppression by their fight for other freedoms, they saw that they lived in a society that was no more than "a system of sex-slavery for women." This had come about through men's insistence on women's reproductive functions, Christabel Pankhurst wrote, and the "doctrine that woman is sex, and beyond that nothing." Men liked to dress this up as the idea that women were born to achieve a respected role as mothers, but that was eye-wash: "What a man who says that really means, is that women are created primarily for the sex gratification of men, and secondarily, for the bearing of children if he happens to want them, but of no more children than he wants."[18]

These radical views were by no means confined to the iconoclastic wing of the women's rights movement inhabited by the Pankhursts and their supporters. Moderates in the Ladies' National Association inspired by the social reformer Josephine Butler came out wholeheartedly against the sexual abuse of a whole class of women as prostitutes. The exercise of man's "free right" of sexuality was in reality gross exploitation, they argued, creating a false division of women into the "pure" and the "fallen" and thereby destroying the "sisterhood of women." Butler herself was at pains to stress that the "pure," respectable woman was not in fact any less exploited than her "frail" sister; it was simply that her body had been designated for a different sexual purpose, as a "conduit" for the transmission of property by inheritance, not for sexual pleasure.

For attacking "the licentiousness of men," "the galling tyranny of the strong over the weak," Butler was branded "no better than a prostitute" by outraged males scrambling to defend themselves against the idea that they ever had anything to do with such creatures. But women had at last got the bit between their teeth. From America came a characteristic blast from Elizabeth Cady Stanton:

> Man in his lust has regulated this whole question of sexual intercourse. Long enough! Let the mother of mankind, whose prerogative it is to set bounds to his indulgence, rouse up and give this matter a thorough fearless examination.[19]

Unlike her colleagues Lucy Stone and Susan B. Anthony, Elizabeth Cady Stanton had a very active concept of the relations between men and women as a sex war. Although deeply concerned with women's hope of full citizenship and right to vote, she felt a passionate personal anger against the man-made laws and customs that gave men rights of ownership and control over women's bodies. In England, the campaigning "Miss Swiney of Cheltenham" shared Stanton's sense of furious rage coupled with a clear perception that women's exploitation was neither natural nor coincidental, but part of a full-blown sexual *system:*

> For, consider what man-rule, man-made religion, man's moral code has implied to woman. She has seen her female child, Nature's highest development in organic evolution, ruthlessly murdered as superfluous. She has seen her son, the "defective variation" biologically, the outcome of malnutrition and adverse conditions, and thereby imperfect, placed over her as master, Lord and tyrant! . . . Church and State, religion, law, prejudice, custom, tradition, greed, lust, hatred, injustice, selfishness, ignorance and arrogance have all conspired against her under the sexual rule of the human male![20]

Not everyone agreed with Swiney, particularly in her outright declaration of women's unassailable superiority. But in spite of themselves many women thrilled to the fine feminist fury of her attacks on men— the usurping lords of creation were no more than a eugenic disaster, their brains small and weak, their bodies "lustful and diseased," their sperm a "cheesy mess" of "virulent poison." Emboldened by the freedom Swiney took to call a sperm a sperm, women everywhere began to "give this matter" the "thorough fearless examination" that Elizabeth Cady Stanton had called for.

The prevalence of prostitution now became a major concern of feminists; the more so as every fresh legislative onslaught on the problem throughout the nineteenth century invariably resulted in the women being made to suffer more, without taking any account of their exploiters and *raison d'être*, men. Different countries had differing agendas: France was slow to respond to all campaigns against child prostitution, since most of the demand for the young victims of the "white slave trade" that so tortured English reformers originated there; meanwhile French campaigners were striving in vain to arouse the nation's conscience to the plight of adult women regularly beaten through the streets by the police for public amusement: "filthy with dust or mud, their skirts and blouses in ribbons, they are kicked, punched, and dragged by the hair . . . "[21] In England, official violence against prostitutes took the form of regularly enforced, brutal and degrading internal examinations for venereal disease, under the Contagious Diseases Acts which solemnly assumed that only females could harbor or transmit sexual infection. But national differences were harmonized by the underlying mission of all the reformers to withdraw from men the sexual *droit* that every one, *seigneur* or not, seemed to feel entitled to claim. And as the struggle took shape, two major themes emerged, both of which were to change the way that women were able to live their lives in the twentieth century.

The first of these derived from what is arguably the most basic physical right of all: *the right to refuse*. Before the Industrial Revolution, there were few creatures more pitied and despised than the "old maid." She was generally assumed to be dying for a man and worthless without one; should any come her way he would be accepted sight unseen; and the idea that any woman would choose this state of single misery over wedded bliss would have been a pure anachronism. By offering single women a purpose in life and the work to accomplish it, the women's movement of the nineteenth century raised their sights and their self-esteem. In the varied programs of law reform, suffrage, education for girls, temperance, abolitionism and the rest, unmarried women found the exultation of personal achievement and with it the confidence to question the notion that marriage was all-in-all. After her heroic stint in the Crimea, Florence Nightingale became the world's most famous spinster. Her refusal to marry was a plain statement of the value she placed on her autonomy, her individuality and the integrity of her body. She also made her rejection of marriage quite explicit with her pronouncement that "women must sacrifice all their life if they accepted *that* [a marriage proposal from a man] . . . behind *his* destiny woman must annihilate herself."[22]

The newly awakened spinster, therefore, did not need men. But that did not mean that she wanted to live in an unawakened, virgin or celibate state. Along with the sexual right to refuse, comes the right to choose. Free to choose to please themselves, many women made the obvious choice of another woman. In addition to the shocks it had already suffered, conventional morality now had to take on board the full-blown reality of lesbian love. By the nineteenth century, this was hardly a historical novelty. In the past, though, like so much else of women's private, domestic activity, it had simply been largely invisible to "real," i.e. male, society. Those men who were familiar with lesbian practices as a known feature of their society generally regarded them with self-flattering complacence: the Abbé de Brantôme, writing of the ladies at the court of Henri II in the seventeenth century, defended sex between women as "nothing but an apprenticeship for the greater love of men," and acceptable to husbands as there could be no risk of "horns" involved.

The self-indulgent attitude of a sophisticated courtier was hardly that of the Church, however. Although the Bible contains only one reference to lesbianism (in the proscriptions of Paul, where else?) Christianity developed a rabid loathing of this "unnatural vice," for which death was made the penalty. As late as 1721 in Europe, a German woman, Catharina Margaretha Linck, was burned at the stake for attempting to pass as a man, and marrying another woman. This case illustrates the true nature of the patriarchal outrage, however, which emerges equally clearly from all other comparable examples. Linck's offense was not to have made love to her "wife," but to have usurped male attire to do so. Similarly, within the Church itself, nuns or laywomen caught using "sodomitical devices" (dildoes), that is, usurping the male member, could expect no mercy. In the minds of churchmen, fathers and husbands, women kissing, fondling, sharing a bed and masturbating each other to orgasm did not seem so terrible, because it consorted with their own ideas of women's sexuality, and even fed their phallocentric fantasies, as the "two lesbians and one man" scenario, familiar to pornography from the classical period, continues to do even today.

With the emergence of women who had made the conscious political decision to separate themselves from the mainstream of their contemporary society, the question of women's love had to be seen in a new light. When in 1892 a young Tennessee woman, Alice Mitchell, murdered her lover, Freda Ward, "to make sure that no one else could get her," respectable Americans could no longer maintain that such behavior only happened in the Old World, and then only in French pornography. European lesbians, moreover, were now gathering and finding, as early as 1900, the beginnings of gay pride, like this turn-of-the-century German scientist:

Take this courage, my sisters, and show that you have as much right to love as the "normal" world! Defy this world, and they will tolerate you, they will acknowledge you, and they will even envy you.[23]

Her confidence was premature. With little experience and with a perverted, phallo-flattering understanding of lesbian women, both Europe and America had freely tolerated women's "romantic friendships," "sentimental attachments," "the love of kindred spirits," even the "Boston marriage." When women no longer disguised the true, sexual base of these unions, the reaction was immediate. For if two clitorises could manage happily without even one penis, the assumption of phallic supremacy was cut off at the root. Suddenly men were forced to face the idea that a finger, a tongue, a *woman*, could do better than their sacred organ. Taken with the economic and political equality women were seeking, they could even dispense with men altogether.

This was armageddon. Women fighting their way out of the closet found the door not just slammed in their faces, but the opening bricked up. In the Britain of 1928, the writer Radclyffe Hall published her passionate plea for tolerance, *The Well of Loneliness*. Christened Marguerite but always known as John, Radclyffe Hall has come under fire from later lesbian feminists because of her predominantly negative view of what she saw, in the psycho-babble of her time, as a "sexual inversion." "I am one of those whom God has marked on the forehead," her heroine declares to her lover. "Like Cain I am marked and blemished." But the lesbian protagonist speaks for all her sisters in an unforgettable final cry, "Acknowledge us, oh God, before the whole world. Give us also the right to our existence!"[24] The cry went unheard. In a savage and protracted prosecution, Radclyffe Hall was ruined both socially and financially as her man-made society demonstrated that it only had to perceive any challenge to its authority to fall upon it with all the fury at its command.

It cannot be said, though, that the patriarchs were giving too much attention to the unfamiliar sound of lesbian demands for tolerance and acceptance. They had another battle on their hands in every industrialized society of the world, and no neck so red but it felt the wind of change. From the mid-century, men had had to see their sexual rights chipped away, one by one, as prostitution, child sex, and violence against women had all come under the scathing scrutiny of feminists. Now all the battles over sexuality, the struggle by women to break or even to lessen men's power over female bodies, came to a head in the fight for contraception. Modern "birth control," as it was called in Margaret Sanger's phrase, became the symbol and center of the campaign for physical emancipation, as the vote was of the clamor for citizenship. Both triggered the same reactions of fury, paranoia and resentment, and both called for the same conviction and tenacity in their campaigners. Of the two, though, the question of birth control had the power to touch each individual most intimately, in the heart of their private space; for a couple who could honestly feel that votes for women would make little difference to their existence could hardly hold the same view of something which threatened to change everyone's sex life, for better or for worse, for ever.

What made the new techniques different from all the old historical potions and devices was that, for the first time, they would work. Notions of the cervical and penile barrier, cap or sheath, had been around for as long as humanity; now, for the first time, the technology was available to produce a reliable, inexpensive reality of what had formerly been a fantasy. The key development was the vulcanization of rubber in the 1840s, making possible the modern condom, and humanizing and disseminating the invention of the German physician Wilde, of caps of iron and silver. With the patenting of the douche syringe in the 1870s, which had the added advantage that it could be purchased by women as if for personal hygiene with no intention of interfering with "nature's way," then the rout of the sperm was well and truly in hand.

In this, however, science moved faster than the opinion of the public it was to benefit. From the first stirrings of the discussion in modern times, when the reformer Francis Place had sung the praises of "a piece of sponge, about an inch square, placed in the vagina prior to coition and afterwards withdrawn by means of a double twisted thread," the reaction was hysterical. Medical men on both sides of the Atlantic, trapped as they were in their own parallel struggle to make their profession respectable, drew back in horror from this "vile perversion of nature." Sex for its own sake, with the deliberate intention to avoid conception, was no more than "conjugal onanism," and every "choked germ" constituted "indirect infanticide." "But like all crimes, it is not and it cannot be practiced with impunity," thundered the Jeremiah of the British Medical Association, Dr. C. H. F. Routh:

> . . . chronic metritis . . . leucorrhoea . . . menorrhagia . . . and haematocele . . . hysteralgia and hyperaesthesia . . . cancer in an aggravated form . . . ovarian dropsy . . . absolute sterility, mania leading to suicide and the most repulsive nymphomania are induced thereby . . . [25]

Nor was this chronic logorrhoea all that the reformers had to fear. In 1877 the British campaigner Annie Besant was sentenced to prison; she escaped jail but lost custody of her daughter as an "unfit" mother. Ten years later, a British doctor, H. A. Allbutt, was struck off the professional register for writing about birth control in *The Wife's Handbook*. But beneath the fury of the aroused patriarchs, the tide was on the turn. In 1882, Aletta Jacobs, Holland's first woman doctor, opened the world's first birth control clinic. The next generation of women campaigning for this issue, Marie Stopes in Britain and Margaret Sanger in the USA, found the worst force of the opposition spent and the victory in sight. The decisive link between sex and reproduction had been broken. To Sanger and Stopes, who had entered the struggle with the same aim, but different motives, the future was assured. Sanger saw the hopeless poverty and physical suffering of the over-breeding mother lifted from her shoulders, while Stopes waited to welcome the women whom contraception would liberate into the paradise of "married love." Both, however, saw women as the victors. At the height of the camp battle, Sanger had named her campaign journal, the *Woman Rebel*. The revolution was over, its objectives achieved. The "woman rebel" would now only have to live and learn to exploit the advantages of her new situation.

Doubtless she could: doubtless she would have, if given the chance. But this she was not to be. For the same set of historical circumstances that gave rise to nineteenth-century feminism produced also the masculine response to it. Throughout the West, wherever a father god, legal, professional, domestic, had been kicked off his throne, men lay on the ground, howling with injured pride, screaming to be reinstated. The hour found the man. From Vienna, Sigmund Freud set about the vital cultural work of restoring man to his rightful place at the center of the universe.

The first cosmic misfortune for women was Freud's birth into German bourgeois society just at the midpoint of the nineteenth century—for a man destined to reshape the world's notion of the female sex, Freud could hardly have had a worse model of social organization than this stultifying, narrow, reactionary and destructive framework which reduced women to empty-headed dolls or drove them into hysterical fugue. Freud's own attitudes had been quite unaltered from the paths of Jewish patriarchy by any of the great women's campaigns of his time, as this scolding letter to his fiancé makes clear:

> It really is a stillborn thought to send women into the struggle for existence exactly as men. If, for instance, I imagined my sweet girl as a competitor it would only end in my telling her . . . that I am fond of her and that I implore her to withdraw from the strife into the calm uncompetitive activity of my home. . . . I believe that all reforming action in law and education would break down in front of the fact that, long before the age at which a man can earn a position in society, nature has determined a woman's destiny through beauty, charm and sweetness. Law and custom may have much to give women that has been withheld from them, but the position of women will surely be what it is: in youth an adored darling, and in mature years a loved wife.[26]

With Dame Nature reappearing on the primal scene to prop up the rightful disposition of power between males and females in the status quo, it is no surprise to see another former leading man thrusting back into his old role center stage. With sublime unselfconsciousness, as if all the years, the work and the successes of the women's movement had never been, Freud brought back the phallus. In reality, of course, the great snake had never been away. But he was beginning to hide his head, as the women's attacks on unbridled masculine sexual prerogative had begun to beat him down. Now though, there was a new play by the new German *dramaturg*, and he had the principal part.

The plot was simple. A little boy grows up loving his mother. One day he discovers a great wonder, the adult male dong. Regrettably it is not attached to him—small boy collapses in confusion. Meanwhile his sister has also seen this great sight—she too burns with rage because she does not have it. Little brother will at least overcome his parricidal hatred and castration fears, and grow up to get a plonker of his own to play with. Small girl would however be stuck for always in her immature envy of the sacred object. The moral of the Oedipal drama is therefore simple, too: it is better to be a boy than a girl, and there is nothing in the world so wonderful, powerful, important and worth having as a penis.

From this starting-point, there could be no getting away from the logical extension of it: woman as a sex was inferior because of her "poverty of external genitals": simply to be woman was to be defective. Then again, stuck himself at the "mine's bigger than yours" stage of development Freud could not help but find the "woman's penis," the clitoris, pathetically inadequate. Recognizing that the clitoris is richly sensitive despite its apparently unimpressive size, Freud decided that it was suffering from a kind of retardation, a "childish masculinity." Only if the "excitability" transferred itself from the clitoris to the vagina was a woman sexually mature. The vaginal orgasm was the mark of a real woman, the clitoral meant "go back and start again." The impact of this has been summed up by a modern American biologist:

> Freud's theory of the vaginal orgasm required women to deny their own senses and knowledge about their own eroticism in order to be mature and female, a truly debilitating and depressing enterprise. The effects were profound and far ranging. For many women it was a fruitless effort that only deepened a sense of inferiority, inadequacy and guilt. As a theory to explain and cure "frigidity," it ensures lack of orgasm by requiring women to have sex in precisely the way it is most difficult for them to experience an orgasm. . . . It reinforced the phallocentricity of sexuality by defining women's sexuality in terms only of the penis.[27]

The legacy of Freud ensured that women's most personal and intimate part, her sex, was from now on to be hijacked by male "experts"—men who, while they never asked women how they thought or felt, nor listened to the evidence women gave anyway, could still have the authority to know better than women what their sex, at every level, was and should be. For men, this was a rich new terrain where old Mother Nature could be brought into the service of the new father god of science. And screwed out of her skull, what would she do but replay the story as before: man strong, woman weak, man active, woman passive, man dominant, woman submissive, even exquisitely so, as in this description of the "true woman" by one of Freud's female acolytes, the Princess Marie Buonaparte in her work on *Female Sexuality:*

> For the role of *everything female,* from the ovum to the beloved, is a waiting one. The vagina must await the advent of the penis in the same passive, latent and dormant manner that the ovum awaits the spermatozoon. Indeed, the externally feminine myth of the Sleeping Beauty is the retelling of our first biological relation.[28]

It was a good trick. And it came just at the right time. With the spread of contraceptive knowledge and techniques, women had been on the brink of taking control of their bodies. From now on it would be harder, for men in the West at any rate, to keep their women down through multiple child-bearing, ensuring that they stayed "barefoot, pregnant and in the kitchen." But this was not to be, as the gallant campaigners had hoped, the end of the oppression of women through their sex. For when they could no longer be imprisoned and beaten down for it, when they were not trapped by too many babies to be able to refuse it, the powers-that-always-were came up with this, in some ways their finest card—women were to be psychologically coerced into it, intimidated by fears of frigidity, of not being a "true woman," of being an "immature man" or an incomplete child. It was flawless. Everywhere the word of the Viennese fabulist spread, women, made anxious, struggled to comply. "No woman can call herself free who does not own and control her own body," said Margaret Sanger. And as the spirit of the Father looked upon his works and found them good, he could only agree.

12

DAUGHTERS OF TIME

Truth is the daughter of Time, not of Authority.

FRANCIS BACON

History, if you read it right, is the record of the
attempts to tame Father . . . the greatest triumph
of what we call civilization was the domestication
of the human male.

MAX LERNER

How are men and women to think about their maleness and femaleness in this twentieth century, in
which so many of our old ideas must be made new?

MARGARET MEAD

On August 4, 1914, Sir Edward Grey, Britain's Foreign Secretary,
looked down Whitehall over a darkening London. "The lamps," he
said "are going out all over Europe. We shall not see them lit again
for our lifetime." This was hardly to be wondered at—after the hostilities, none of the countries involved could have afforded to pay a
gas or electricity bill. Fighting this war had cost Britain alone over
£50,000 million, and the cost of putting to rights all the devastation
it had caused came to about twice as much again.[1] Money that could
have been spent on better housing, public services, food supplies, went
into a conflict that left millions of people throughout Europe without
a roof over their heads or a crust of bread.

They were the lucky ones. In four years, over ten million people
lost their lives in the service of this god of war, who to this day demands
hecatombs of human sacrifices. What drives old men in government
to send the choicest of their youths to murder the youth of an enemy
state, and/or be murdered themselves? Whatever the reason, when the
women who had lost lovers, husbands, sons or the prospect of all of
these were told that their sterling war service had brought them an
enhanced social and legal status, they must have thought the price was
rather high. And even then, the twin goals of freedom and equality
were as far away as ever. During the course of the hostilities, the

British nurse Edith Cavell was shot by the Germans for helping wounded soldiers to escape, and the Dutch dancer Mata Hari by the French, allegedly for being a German spy.[2] This brutal extension of the equality of the firing squad, when in all other respects women were still excluded from the privileges men awarded themselves, was a chill reminder of how little circumstances, or men, had changed.

This lesson of the First World War was only repeated and reinforced in the Second World War. There the rise of fascism, with its unbridled stress on virility and exaggerated masculinity, undermined almost all the gains won by women in the previous century of struggle. Nazism in particular was wedded to the "Gretchen image" of womanhood, Hitler calling the emancipation of women a symptom of depravity produced by frustration and malfunctioning sex glands, while Goebbels announced that "the female bird preens herself for her mate and lays her eggs only for him." The kernel of Nazi thinking on the woman question was a doctrine of inequality between the sexes as immutable as that between the Aryan and non-Aryan races. As always throughout women's history, though, this inequality took a great deal of brute force to sustain. As historian Richard Grunberger explains:

> The Weimer constitution gave women the vote, and a feminist elite, ranging from Rosa Luxemburg and Clara Zetkin on the far left, through to some National Reichstag deputies on the right, had helped shape the political postwar scene. Interposed between these political figures and the army of working women was the professional vanguard of the second sex: nearly 100,000 women teachers, 13,000 women musicians, and 3000 doctors.[3]

These were the women who were now to be dismissed from public life—one of the earliest Nazi party ordinances of January 1921 excluded women in perpetuity from holding any office in the party. What women were to do, of course, for their party and war work, was to breed, in numbers, the child of the future, the Aryan dream. In return for reverting to the old formula of *"Kinder, Kirche, Küche,"* women were promised "the esteem they deserved for their essential dignity."

Only some women, however. How far the Nazi reverence for women went was clearly illustrated by episodes like this, where the system conformed to the party ideology with typical Nazi efficiency:

> In Auschwitz there was a bordello of forty rooms in block 24 for the black triangles, German inmates, and a few select sycophants with green triangles. Tickets were handed out as a reward by the SS to this "Puff Haus." The madame was called the "Puff Mutter." The girls worked a two-hour day and three times a week . . . . The Puff Mutter rang the bell each twenty minutes (same time as the burning shift in the ovens) . . . [4]

With that ingenuity of cruelty for which the regime became notorious, the Nazis even discovered a new and hitherto untried use for prostitutes—they were strapped to the bodies of male concentration camp inmates who had been immersed in icy water until they died, to discover if the application of their body heat could restore any life to the dead man. The point of these "scientific experiments," by Dr. Sigmund Rascher of the Luftwaffe at Dachau, was to discover if a Luftwaffe pilot who had come down in icy seas could survive the ordeal. Sunlamps, hot water bottles, even electro-convulsive therapy were all tried before the idea of female "animal warmth" occurred to the experimenters. Himmler's only stipulation in his directive to Pohl, his deputy for concentration camps, was that the women should not be *German* prostitutes.[5]

By the standards of the Holocaust, these women were fortunate. Outside the camps, a handful of women were swimming against the tide of the wild female enthusiasm for Hitler that had been one of the key factors in his rise to power, from the unknown schoolgirl Hiltgunt Zassenhaus, who thrust her arm through a pane of glass rather than give the Nazi salute, to the now-famous heroines of the Resistance. Given their exclusion from the armed forces, the women's anti-fascist activity had to be expressed through intelligence or guerrilla activity. This was nothing new, for women have a history of covert operations against the enemy dating back to Delilah and Jael. Although generally obscured in times of open war, when the mythologizing of the conflict demands the repetition of the old lie that men are only fighting to protect and defend "the weaker sex," the contribution of women cannot be disguised or denied in times of internal conflict or revolutionary upheaval. Revolutions of the modern period have in fact been crucially dependent for their success upon women; who, when they throw off the conservatism which voting patterns suggest are more characteristic of the sex than violence, often prove themselves, in Fidel Castro's words, "twice as revolutionary as the men."

There was of course nothing exceptional in the association of women with radical activity. Most revolutionary movements begin with the highest ideals on women's behalf: the T'ai-P'ing Rebellion that brought China to its knees between 1850 and 1864 originally planned to give full social and educational equality to all females, in that context a proposal even more revolutionary than the primitive communism for which the movement is remembered. But no matter how much revolutions can, like war, be presented as *for* women, they are always *of* and *in* it too, deeply committed at every level. Six hundred women died at the last stand of Piribebuy in the struggle of Paraguay against Brazil, this bloody massacre only one of a number of engagements fought by women in the Paraguayan War of 1864–70. Their prominence was due to the devastating casualties inflicted on the men, as well as a pitiful shortage of ammunition—at Piribebuy in 1868 the women went down still firing volleys of stones, sand and empty bottles at the enemy, in one of the most sublime yet futile acts of defiance in military history.[6]

As this shows, under the topsy-turvy conditions of revolution, women found themselves once again serving as soldiers in the front line. The last known female regular soldiers had been abolished in Ireland in the seventh century AD, but the tradition, stretching all the way back to the old matriarchies, had never entirely disappeared. In Africa, for instance, the "fighting Amazons" of Dahomey had attracted the derision of Sir Richard Burton in 1863—". . . mostly elderly and all of them hideous . . . the officers decidedly chosen for the size of their bottoms . . . they maneuver with the precision of a flock of sheep . . ."[7] But Burton also recorded that this army, 2500 strong, was well armed and effective in battle. Nor could they all have been old and ugly, since all 2500 of them were official wives of the king.

Despite the official refusal to use women in the front line, a surprising number from the early modern period onwards have managed to see active service of one sort or another. The Spaniard Catalina de Erauso in the sixteenth century escaped from a convent the night before she was due to take her vows, and fought for the Spanish all over South America; "Kit" Cavanagh joined the British army in 1693 to find her husband, who had been press-ganged, fighting the French so successfully that she was promoted to the cavalry; Hannah Snell, who received twelve wounds fighting at the British naval assault on Pondicherry in 1748, extracted a ball from her groin herself, to prevent discovery of her sex; Loreta Velasquez of Cuba joined the Confederates to fight in the American Civil War after her three children all died of a fever; and English vicar's daughter Flora Sandes captained a Serbian infantry unit against the Bulgarians in the First World War. There were many, many more women soldiers, whose war service formed a violent contrast to women's essentially passive wartime role of nursing the injured and mourning the dead.

For as combatants shoulder to shoulder with men, women had a position of strength denied them in their traditional roles—Trinidad Tescon, the Filipina who fought against the Spanish in all the key engagements of the Phillipine Revolution after 1895, used her reputation as a warrior-heroine to set up hospitals for the wounded, where she was known to the men simply as "Ina" (Mother). Equally brave though less compassionate (her milk of human kindness curdled somewhat by experiences of childhood prostitution and a gynocidal spouse) was the Russian Bolshevik soldier Mariya Bochkareva. After outstanding military service rewarded by many decorations for valor, Bochkareva founded an all-woman crack corps of 2000 high-grade volunteers in a "Woman's Battalion of Death." These shock troops were so successful that similar units were organized all over Russia, with as many as 1500 women enlisting in one night, so great was their eagerness for the fray.[8]

In general, though, women made their greatest contribution to revolutionary movements as freedom fighters rather than as soldiers on the masculine pattern. This tradition was particularly marked in Latin America, where Gertrudis Bocanegra created and ran an underground network of women during the Mexican War of Independence, dying after government arrest and torture in 1817. The same fate overtook the Chinese revolutionary Ch'iu Chin, a conscious feminist who took Joan of Arc as her model when she launched herself into the struggle against the Manchu dynasty in 1898. After the failure of her planned uprising, Ch'iu Chin's life work seemed to be destroyed with her execution in 1907. But her network survived, through her heroic resistance to her torturers (she refused to implicate anyone else, writing only the seven Chinese letters, "The autumn wind and rain sadden us"), and her bravery in itself inspired her successors and helped to ensure the final victory of the cause for which she died.

To the eye of history though, the cause often seems to be the true winner, not the women who fought for it. Many died who might have lived, like the Russian Sofya Perovskaya; the clarity and conviction with which she planned the assassination of the Tsar Alexander II in 1881 deserted her when her lover was arrested, and careless of all safety, she threw her life away. Even those who survived paid an appalling price: Perovskaya's co-worker and friend Elisaveta Kovalskaya spent twenty years in Siberia, the same sentence as that served by another of the group, Vera Figner, in the terrible island fortress of the River Neva, where, as Figner later put it in her memoirs, "the clock of life stopped." Most poignant of all, perhaps, was the story of Vera Liubatovich, who escaped to Geneva with her lover, where they had a child. When he was subsequently taken by the secret police, Liubatovich left her baby to search for him, was arrested herself and banished to Siberia, and so lost everything.[9]

Yet the risk has never deterred the true revolutionary. In the last of the major upheavals involved in the remaking of the modern world, China's revolution was distinguished by a long history of preparatory activity by women, and female volunteers were among the first to join the final strike of this epic struggle, some, like K'ang K'o-ch'ing taking up arms as a very young teenager. Like K'ang K'o-ch'ing again, Teng Ying-ch'ao was one of the only 35 women who made the Long March of 1934–5, abandoning her home and family for the 8000-mile trial of endurance to "plant Communism in China" with her husband Zou Enlai. Teng Ying-ch'ao lived to see her husband as premier of the new China, herself holding a series of the highest political offices; Ho Hsiang-ning, one of the first Chinese feminists to adopt the revolutionary gesture of bobbing her hair in the 1920s, lost her husband to the struggle when he was assassinated in 1925; Xiang Jingyu, who had originated the vogue for bobbing hair as a gesture of feminist defiance, lost her life in the 1927 "White Terror" purge of the Communists, shot in a gag to prevent her final speech. Yet the roll call continues, through the revolutions of the 1930s, 1950s, 1970s: in Spain, Dolores Ibarruri, "La Pasionaria," who inspired a whole generation with her powerful anti-fascist slogan, *"No pasaran!"* (They shall not pass); Algeria's Djamila Boupacha and Haydee Santamaria of Cuba, both of whom suffered appalling sexual tortures that awakened the conscience of the whole world; and Joyce "Teurai Ropa" (Spill-Blood) Nhongo, who fought off a Rhodesian attack intended to capture her for propaganda purposes, two days before giving birth to her daughter.

The cost was high, but then so were the gains. In pre-revolutionary China, any man refusing to beat his wife every night, against the order of his father, could be thrown into the dungeon of the local magistrate or landowner. The Revolution forbade it, and the women immediately seized the chance to escape from the misery of 5000 years, as one aggrieved husband complained:

> All my friends beat their wives, so I was only observing custom. Sometimes I didn't have any reason except that I hadn't beaten her recently. . . . Right after liberation it was difficult for me to beat her any more. I would sometimes lose my temper and raise my elbows to beat her, and she and the children would restrain me, reminding me that Chairman Mao wouldn't permit it, so I refrained. . . . They maintained a spirit of revolt and if we mistreated our wives, all would protest. It was impossible.[10]

For him, maybe. For her, this was the real revolution. And she did not owe it all to Chairman Mao. Although the ban of the Central

Committee of the Chinese Communist Party on wife beating was crucial, what ensured its success was the strength of the Chinese Women's Association. In an early forerunner of the "consciousness-raising" groups developed by the women's movement in the late 1960s, Chinese women were encouraged to come together to "speak bitterness," to confront their situation and their husband's abuse of his power, and to challenge (and even physically punish) any men who refused to give up their bad old ways.

The overthrow of one regime for another does not always produce such clear and immediate benefits for women. For rural women or the urban poor, life may change little from the round of endless childbearing and the struggle for survival. Often the real events destined to change women's lives seem at first to be remote or insignificant. When in 1955 an American researcher at the Worcester Institute for Chemical Biology, Massachusetts, announced that he had isolated a group of chemical steroids of the progestagen type, the average woman neither knew of it nor cared. But Gregory Pincus had in fact discovered the philosopher's stone of genetic science, the element with the power to turn centuries of wishful dreaming into reality. For progestagens, Pincus had discovered, had the power to prevent ovulation when taken orally. Without fanfare, then, "the Pill" was born, an insignificant compound of naturally occurring chemicals, yet in its impact due to change as many lives as any other of this century's revolutions.

The 1955 meeting of research scientists in Tokyo at which Pincus reported his findings was in itself a moment of profound change. Another of its revelations was the quite unexpected reappearance of the intra-uterine contraceptive device. This had first been developed in Germany and Israel in experiments of the 1920s and 30s, based on much older medical knowledge—every Indian bazaar *dhai*, however ignorant, knew that if she could wedge a seed pod, stick of vanilla or licorice root up through the vagina into the womb itself, a woman would not conceive. But the early results were disappointing and even disastrous. The technology was simply not available either to introduce the device safely, or to develop a material that the womb would not try to break down, with the often fatal result of pelvic inflammatory disease. Now the Japanese, fresh from their technical triumph in revolutionizing radio, succeeded in transistorizing contraception. A miniaturized squiggle of indestructible plastic, soon to be known familiarly as "the coil," when placed in the uterus, ensured no babies.

Within 15 years, over 20 million women were using the contraceptive pill, and over 10 million women the coil.[11] It is not difficult to see why women embraced these new contraceptives in such numbers, and with such speed. After some initial teething troubles, both had a significantly increased reliability rate over the existing devices. Both had the advantage that they were in the sole and entire control of the woman, unlike the sheath—a wife no longer had to lie there wondering *if* her husband would submit to one of "them things" that "spoiled his pleasure," *if* he would still be sober enough to get it on, and if he could keep it in place.

The pill and the IUD had another advantage over the cervical cap, too. This lay in their 24-hour, all-the-year-round capacity. The cap, with the addition of the spermicidal jelly that had emerged from the unlikely source of the dreaming spires of Oxford in 1932, required forward planning for sex, making it feel uncomfortably like an act of calculation or a routine that often missed its point—"just slip it in every night when you brush your teeth, and leave the rest to your husband," warbled a British birth control leaflet of the innocent 1950s. Now, whether moved by some romantic myth of spontaneous passion, or an impulse of hypocrisy generated by the patriarchal double standard, women could distance themselves from the direct practice of contraception. Contraception itself had separated sex from reproduction—the new technology now divorced contraception from sex.

In doing so, it brought to a head the argument that had been part of the fabric of human existence since humanity realized that it had existence, the question that as much as anything else created the war between the sexes, even the sex war within individual couples—who controls a woman's body? For the first time in history, Western societies found themselves grappling with a situation that would have seemed an unthinkable blasphemy to earlier ages, the prospect that a woman could use and take sex in exactly the way that men had always been able to do, casually, at will, without premeditation and—perhaps worst of all—*without consequences*. This last took on a new edge with the liberalization of Western laws regulating abortion during the course of the 1960s.

The history of abortion in itself forms a microcosm of the way that social and legal controls over women's bodies have, until very recently, *always* reflected patriarchal imperatives and paranoias, never women's needs. As late as 1939 in Britain, a government committee chaired by Lord Birkett was still reaffirming the state's right to control women's reproduction in order to keep the birth rate up. A profound shift took place in the West when the state's *political* interest in having control, gave way to a *legal* recognition of the individual right to personal autonomy.

In countries with a strong Roman Catholic tradition where abortion was not simply illegal but inconceivable, the conflict was bitter, the battle prolonged, the hostilities ongoing. Success there came as it did everywhere, from strong and concerted feminist action. In Ireland, a large number of women travelled together from Dublin to Belfast (in the north of the island, and as such part of the UK and subject to British laws) to buy contraceptives. When the so-called "contraceptive train" returned to Dublin, crowd support was very marked, and customs officers turned a blind eye to the illegal importations. In France, a group of women, including leading luminaries like Simone de Beauvoir, signed and circulated the *Manifeste des 343*, a document admitting that all the signatories had had illegal abortions, and challenging the authorities to prosecute them. From this came the pro-abortion organization "Choisir" (Choose), founded by Gisela Halimi, the lawyer who acted for the tortured Algerian freedom fighter Djamila Boupacha. The campaigns of Choisir resulted in the epochal laws on contraception and abortion carried through the French parliament by Simone Veil in 1974.

By the end of the 1970s, key legal decisions on both sides of the Atlantic had turned the tide for the women of Europe and America. In 1973, the Supreme Court of the United States pronounced that "the right of personal privacy includes the abortion decision," later confirming this in a landmark pronouncement:

> Inasmuch as it is the woman who physically bears the child and who is the more directly and immediately affected by the pregnancy, as between the two (male parent and female parent) the balance weighs in her favor.[12]

In a similar British decision, confirmed on appeal to the European Court of Justice in 1981, the court was even more specific: the law of England "gives no right to a father to be consulted in respect of the termination of a pregnancy."

No right to father? Women demanding control of their own bodies, and receiving the support of the courts? How had this come about? Only through almost twenty years of the most intensive feminist activity that women had ever generated. It is important to understand that the women of industrialized societies had not simply crept back into their homes, tugging a grateful forelock to their lords and masters, after the successful climax of the suffrage campaign. In the words of

Dora Russell, a life-long activist, to Dale Spender, "There's always been a women's movement this century!" The inter-war period produced, too, one major feminist text, Simone de Beauvoir's dazzling analysis of the web of women's oppression, *The Second Sex* (1949).

But through women's perennial absence from the history books, from the records of contemporary experience, from vigorous and self-renewing contact with each other such as men have always enjoyed through work and public activity, there has never been a visible, continuous, accepted tradition of women's political action. Only when the inevitable claw-back by the undefeated patriarchs of male power and privilege in new and usually unsuspected disguises produces the next generation of revolt, do women look back and discover their strength, their solidarity, their political history. And on each of these occasions, everything has to be rediscovered, reinvented, usually in the teeth of men's assurances that women have never had it so good. So powerful is this denial of women's oppression that the bad feeling it produces becomes for each woman, "the problem without a name." In this justly famous phrase, Betty Friedan, the mother of modern feminism, initiated in 1963, with the publication of *The Feminine Mystique*, the crucial post-suffrage phase of the women's struggle:

> It was a strange stirring, a sense of dissatisfaction, a yearning that women suffered in the middle of the twentieth century in the United States. Each suburban wife struggled with it alone. As she made the beds, shopped for groceries, matched slip cover material, ate peanut butter sandwiches, chauffeured Cub Scouts and Brownies, lay beside her husband at night, she was afraid to ask even of herself the silent question, "Is this all?"[13]

Betty Friedan's achievement lay in blasting to smithereens the myth of the happy housewife. She thus made it possible for women to break the candy bars of their imprisonment within the "domestic sphere" and share with one another their frustration and their rage. A powerful anger was flowing in from another source, too, at very much the same time. The radical politics of the 1960s attracted many strong and committed young women to the fight against racism and the Vietnam war. Inside every "revolutionary" movement, however, they found that "men led the marches and made the speeches and expected their female comrades to lick the envelopes and listen." When the black leader Stokely Carmichael was heard to say that the only place for women in the movement was "prone," activist women saw that there was a subject class more in need of liberating than the occupied Vietnamese, nearer to them in oppression than the blacks—themselves.

The explosion of women's anger and action clearly emerges from an indication of the principal events of the years that followed:

1966	The founding of America's National Organization of Women, with Friedan at its head
1969	"The Myth of the Vaginal Orgasm," a "landmark paper by [Anne] Koedt that unhooded the clitoris from generations of oblivion and mystery, and used it as a rallying cry for women's sexuality"[14]
1970	The publication of Kate Millet's *Sexual Politics*, Germaine Greer's *The Female Eunuch*, Shulamith Firestone's *The Dialectic of Sex: The Case for Feminist Revolution*
	First National Women's Liberation Conference in Britain
1971	The founding of the US National Women's Political Caucus
1973	International Feminist Congress
1975	UN Decade of Women's rights
1960s–80s	Programs of law reform, equal opportunities legislation, and positive action throughout the industrialized world.

From its puzzled and uncertain beginnings, then, the new women's movement swelled into a commanding political force, enlisting the commitment of individual males and entire governments, not merely the women's franchise. A new note in the voice of protest, a new dimension in the analysis, gave the movement an authority and authenticity that did not merely demand attention, but commanded it:

> Women are an oppressed class. . . . We are exploited as sex objects, breeders, domestic servants and cheap labor . . . our prescribed behavior is enforced with threats of physical violence. *Because we have lived so intimately with our oppressors, in isolation from each other, we have been kept from seeing our personal suffering as a political condition.*[15]

Out of this original, and once understood irresistible insight sprang the most powerful of the new movement's slogans: the personal is political. For the first time, large numbers of women took on board the concept that the enemy was not the Church, the state, the law, the government, "them"—but the agent and representative of all these, the man in their bed—*him*.

Millions of women heard this as the statement they had been waiting for all their lives; an account of the way social reality works that finally explained their experiences to them. For some of these women, one course of action seemed obvious. If women could succeed in taking the feminist slogan to the next stage and make the personal political, then they would have the power to turn back at least some of the tides that have flowed against women in the past. The advent of women into politics and power worldwide was scattered and slow. When Sirimavo Bandaranaike of Sri Lanka became the world's first woman prime minister in 1960, it did not look like much of a portent. But her appointment was the harbinger of a new race of women politicians, tough, able, hungry for office and above all committed to living out the truth of the American Jill Johnston's dictum, "No one should have to dance backwards all their life."

Dancing at all in the wholly male arena of power politics called for nifty footwork and enormous stamina, both emotional and physical. When Nancy Astor was elected as the first woman to enter the British parliament in its 1000-year history, she described her first six months as "sheer hell." Even to win the right to stand for election had been, in most countries, a hell of its own—the French Socialist Jeanne Déroin had incurred ridicule and persecution in 1849 for her attempt to enter the French parliament at a time when the only public offices open to women were those of postmistress and schoolteacher. Yet women persisted with their candidatures, often showing an unshakable refusal to accept the limitations placed upon their sex: in 1872, the kaleido-scopic Victoria Claflin Woodhull became the first woman in the history of the United States to run for the presidency. Woodhull, who with her sister also set up the country's first female professional stock-brokerage business, was so far in advance of her time as to become a national scandal and laughing stock.

But within a century of Claflin's audacious challenge, the "firsts" for women in previously all-male posts, often in highly conservative countries, were beginning to happen every year. In 1966, Indira Gandhi became India's first female prime minister; in 1969, Golda Meir triumphed in a stronghold of the patriarchs, Israel; in 1974, Eleanor Grasso became America's first woman governor to be elected in her own right, the same year that France's newly appointed health min-ister, Simone Veil, had her own triumph in piloting abortion reform through her parliament; 1979 brought Benazir Bhutto of Pakistan, Hao Tianx'u of China and Margaret Thatcher of Britain to power in their respective countries, to be followed by other exhilarating "role-busters," as the American press soon dubbed these women: Vigdís Finnbogadóttir, in 1980 Iceland's first woman head of state; in 1984 Geraldine Ferraro of New York, a serious contender for the US vice presidency where she would have been only a heartbeat away from one of the most powerful positions in the Western world. Repeat these successes worldwide at parish and *département* level, in civil services and executive wings of their administrations, and it is easy to feel the substance of one American business-woman's claim that "the women are coming—with a great orgasmic roar!"

Not all feminists are impressed, however, with women's undoubted success in penetrating the structures of the male world of power. Suspicious of the ease with which masculine systems absorb women without changing their own essential nature, separatists have argued that "the Master's tools will never dismantle the Master's house," in the words of the black American poet Audre Lorde. The growing conviction that men and women have not merely distinct but *opposed* political needs and imperatives has fuelled the formation of women-only parties and groups, to lobby or fight for woman-identified issues. In the decades since the 1960s' rebirth of modern feminism, these have included some radical new approaches to age-old but unidentified social problems (unidentified often because women's problems) like Women's Aid Refuges and Rape Crisis Centers. Conservation and "Green" issues are also high on very many women's agenda for political action, as historian Amaury de Riencourt notes: "Having fouled his planetary nest, Western man now has to contend with the aroused spirit of Mother Earth—generator, like the multifaceted goddess Kali, not only of civilized stability, but occasionally of revolutionary anger."[16] The sense of "Women for Life on Earth" is the moving spirit of what has become the world's most enduring peace camp, the Women's Peace Camp at Greenham Common in the South of England. Despite continual harassment from the US army occupiers of the nuclear missile base, the British courts, the local police, random gangs of violent men, and the seamy underbelly of the British tabloid press, the Women's Camp has continued since 1981 as a living embodiment of the song of the women's peace movement:

> Oh sisters, come you, sing for all you're worth,
> Arms are made for linking,
> Sisters, we're asking for the earth.

For the earth has still to be won. The removal of most of the more blatant of the injustices against women has served to concentrate attention on those that remain. After the euphoria of the first handful of spectacular triumphs, late twentieth-century feminism had to come to terms with the fact that, with every battle won, the enemy regroups elsewhere; new oppressions emerge, which like their predecessors are only symptoms and expressions of more fundamental inequalities whose roots are hard enough to identify, let alone remove. With a sense of history sharpened by repeated disappointment, women are coming to see the essentially repetitive nature of their struggle; to understand, too, that the circumstances under which they win rights and freedoms *in themselves* can undermine those very rights and freedoms so painfully won.

For women make progress in times of social change, when older, established power blocks shift and crack, allowing women (and others previously excluded) to penetrate structures where before they were denied. Women's advance in the public sphere, or in the world of work, is connected therefore with times of upheaval: frontier women fight and shoot, immigrant women work in business, run for office in the city or the trades union. The post-1960s phase of the fight for emancipation is the twin sister of the world recession that has pushed up women's participation in the workforce just as the Great War did, when women in their millions abandoned the feather duster for the lathe and vowed never to go back into "domestic service" again.

They did, of course. Domestic service was soon given another name, and a whole generation of budding engineers and skilled workers, the riveting Rosies of two world wars, found themselves back in the home. For no matter how vital it is *at the time* for women to work, to drive cars, to have crèches and nursery schools for their babies, these signs of emancipation are seen as a response to crisis, and are fatally undermined by this. The atmosphere of uncertainty, dissatisfaction and fear, though caused by the larger crisis, becomes associated with the fact that women now have jobs or are no longer in the home as a warm and welcoming presence. Identified then with the bad feelings of change, women come to be seen as the *cause* of the badness. And not only to men—to women too, these strains and dissatisfactions, and being made to take responsibility for being the cause of them, often seems too high a price to pay for their new freedoms.

The root causes of dissatisfaction with women's progress towards freedom have in fact proved quite constant over many hundreds of years:

- women working while men are unemployed ("taking men's jobs")
- women getting out of the isolation of the home and developing solidarity with other women in factories or other groups
- women getting cash of their own and the independence that confers
- women getting public rights instead of their previous domestic privileges
- women learning "masculine" skills (to ride, to shoot, to run a

business), so demystifying masculine competence, and challenging the implicit masculine right to lead
- the absence of the "angel at the hearth": domestic management suffers when women do other things.

Marry these stresses to the underlying and very human impulse of nostalgia for a return to the way it used to be—"when we all get back to normal, it will all be all right again" . . . "when this lousy war is over . . ."—then it is easy to see why the gains that women make they do not hold. There is always, often almost unseen, a creeping patriarchal clawback. "We discovered to our astonishment that when you got the vote you were not thereby made a full citizen. It was a horrible discovery," mourned one former suffragette, fifty years after that battle had been thought won.[17]

It was also a discovery that has had to be made again and again. Women have had to learn, often painfully and always with reluctance, that their freedom will not simply come of its own accord. In the nineteenth century, high expectations were pinned on the vote, on education, on women's access to the professions. In the European revolutionary struggle, Clara Zetkin, founder of the International Socialist Women's Congress in 1907, was instrumental in all these, and internationally distinguished for the brilliance of her critical analysis and the breadth of her understanding.

Yet like a great many others both before and since, Zetkin sincerely believed that women's full participation in the labor force, and full legal equality, would automatically lead to their political and social emancipation. In addition, the extreme bitterness of this particular conflict, in which Zetkin's friend and colleague Rosa Luxemburg was like Hypatia, seized by opponents, beaten and killed, drove women's special interests to the wall. Neither Zetkin nor Luxemburg trusted Marx to revolutionize the future for women with the ardor he applied to the revolution for men; and after a few halfhearted changes like the extension of abortion and divorce, the Russian woman found herself worse off than ever. Now she was to be an economic tool of the regime, as well as a sexual object for her man, compelled to work all day *and* carry the entire burden of childcare and domestic work in her "leisure" hours at night.

The result was inevitable. At the turn of the century, the average life span of the Russian woman was two years less than that of the average man, despite women's biological tendency to greater longevity. By the early 1960s, women's life span was *eight years* less than their males.[18] Yet the Party line retained this manifestly unjust division of labor, by embracing the most archaic notion of sex roles that the new patriarchs could devise:

> A boy must be prepared for service in the Red Army while he is still at school. He receives special physical and purely military training for a stern soldier's life. . . . What of the girl? She is essentially a mother. School must give the girl special knowledge of human anatomy, physiology, psychology, pedagogy and hygiene.[19]

This crippling sex segregation continues to be found in the deep structures of every society, because it continues to flourish in the deepest recesses of the human mind. For women, the life choices (which by and large are made for them by their societies) come down to one of two evils—either the overloaded worker/wife/mother with her double burden, or the under-occupied housewife/drone with her half-life of deprivation and despair. In truth there is little to choose between them. Of the two, the role of full-time homemaker may seem to be preferable in terms of offering individual women marginally more control over their own lives than industrial organization, and a less onerous lot than that of the wage slave. This is an illusion, for the houseworker has little or no control over a job that eats away at all her waking hours, and whose chief characteristic is that it is "never done."

And during the course of the crowded century and more that has elapsed since Charlotte Perkins Gilman crisply pointed out that "a house does not need a wife any more than it does a husband," women's work of domestic labor has shown no sign of diminishing. Vacuum cleaners, washing machines, fridges, dishwashers, food processors and microwave ovens have poured from the laboratories and factories in a continuous stream since the mid-nineteenth century—gas ranges came from Britain in 1841, electricity in 1881, and the first vacuum cleaner was patented in 1908—without making any impact on the number of hours women spent in cooking, cleaning, and caring for a family. Time saved on one chore was simply taken up by another as domestic work itself became more sophisticated and demanding, and women had to work harder to meet the higher expectations of improved service that the brave new technology had created.[20]

On the theoretical side, suggestions to reduce or redefine housework met with a similar lack of success. Charlotte Perkins Gilman, recognized that social inequality begins in the home, proposed the abolition of housework. The labor of cooking, cleaning and childcare could be communal, she argued, and performed by both men and women like any other kind of job, leaving the home as a place of private rest and recreation. The male sex, however, showed no enthusiasm for ending the division between men's work and women's work, and confined their efforts to inventing more and more domestic machinery whose only certain benefit, due to the extra work they entail, is to their manufacturer.

The proliferation of machines for housework has also helped to make it the solitary, mechanical and marginalized activity it has become in the second half of the twentieth century. This in turn makes it irredeemably low status work, in the eyes of those who do it no less than those who benefit from it ("I'm only a housewife" has become a classic self-deprecation of the post-1960s). Undervalued, unseen (except by advertisers), alienated and despised, the "housewife" is no more than an unwaged household slave, frequently reliant, as the West's soaring incidence of female alcoholism and tranquilizer consumption indicate, on drugs to keep herself going.

The so-called "working woman," as if what the "housewife" does is not work, performs all this unpaid labor on top of her occupational labor for which, at best, she will only be getting three-quarters of what her male equivalent is paid. Equal pay legislation in many parts of the world has produced only a minimal impact on this most entrenched and immovable of injustices. Women constitute one-third of the world's formal labor force. For this they receive only 10 percent of the world's income, and own less than 1 percent of the world's property.[21] Further, within the world of work, women are systematically held in low grades and denied access to promotion, or to the kind of work which brings status and reward. In many societies, the fact that women perform certain occupations is enough to ensure their designation as "woman's work," in itself a guarantee that this work remains a low-paid ghetto activity. Through the ensuing combination of all these factors, women are then excluded from the crucial resources that would enable them to better their circumstances, and to wield more power within their family and community.

Yet the fact that women in Western industrialized societies are now doing well enough in the occupational world to want to do better, in itself argues considerable progress. In the past, the exclusion of women from top jobs was never a problem; now, the bands of aware and angry women gathering in the corridors of power are not simply griping about the barriers obstructing them, but setting about the task of breaking them down. From the 1970s, however, it began to emerge more and more clearly that gains like this had by and large been won by and for women of the white middle classes. Even when white feminists had attempted to relate to the needs of women of color, their overtures often struck black women as inappropriate, patronizing and racist. To the blacks, attuned as they were to all the fine nuances of oppression, there was an uneasy whiff of old style colonization about the whites' attempts to enroll black women in the liberation movements. Explaining "What the Black Woman Thinks about Women's Lib" in 1971, Toni Morrison wrote, "Too many movements and organizations have made deliberate overtures to enroll blacks and have ended up by rolling them. They don't want to be used again to help somebody gain power—a power that is carefully kept out of their hands."[22]

For some black women activists, feminism was a sideshow, a distraction from the real battle, the real enemy: racism. Others, like Bell Hooks, argued for an understanding that would encompass the interlocking of the various different forms of oppression; those all cast alike as worms beneath the boot of white male supremacy should use their strength to strike together against the common enemy, not to turn against each other. What the black women are saying is very clear: that although all women share a common oppression as women, not all women are equally oppressed. And it is difficult, if not impossible, for an outsider to grasp the complex web of allegiances and associations that can bind a woman to a man, or a way of life, that clearly relegates her to an inferior place. Among the native American women of the Lakota, or Sioux, submission to the *bloka* (maleness, male dominance) of this warrior society is part of its most ancient tradition. To strike out for the more assertive behavior of American women towards men would mean Lakota women rejecting the "native" half of their selves in favor of "American," to the prejudice of their personal integrity.

Where racism crosses sexism, the experience of the individual woman victim has always been of this kind of fragmentation. In the American south, a gentleman would always stand for a lady—but it was a well-known fact that a nigger couldn't be a lady (every Southern gentleman had a library of books by other scientific gentlemen proving that as one of the "highest animal species" she wasn't even a fully human woman)—so if you were black and a woman, you stopped being half of yourself when you had to stand to give up your seat to a white gentleman. For one woman, it was eventually too much. Rosa Parks has passed into history as the black woman who in 1955 refused to give up her seat on a bus in Montgomery, Alabama, at the order of a white man. Her action inspired a widespread black boycott of the buses throughout the South of America, and so the civil rights movement was born. "A miracle has taken place," said Martin Luther King, blessing the birth of the overthrow of the psychological slavery that had replaced almost unnoticed the physical chains of legalized subordination.

It is, however, a classic tenet of racism that ethnic groups, problematized by their adopted nations, would be "better off in their own country." The recent experience of many women in their own countries suggests that freedom may be coming—but "not here, not yet, and not for us," in the Iranian women's phrase. There the enforced Westernization of the late Shah gave way to the fundamentalist fanaticism of the Ayatollah Khomeini without a momentary interruption in the tyranny of men over women. A Western observer summed up the contradictions inflicted on Iranian women from both sides of the religious and political spectrum:

> In 1978–9, educated women donned the *chador* as a protest against the Shah, while Ayatollah Khomeini denounced the Shah's attitude to women. . . . "The Shah declared that women should only be objects of sexual attraction. It is this concept which leads women to prostitution and reduces them to the status of sexual objects."
>
> Today, women who expose too much hair can be sent to camps for "corrective moral re-education." The veil is seen as the symbol of independence from the Western values that the Shah used merely to consolidate his family's power. Failure to observe correct wearing of "hejab" (correct religious dress) is counter-revolutionary.[23]

This attack on the "romanticization of Islam," though made by a Western male, is abundantly supported by the testimony of Iranian women themselves. Writer Mashid Amir Shahi has publicly attacked Khomeini's decree that women are "unequal, and biologically, naturally and intellectually inferior to men." What this has meant in practice was illustrated by an anonymous speaker at a London conference:

> Wedding day, well, is compulsory. Political women are tortured and raped before execution. Especially young women. They rape nine-year-old women in the prison because it is against God if they execute a virgin woman. Women are attacked in various horrific ways, such as acid being thrown in their faces, their hair being burnt if it is not covered. It means that just to be a woman in Iran is a political crime.[24]

Plus ça change . . . In the course of history, to be a woman had been a sin against nature and a crime against God. Now it has become an ideological deviance into the bargain. Under this system, the woman who dared to question the ideology by which she was judged would find herself among the "daughters of the Devil" whom the men of God, or the God of men, had determined to destroy. For the woman who argued, questioned, challenged, was not a woman. Woman was designated by nature to please and complement man, to love and serve her lord and master. After all, what else are women for?

In this baseline demand lurks the eternal myth of womanhood, and the eternal unsatisfied fantasy of the self-deluded male. To them, the answer was simple—women were for men, and should be grateful. Nowhere has this egregious exaction been more visibly expressed, nor more extensively fostered, than in the world's dream factory of the twentieth century, the Hollywood film industry. Hollywood's idiosyncratic vice and overriding obsession, the sexualizing of the female, in fact is wholly characteristic of all the other mass media, and indeed the secret of their commercial success. But although advertising has now taken over as the prime site of sexual stereotyping in the Western industrialized societies, Hollywood led the way. Whatever ideas the inhabitants of the postwar world nurse about male and female, love and work, they will have derived a high proportion of them from the dreamworld of Hollywood fiction.

And what did Hollywood have to tell a breathless world through the undying magic of the silver screen? What was the message of the moguls who knew All About Eve, how women became Notorious, feared a Psycho and longed for King Kong and a grapefruit in the face? What else but that there were bad girls and good girls, girls you screwed and girls you married, little women to boil some water (lots of it). Study on this, sister, Gentlemen Prefer Blondes. Without knowing how, for it was always very respectful towards religion (Jesus of Nazareth, the Man Born To Be Box Office), Hollywood became the Church of America, every film the new covenant, every picture told a story and the story was the greatest, oldest, cruellest, dumbest story every told, the man born to be man.

For boys will be boys, and nowhere more so than in the all-American playground of the Hollywood movie. As film after film rolled off the cameras under the beady scrutiny of the first generation movie moguls, patriarchs of the purest water to the last man, the father gods must have been hugging themselves with glee. For who needed physical restraints, savage laws, exclusion from education, from work and from society to keep women in their second-rate "sphere," when you could show them a film that did the same job, *and* sent them away happy into the bargain?

The extent to which the mass media of the twentieth century have served to replace the older instruments of dominance and restraint in the perennial patriarchal work of keeping women subordinate has yet to be fully acknowledged. But in its groping, voyeuristic response to the female, its tireless recycling of the same old female archetypes of mother, maiden, whore, its unreeling of ideal scenarios contrasted with the threatening accounts of the "girls who went wrong," Hollywood has to take its proud place alongside the "morals police" of the Ayatollah Khomeini for its valuable work in keeping women in line and training them to be everything a regular guy could ever hope for as his wife and the mother of his children.

As these pseudo-modern industries, the mass media, lead us firmly by the genitals backwards into the future, we can recognize the new arena in which the next stage for the freedom and equality of women will be fought out. Over the millennia of civilization, the source and site of women's inferiority has been located in nature, biology, religion, physiology, brain size and the female psyche. Women have fought back, for the right to read, to own money, to vote. One by one those oppressions have gone down in some parts of the world, thereby undermining the "natural" and inevitable status of those that remain. But underlying patterns change slowly. This is in no way to belittle the fruits of the struggle to date. It is simply to insist that in the deeper struggle which feminists worldwide now realize that they face, changing the world takes longer.

For there is much to do, amounting in fact to a remaking of modern society. *All democratic experiments, all revolutions, all demands for equality have so far, in every instance, stopped short of sexual equality.* Every society has in its prestige structures a series of subtle, interacting codes of dominance which always, everywhere, finally rank men higher than women. Nowhere has any society successfully dispensed with the age-old sex-role division of labor and the rewards in goods and power that accompany it. Nowhere do women enjoy the rights, privileges, possibilities and leisure time that men do. Everywhere men still mediate between women and power, women and the state, women and freedom, women and themselves.

This story has no ending, as the history of women, so long in the making, is in one sense only just begun. Women have always fought not just for survival, but for the meaning of the struggle—now, they are organized, grouping and pushing forward, not merely for new definitions, but for the *right to define*. What will the writing of history be like, Gerda Lerner wonders, "when that umbrella of dominance is removed and definition is shared equally by men and women?" In her vision of the future, "we will simply step out under the free sky":

> We now know that man is not the measure of that which is human, but men and women are. Men are not the center of the world, but men and women are. This insight will transform consciousness as decisively as did Copernicus's discovery that the earth is not the center of the universe.[25]

This will be crucial: the new woman needs a new man. But she will not now make the mistake made by so many women in the past, of trusting her freedom, her future, to him alone. The new spirit of women's self-discovery and self-reliance has permeated every aspect of contemporary life.

This new strength of woman lies in the clear-sighted and untroubled recognition of the oldest truth in the newest voice of young black feminism: "We realize that the only people who care enough about us to work consistently for our liberation is us. Our politics evolve from a healthy love for ourselves, our sisters and our community which allows us to continue our struggle and our work."[26] Love, struggle and work—the history of the world's women, past and future. And if there can be one final certainty it is this: that the love, the struggle and the work will go on, through the one inescapable imperative outlined by Alfred Adler:

> Whatever name we give it, we shall always find in human beings this great line of activity—this struggle to rise from an inferior to a superior position, from defeat to victory, from below to above.

NOTES AND REFERENCES

Chapter 1 The First Women

1 Elizabeth Gould Davis, *The First Sex* (1971), pp. 34–5. The argument that the male chromosome "Y" is no more than "a defective X" has a long pedigree—see Francis Swiney, *Women and Natural Law* (1912). In the modern period it has been vigorously advanced by Valerie Solanas in *The Scum Manifesto* (New York, 1968), and by Gould Davis: "this small and twisted Y chromosome is a genetic error . . . the first males were freaks, produced by some damage to the genes . . ." See also Ashley Montagu, *Sex, Man and Society* (New York, 1969), Ruth Bleier, *Science and Gender* (New York and Oxford, 1984), and the research isolating the Testis Determining Factor (TDF) of the human chromosome at the Whitehead Institute for Biomedical Research at MIT (*Cell*, January 1988).

2 Amaury de Riencourt, *Women and Power in History* (1974, first published in English in 1983), p. 52. For a fuller discussion of "maleness and femaleness," see Joan Wallach Scott, *Gender and the Politics of History* (New York, 1988).

3 Nigel Calder, *Timescale* (1984), p. 10.

4 Accounts of the "gene fount mother" are to be found in the *Listener*, 2/27/86, the *Guardian*, 3/3/86, and *Newsweek*, 11/1/88.

5 For the shortness of the first humans' life span, see Marian Lowe and Ruth Hubbard (eds.), *Woman's Nature: Rationalizations of Inequality* (New York and Oxford, 1983), p. 131.

6 George P. Murdock, *Our Primitive Contemporaries* (New York, 1934); *Social Structure* (New York, 1949); "World Ethnographic Sample," *American Anthropologist* (1957); "Ethnographic Atlas: a Summary," *Ethnology* 6, No. 2, 109–236. Murdock's own work is discussed in Jo Freeman (ed), *Women: a Feminist Perspective* (Palo Alto, California, 1979), p. 94. See also the work of Richard Lee, in *Man the Hunter*, eds. R. B. Lee and Irven De Vore (1968). Lee showed that even failure at the hunt would not induce the !Kung bushmen of Botswana to hunt more than one week in three or four; since hunting was subject to magic outside their control no amount of effort on their part, they believed, could reverse a run of bad luck. Their refusal could go on for a month, or even longer, during which visiting, entertaining and especially dancing were the primary activities of the men, and women's gathering alone sustained the tribe.

7 Women's gathering skills are described by Elaine Morgan in *The Descent of Woman* (1972), p. 184; and see Calder, p. 156, for a description of the botanical and ecological knowledge displayed in the most famous of prehistoric burials, that of "the Flower Man of Shanidar." This unknown Mesopotamian was laid to rest about 60,000 years ago on a bed of flowers like ragwort and hollyhock, all known

to have medicinal properties, and all used to this day in women's traditional remedies. Of course the flower-gatherers could have been men—but if prehistoric Shanidar boasted a man who could tell a hollyhock from a hole in the ground, he failed to hand down the secret of his skill to most of his male descendants.

8 For a discussion of tool-making, see Kenneth Oakley, *Man the Tool-Maker* (1947); R. Leakey and R. Lewin, *Origins* (New York, 1977); G. Isaac and R. Leakey, *Human Ancestors* (1979); B. M. Fagan, *People of the Earth: an Introduction to World Pre-History* (1980).

9 Elise Boulding, in *The Underside of History* (Colorado, 1976), p. 78, discusses women's discovery of the technique of fire-hardening and suggests that women thereby invented hunting, by providing the tribe with weapons capable of spearing and impaling.

10 See Sally Slocum, "Woman the Gatherer: Male Bias in Anthropology." This landmark paper is to be found in Rayna Reiter (ed.), *Towards an Anthroplogy of Women* (New York, 1975), and in Mary Evans (ed.), *The Woman Question: Readings in the Subordination of Women* (1982). The importance of the swag bag is also discussed by Sheila Lewenhak in *Women and Work* (1980), pp. 20–1.

11 Slocum, above.

12 The story of Man the Hunter is to be found everywhere, in scholarly and popular books for adults and children—see Lee and De Vore (above); S. Washburn and C. S. Lancaster, "The Evolution of Hunting," in Lee and De Vore (eds.), *Kalahari Hunter-Gatherers* (Harvard, 1976); Sol Tax (ed.), *Evolution After Darwin*, vol. II: *The Evolution of Man* (Chicago, 1960); Josef Wolf and Zdenek Burian, *The Dawn of Man* (London and Prague, 1978); Robert Ardrey, *African Genesis* (1961) and *The Hunting Hypothesis* (1976); and many, many more.

13 Ardrey (1976), pp. 91–2.

14 W. I. Thomas, *Sex and Society: Studies in the Psychology of Sex* (1907), p. 228.

15 Calder, pp. 142–3.

16 Morgan, pp. 58–63. The human male's super-sized penis is also examined at length by Desmond Morris in *The Naked Ape* (1967), p. 65 and p. 75.

17 Boulding, p. 83.

18 Vonda McIntyre's argument is to be found in Joanna Russ, *How to Suppress Women's Writing* (Texas, 1983), pp. 51–2.

19 Elaine Morgan, p. 116, describes the hygiene routine of female monkeys; Sheila Lewenhak (p. 20 and pp. 23–4) the Stone Age sling-makers; and Paula Weideger, *History's Mistress* 1985), pp. 133–4, the experiments with tampons.

20 Donald C. Johanson and Maitland A. Edey, *Lucy: The Beginnings of Humankind* (London and New York, 1981), p. 340.

21 H. G. Wells, *The Outline of History* (1920), p. 94 and p. 118.

22 Ardrey (1976), p. 83.

23 Morris, p. 65 and p. 75.

24 Ardrey (1976), p. 100.

25 Charles Darwin, *On the Origin of Species by means of Natural Selection* (1859), and *The Descent of Man* (1871); Thomas Huxley, *Ethics and Evolution* (1893); Herbert Spencer, *Principles of Biology* (1864–7); Carveth Read, *Origins of Man* (1925); Raymond Dart, "The Predatory Transition from Ape to Man," *International Anthropological and Linguistic Review* V.i., n. 4 (1953).

26 Robert Ardrey (1961), p. 316; Konrad Lorenz, *On Aggression* (1966); Anthony Storr, *Human Aggression* (1968) p. i.

27 Wells, pp. 77–8; Ardrey (1978), p. 91.

28 Washburn, and Lancaster, p. 303; Johanson, p. 65; John Nicholson, *Men and Women: How Different Are They?* (Oxford, 1984), p. 5.

29 De Riencourt, p. 6.

30 Myra Shackley, *Neanderthal Man* (1980), p. 68.

31 Peter Farb, *Man's Rise to Civilisation as shown by the Indians of North America from Primeval Times to the Coming of the Industrial State* (1968), pp. 36–7.

32 Shackley, p. 68.

33 J. Constable, *The Neanderthals* (1973).

34 Shackley, p. 206.

35 Shackley, p. 94.

36 Lowe and Hubbard, pp. 114–15. For a full and fascinating bibliography of this whole debate, see Barbara Sicherman, E. William Monter, Joan Wallach Scott and Kathryn Kish Sklar, *Recent United States Scholarship on the History of Women* (Washington, D.C., American Historical Association, 1980).

38 Robert Graves, *The New Larousse Encyclopaedia of Mythology* (1959), p. 6; and see G-H Luquet, *The Art and Religion of Fossil Man* (Oxford, 1930).

39 Lewenhak, pp. 19–36.

40 Graves, Larousse, p. 7.

Chapter 2 **The Great Goddess**

1 The fullest examination of the historical phrase when the supreme deity was female has been carried out by Merlin Stone, *The Paradise Papers: the Suppression of Women's Rites* (1976), and *Ancient Mirrors of Womanhood* (1979); see also the work of Elizabeth Gould Davis (above), and Elizabeth Fisher, *Woman's Creation: Sexual Evolution and the Shaping of Society* (New York, 1979). But this idea has been established among scholars for many years through the work of Erich Neumann, *The Great Mother: An Analysis of the Archetype* (New York and London, 1955); E. O. James, *The Cult of the Mother Goddess: An Archaeological and Documentary Study* (1959); Robert Graves, *The White Goddess: A Historical Grammar of Poetic Myth* (1948); C. Kerényi, *Eleusis: Archetypal Image of Mother and Daughter* (New York and London, 1967); and many others.

2 For a discussion on Inanna and her poet-priest Enheduanna, see Paul Friedrich, *The Meaning of Aphrodite* (Chicago and London, 1978), p. 13–15.

3 The vision of L. Apuleius is to be found in *The Golden Ass*, translated by Robert Graves (Penguin, 1950), pp. 228–9. As Apuleius insists here, the goddess had different titles and was worshipped by rites which differed from place to place, but she was one deity, "the Goddess of ten thousand names," as Plutarch describes her: Isis, Ishtar, Ashtoreth, Astarte, Athar, Aphrodite, Inanna, Cybele, Demeter, Au Set, Allat, and hundreds, if not thousands more. Her titles were equally varied, and often strangely familiar: Our Lady, the Queen of Heaven, the Holy One, Divine Ruler, the Lady of the High Place, the Lioness of the Gods, the Lady, the White Lady, the God-Mother of the Country, Holy Mother.

4 Sir Arthur Evans, *The Palace of Minos at Knossos* (4 vols., 1921–35), *passim*, and de Riencourt, pp. 26–7 and p. 30.

5 Neumann, p. 94.

6 The sacred status of women, and the anthropological and archaeological evidence to support it, is to be found in James (1959), Neumann, Wolf and Burian (above), Stone (1976), particularly pp. 19, 34, 46, 172, and numerous other sources.

7 "According to women archaeologists, there are far more representations of women's thighs and vulvas in Paleolithic cave art than has ever been reported in the literature. Not only the Abbé Breuil, who played such an important part in publishing this art, but several of the other early researchers in the field were members of the Catholic clergy, and they tended to ignore these disquieting reminders of the dangerous female"—Fisher, p. 143. One honourable exception was *The Art of Prehistoric Man in Western Europe* (1967), by André Leroi-Gourhan. The frieze at Angles-sur-l'Anglin is discussed by John Coles in *The Archaeology of Early Man* (1969), p. 248.

8 The mystery of birth in prehistoric cultures, and complete ignorance of the masculine part in reproduction, are documented in Sir James Frazer, *The Golden Bough* (1922); Margaret Mead, *Male and Female: A Study of the Sexes in a Changing World* (1949); Jacquetta Hawkes, *Dawn of the Gods* (1958), *Prehistory* (New York, 1965), *The First Great Civilisations* (1975); S. G. F. Brandon, *Creation Legends of the Ancient Near East* (1963), and elsewhere.

9 James (1959), pp. 42–3; and see the work of Graves (1960); Frazer; and Brian Branston, *The Lost Gods of England* (1974).

10 Allen Edwardes, *The Jewel in the Lotus: a Historical Survey of the Sexual Culture of the East* (1965), pp. 58–9.

11 Penelope Shuttle and Peter Redgrove, *The Wise Wound: Menstruation and Everywoman* (1978), p. 178.

12 Graves, Larousse, p. 58.

13 Friedrich, p. 31.

14 Graves, Larousse, p. 60.

15 *The Epic of Gilgamesh*, translated by N. K. Sandars (London, 1960).

16 Helen Diner, *Mothers and Amazons: The First Feminine History of Culture* (1932), p. 15.

17 M. Esther Harding, *Women's Mysteries, Ancient and Modern: A Psychological Interpretation of the Feminine Principle as Portrayed in Myth, Story and Dreams* (New York, 1955), p. 138.

18 See Diner, p. 174; Frazer, p. 267 and p. 270; James (1959), p. 101; and Harding, p. 128.

19 Shuttle and Redgrove, p. 182.

20 The first serious work on matriarchy was done by the Swiss scholar J. J. Bachofen in *Das Mutterrecht* [The Mother-Right] (1861); see the English version, *Myth, Religion and Mother-Right* (Princeton, 1967). The theory of the existence of a world-wide matriarchy before the emergence of the "patriarchal revolution" was also accepted by Engels in *The Origin of the Family* (1884); and by Mathilde and Mathias Vaerting in *The Dominant Sex: A Study in the Sociology of Sex Differences*

(English translation 1923). Other early contributors to the discussion included Matilda Joslyn Gage, *Women, Church and State* (1893), Robert Briffault *The Mothers* (1927), and Helen Diner (above). Later work includes that of Evelyn Reed, *Woman's Evolution* (New York, 1975), Fisher and Gould Davis (above). See too Paula Webster, "Matriarchy: A Vision of Power," in Reiter (q.v.), which includes a helpful review of the literature.

21 *The Second Sex* (English edition, 1953), p. 96; but see "And then the Great Mother was dethroned" (p. 101), and other similar references in chapters 11 and 12 that tend to undermine de Beauvoir's own dismissal of the subject. However, hers is still substantially the position of modern feminists—see Mary Lefkowitz, *Women in Greek Myth* (1987).

22 Diner, p. 169.

23 Diner, p. 169.

24 Melanie Kaye, "Some Notes on Jewish Lesbian Identity," in *Nice Jewish Girls*, ed. Evelyn Torton Beck (Mass., 1982), pp. 28–44.

25 John Ferguson, *The Religions of the Roman Empire* (1970), p. 14.

26 Charles A. Seltman, *Women in Antiquity* (1956), p. 82; C. Gascoigne Hartley, *The Position of Women in Primitive Society* (1914), pp. 206–7; and Boulding, p. 186.

27 Diner, p. 170.

28 Diner, p. 170.

29 *The Oxford Classical Dictionary* (Oxford, 1970), p. 254.

30 For Tamyris, see *The Macmillan Dictionary of Women's Biography*, ed. Jennifer S. Uglow (1982), p. 457; and Eilean Ní Chuilleanáin (ed.), *Irish Women: Image and Achievement—Women in Irish Culture from Earliest Times* (1985), p. 14.

31 Ní Chuilleanáin, p. 14.

32 Nora Chadwick, *The Celts* (1970), p. 50.

33 The Athenian festival of *Boedromion*, for example, was held to commemorate the defeat of the Amazons by Theseus, and the ceremonial ritual in honor of the dead at Panopsion was believed to honor the fallen Amazons. But see G. D. Rothery, *The Amazons* (1910), for the kind of unhistorical treatment that undermined the whole concept.

34 *Macmillan Dictionary of Biography*, pp. 459–60, and *Oxford Classical Dictionary*, p. 1041.

35 Diner, p. 172.

36 Chadwick, p. 55.

37 Boulding, p. 318.

38 The Cogul figures are described by James (1959), p. 21, and the females of ancient Britain in Seltman, p. 37.

39 Harding, p. 135.

40 Stone, pp. 168–78.

41 Hilary Evans, *The Oldest Profession: An Illustrated History of Prostitution* (1979), p. 33.

42 John Langdon-Davies, *A Short History of Women* (1928), p. 141.

Chapter 3   **The Rise of the Phallus**

1 Robert Graves, *The Greek Myths* (2 vols., 1960), I, p. 28. See Marilyn French, *Beyond Power: Men, Women, and Morals* (1985), p. 49 ff. Gerda Lerner, in *The Creation of Patriarchy* (New York and Oxford, 1986), p. 146, reports that over 30,000 Mother-Goddess figurines have been found in 3000 sites in south-east Europe alone. For the Winnepagos, see Harding, p. 117.

2 Shuttle and Redgrove, p. 66; de Riencourt, p. 30. For a questioning of this concept of sexual polarity, however, see E. M. Denise Riley, *"Am I That Name?" Feminism and the Category of "Women" in History* (London, 1988).

3 Shuttle and Redgrove, p. 139; E. O. James, *Sacrifice and Sacrament* (1962), *passim*.

4 Farb, p. 72 and Lewenhak, p. 36. "Sub-incision" is also discussed by Freud and Bettelheim, among others.

5 Ian D. Suttie, *The Origins of Love and Hate* (1960), p. 87.

6 Margaret Mead, *Male and Female: A Study of the Sexes in a Changing World* (New York, 1949), p. 98.

7 Joseph Campbell (ed.), *Papers from the Eranos Year Books*, vol. V, *Man and Transformation* (1964), p. 12.

8 Jean Markdale, *Women of the Celts* (Paris, New York, and London, 1982), p. 14.

9 Lee Alexander Stone, *The Story of Phallicism* (first published 1879; Chicago, 1927 edition), p. 12–13; and G. R. Scott, *Phallic Worship: A History of Sex and Sex Rites in relation to the Religion of all Races from Antiquity to the Present Day* (New Delhi, 1975).

10 Gould Davis, p. 98. For further details of the numerous and varied Indian rites of phallus-worship see Edwardes, pp. 55–94.

11 Edwardes, pp. 72–5.

12 Gould Davis, p. 99.

13 Lee Alexander Stone, p. 75.

14 The phases of the dispossession of the Great Goddess are described by Joseph Campbell in *The Masks of God: Occidental Mythology* (New York, 1970).

15 Graves (1960), pp. 58–60.

16 Ní Chuilleanáin, p. 16; James (1959), p. 53.

17 Calder, p. 160.

18 For a wider discussion of these key historical developments of the agricultural revolution and the massive migration of peoples over all the known world from about 3000 BC onwards, see *The Times Atlas of World History* (revised edition, 1986); and J. M. Roberts, *The Hutchinson History of the World* (1976).

19 Fisher, p. 122.

20 Geoffrey Parrinder, *Sex in the World's Religions* (1980), pp. 105–6.

21 De Riencourt, p. 35 and p. viii.

22 *Macmillan Dictionary of Biography*, p. 54. According to some sources (the later Graeco-Roman historians Appian of Alexandria, and Porphyry), Ptolemy succeeded in marrying Berenice in 81 BC, and killed her 19 days after the wedding.

23 Fisher, pp. 206–7.

24 Boulding, p. 20.

25 Julia O'Faolain and Laura Martines, *Not In God's Image: Women in History* (1973), p. 57; and see Livy's *History*, Book 34.

26 Plutarch, *Dialogue on Love*.

27 Farb, p. 42.

28 O'Faolain and Martines, p. 62.

29 *The Illustrated Origin of Species*, ed. Richard A. Leakey (1979), p. 58.

30 "Kingsworthy: a Victim of Rape" describes the excavations at Worthy Park, Kingsworthy, Hampshire, England, by Sonia Chadwick Hawkes of Oxford University, and Dr. Calvin Wells for the Department of the Environment. It is reported in *Antiquity* and *The Times*, 7/23/75.

31 James (1962), pp. 80–1.

32 C. P. Fitzgerald, *China: A Short Cultural History* (1961), p. 52.

33 Lynn Thorndike, *A Short History of Civilization* (1927), p. 148.

34 For Agnodice's Story, see the *Macmillan Dictionary of Biography*, p. 7.

35 Mead, p. 206.

36 *Macmillan Dictionary of Biography*, p. 464.

37 It is only fair to the unknown band of female medics who practiced before Fabiola to stress that she is the first woman doctor to be known *by name*. Women were practicing medicine as early as 3000 BC in Egypt, where an inscription on the medical school of the Temple of Sais, north of Memphis, records: "I have come from the school of medicine at Heliopolis, and have studied at the Women's School at Sais, where the divine mothers have taught me how to cure disease." In addition, the Kuhn medical papyri of *c.* 2500 BC established that Egyptian women specialists diagnosed pregnancy, treated infertility and carried out all branches of gynecological medicine, while women surgeons performed caesarean sections, removed cancerous breasts, and operated on broken limbs—see Margaret Alic, *Hypatia's Heritage: a History of Women in Science from Antiquity to the late Nineteenth Century* (1986).

38 Wu Chao (ed), *Women in Chinese Folklore*, Women of China Special Series (Beijing, China, 1983), p. 91, and pp. 45–60.

39 Joe Orton, the *Guardian* (London) 4/18/87.

40 Marcel Durry (ed.), *Eloge Funèbre d'une Matrone Romaine: Eloge dit de Turia* (Collection des Universités de France, 1950), p. 8ff.

41 For Hypatia's work and death, see Alic, pp. 41–7. See also the novel by Charles Kingsley, better known as the author of *The Water Babies* (1863). His *Hypatia* (1853) presents a sympathetic portrait of its heroine, contrasting her subtle and humane intelligence with the vicious bigotry of the early Christian Fathers.

Chapter 4 **God the Father**

1 For a detailed investigation of the anti-feminism of Christianity, see the work of Mary Daly, *The Church and the Second Sex* (1968) and *Beyond God the Father: Towards a Philosophy of Women's Liberation* (1973).

2 The story of Felicitas is to be found in Herbert Musurillo (ed.), *The Acts of the Christian Martyrs* (1972), pp. 106–31.

3 Karen Armstrong, *The Gospel According to Woman* (1986), p. 256.

4 Jeremiah 7, 17–18.

5 For the ancient Chinese power-shift from Mother Earth – > phallus – > abstract male power, see C. P. Fitzgerald, *China: A Short Cultural History* (1961), p. 44 and pp. 47–8. For the worldwide usurpation of Goddess worship, see Raphael Patai, *The Hebrew Goddess* (New York, 1967); the work of Merlin Stone (q.v.); and John O'Neill, *The Night of the Gods* (2 vols., 1893), for the continued existence of the Great Goddess's symbolism from Persian horned moons to Roman Catholic veneration of Mary as "Our Lady" and "the Queen of Heaven".

6 R. F. Burton, *Personal Narrative of a Pilgrimage to Al-Madinah and Meccah* (2 vols., 1885–6), II, p. 161.

7 For the full story of the Ka'aba at Mecca, see Harding, p. 41, and O'Neill, I. p. 117.

8 Bertrand Russell, *History of Western Philosophy, and its Connection with Political and Social Circumstances from the Earliest Times to the Present Day* (1946), p. 336.

9 For the role of women in the early church see the discussion by the Professor of Ecclesiastical History at the University of London, *The Times*, 11/1/86; Boulding, p. 360; and J. Morris, *The Lady was a Bishop* (New York, 1973).

10 Julia Leslie, "Essence and Existence: Women and Religion in Ancient Indian Texts," in Holden (q.v.), pp. 89–112.

11 Nawal El Saadawi, "Women in Islam," in Azizah Al-Hibri, *Women and Islam* (1982), pp. 193–206.

12 Azizah Al-Hibri, "A Study of Islamic Herstory, or, How Did We Ever Get Into This Mess?," in Al-Hibri (1982), pp. 207–19.

13 El Saadawi, p. 197.

14 Fatnah A. Sabbah (pseud.), *Woman in the Muslim Unconscious* (London and New York, 1984), pp. 104–6.

15 II Chronicles 15, 16–17.

16 E. L. Ranelagh, *Men on Women* (1985), p. 49.

17 Numbers 5, 14–31.

18 Sabbah, p. 108.

19 Edwardes, p. 32.

20 Gabriel Mandel, *The Poem of the Pillow: The Japanese Methods* (Fribourg, 1984), p. 17–18.

21 Mandel, p. 77 and p. 78.

22 Edwardes, p. 50.

23 Armstrong, p. 43 and p. 23.

24 Fitzgerald, pp. 48–9.

25 De Riencourt, p. 82; and see Sara Maitland, *A Map of the New Country: Women and Christianity* (1983), where Maitland argues that Christianity divides creation into a dualistic opposition of "good" (spirit) and "bad" (flesh), and that such dualistic splits are the root cause not only of sexism, but also of racism, classism and ecological destruction.

26 Ní Chuilleanáin, p. 14.

27 Sabbah, p. 5 and p. 110.

28 Sabbah, p. 13.

Chapter 5   **The Sins of the Mothers**

1 D. Martin Luther, *Kritische Gesamtausgabe* Vol. III. *Briefweschel* (Weimar, 1933), pp. 327–8.

2 O'Faolain, p. 134.

3 Mead (1949), p. 343.

4 Chaim Bermant discusses the Talmudic prescriptions in *The Walled Garden: The Saga of Jewish Family Life and Tradition* (1974), p. 60; for St. Paul, see I Corinthians, 11,5.

5 Armstrong, p. 56. It is noteworthy that the patriarchal religions did not *invent* these new stringencies increasingly applied to women from Christian times onwards; as early as 42 BC a Roman husband, C. Sulpicius Gallus, had divorced his wife because she was seen out of doors with her face unveiled. But this procedure was condemned by his own contemporaries as "harsh and pitiless" (see Valerius Maximus, *Facta et Dicta Memorabilia*). We know too from other sources that the vast majority of Roman women suffered no such restrictions.

6 Renée Hirschon describes the Greeks in "Open Body / Closed Space: The Transformation of Female Sexuality," and Caroline Humphrey the Mongolians in "Women, Taboo, and the Suppression of Attention"; both in Shirley Ardener, *Defining Females: the Nature of Women in Society* (1978).

7 Christopher Hibbert, *The Roots of Evil: A Social History of Crime and Punishment* (Penguin, 1966), p. 45.

8 Gallichan, p. 42.

9 Sabbah, p. 36.

10 All these quotations are taken from Shaykh Nefwazi's *The Perfumed Garden*, translated by Sir Richard Burton (originally published 1876; this edition 1963), p. 201, p. 191, p. 72.

11 Jacob Sprenger, *Malleus Maleficarum* (The Hammer of Witches) (1484); Armstrong, p. 100.

12 Gladys Reichard, *Navajo Religion: A Study of Symbolism* (New York, 1950), p. 31.

13 The deep suspicion that at bottom men are better off without access to or reminder of women's sex organs is evident in the Islamic teaching that when Allah ordained paradise and *houris* to attend on the valiant faithful, he made them *without vaginas*. Many cultures have ritual expressions of their fears of women stealing men's power via their sexual emissions, in the form of taboos on intercourse before major or sacred undertakings—a process not unknown to certain twentieth-century sportsmen and others even today: cf. modern Australian jockspeak, "Bum to mum tonight, boys!"

14 Edwardes, p. 23.

15 Some idea of the range of menstruation taboos, many much more horrific, painful and dangerous than these, can be gained from Frazer, pp. 595–607. For the native American customs, see Lowe and Hubbard, p. 68.

16 Bermant, p. 129.

17 Edwardes, p. 24.

18 Edwardes, as above.

19 The delegation to an older man of the danger of deflowering the virgin bride is

the atavistic origin of the custom of *droit de seigneur*, not as widely believed, the lord's demand to exercise his rights of possession over his female serfs. The latter became in time an accepted "explanation" of what time had rendered inexplicable, then passed into social expectation and even into the law itself in some countries: see the Anglo-Saxon tax called *legerwite* (literally, "payment for lying down"), payable by every bride to her liege lord from the earliest times in England up to the Middle Ages. In effect, it compensated him for the loss of her virginity to another (Katherine O'Donovan, *Sexual Divisions in Law*, 1985, p. 34). Originally though, the lord was *conferring*, not receiving a benefit (Langdon-Davis, p. 99 and p. 118). For the Turkish and Arab brutality on defloration, plus their freedom with the *jus primae noctis*, see Edwardes, pp. 38–9.

20 *The Confessions of Lady Nijō*, translated by Karen Brazell (1975), p. 9.

21 Angela M. Lucas, *Women in the Middle Ages: Religion, Marriage and Letters* (1983), p. 101; Katharine Simms, "Women in Norman Ireland," in Margaret MacCurtain and Donncha Ó'Corrain (eds) *Women in Irish Society: the Historical Dimension* pp. 14–25.

22 For British Army reports on child-brides, see Katharine Mayo, *Mother India* (1927), p. 61; also Pramatha Nath Bose, *A History of Hindu Civilisation during British Rule* (3 vols., 1894), I, 66–7; and H. H. Dodwell (ed), *The Cambridge History of India* (6 vols., Cambridge and New York, 1932), VI, 128–31.

23 Joseph and Frances Gies, *Life in a Medieval Castle* (New York, 1974), p. 77.

24 Pierre de Bourdeille, Abbé de Brantôme, *Les Vies des Dames Galantes* (1961), p. 86. See also Gould Davis, pp. 165–7, and Eric Dingwall, *The Girdle of Chastity* (1931).

25 Edwardes, p. 186–7.

26 Scilla McLean, "Female Circumcision, Excision and Infibulation: the Facts and Proposals for Change," *Minority Rights Group Report No. 47* (December, 1980). See also Fran Hosken, *The Hosken Report—Genital and Sexual Mutilation of Females* (Women's International Network News, Autumn 1979, 187 Grant Street, Lexington, Mass 02173, USA). Note that this practice continues in use today. Over 90 percent of all Sudanese women are still mutilated, despite legislation outlawing it over 35 years ago. Female genital mutilation has indeed spread to the West in the wake of globalization, and all European capitals now boast a surgeon who will perform this operation at the demand of expatriate parents. In 1986 the British parliament refused to pass a bill outlawing this practice in Britain, on the grounds that it would not intervene to restrict the rights of parents.

27 Jacques Lantier, *La Cité Magique* (Paris, 1972), cited by McLean, p. 5.

28 For the Chinese practice of infanticide, see Lisa Leghorn and Katherine Parker, *Woman's Worth: Sexual Economics and the World of Women* (1981), p. 163 and de Riencourt, p. 171. For India, see Bose, Vol. III, and Dodwell VI, 130–1. Even today, argues Barbara Burke, there is worldwide "a relative neglect of girls, through poorer nutrition and general care, which means that mortality rates for females, who are actually hardier than boys at birth, exceed those for males in Bangladesh, Burma, Jordan, Pakistan, Sri Lanka, Thailand, Lebanon and Syria. In parts of South America, mothers wean girls earlier than boys because they fear that nursing them too long will make them unfeminine. Less well nourished, the girls then

tend to succumb to fatal diseases"—"Infanticide," *Science 84*, 5:4 (May 1984), 26–31.

29 Koran LXXXI 1, 8-9, 14.

30 Lesley Blanch, *Pavilions of the Heart: The Four Walls of Love* (1974), p. 102.

31 Geoffrey of Tours, *Historia Francorum Libri Decem*, Bk 6, Chapter 36. It is possible that some of the rage directed at this woman may have been due to her wearing men's clothing, something regarded with particular abhorrence in Western Europe for many centuries by church and laity alike—as late as the seventeenth century one Ann Morrow was blinded by missiles thrown by an unusually vicious crowd when she was pilloried for wearing men's clothing, for the purpose of inducing women to marry her (Hibbert, pp. 44–5). Note that the offence was the same as Joan of Arc's in 1428, i.e., wearing male apparel only, *not*, in this case, trying to contract a false marriage.

32 Cambridge History, VI, 132. Note that in the standard way of euphemizing these practices, disguising their hideous cruelty and sadistic barbarity under obscure and little-understood Latinisms, wife-burning is usually described as "self-immolation". Hardly hurts at all, does it?

33 Cambridge History, VI, 134.

34 This and the details of the English legislation are taken from E. J. Burford, *Bawds and Lodgings: a History of the English Bankside Brothels c. 100–1675* (1976), p. 26, p. 56, p. 73.

35 Master Franz Schmidt, *A Hangman's Diary*, ed. A. Keller, trans C. Calvert and A. W. Gruner (1928), *passim*.

36 Susan Rennie and Kirsten Grimstad, *The New Woman's Survival Sourcebook* (New York, 1975), p. 223.

37 Hibbert, p. 45.

Chapter 6 **A Little Learning**

1 Armstrong, p. 82.

2 Joseph Campbell, pp. 22–3.

3 Diane Bell, "Desert Politics," in Women and Colonisation: Anthropological Perspectives, (eds.) Mona Etienne and Eleanor Leacock (New York, 1980).

4 Lewenhak, p. 32.

5 Basil Davidson, *Africa in History: Themes and Outlines* (1968), p. 119.

6 The sisterhoods of these religions are described in the work of Julia Leslie (q.v.). In Buddhism, although Buddha attacked the idea of women joining male orders, he expressly taught in the *Mahjung Nikaya*, for example, that women could attain enlightenment in their own disciplines. Within Islam, the position of female religious is even more interesting, according to Anne-Marie Schimmel: "History indicates that some women were known as benefactors of Sufi *khanqahs* which they endowed with money or regular food rations. . . . These activities were not restricted to a particular country: we find women patrons of Sufis in India and Iran, in Turkey and North Africa. In medieval Egypt (and possibly other areas)

even special *khanqahs* were erected where they could spend either their whole life or a span of time." Nor was it unknown in Islam for women to lead religious groups which also included or even consisted entirely of men: "We know the names of some *shaykas* in such places as medieval Egypt. We also know the name of an Anatolian woman who . . . was head of a dervish *tekke* and guided the men." "Women in Mystical Islam" in Al-Hibri (q.v.), p. 146 and p. 148.

7 Diner, p. 6; Gould Davis, p. 140; Boulding, pp. 193–4.

8 For a discussion of the surprising range of privileges these women could command, see Julia Leslie in Holden (q.v.), pp. 91–3.

9 Leghorn and Parker, pp. 204–5.

10 Armstrong, p. 122.

11 MacCurtain and Ó'Corrain, pp. 10–11.

12 Anne J. Lane (ed.), *Mary Ritter Beard: a Sourcebook* (New York, 1977), p. 223.

13 Russell, p. 362.

14 Judith C. Brown, *Immodest Acts: The Life of a Lesbian Nun in Renaissance Italy* (Oxford, 1986).

15 Angela M. Lucas, *Women in the Middle Ages: Religion, Marriage and Letters* (1983), pp. 38–42.

16 Lucas, p. 141.

17 De Riencourt, p. 167.

18 *The Lawes Resolution of Women's Rights* (1632), written by the anonymous, "T.E.", p. 141.

19 *Paradise Lost*, Book IV, 635–8.

20 Pennethorne Hughes, *Witchcraft*, (1965), p. 54.

21 Jean Bodin, *De La Démonomanie des Sorciers* (Paris, 1580), p. 225.

22 Reginald Scot, *The Discoverie of Witchcraft*, ed. B. Nicholson (1886), p. 227.

23 O'Faolain, pp. 220–1 and p. 224.

24 Antonia Fraser, *The Weaker Vessel: Woman's Lot in Seventeenth-Century England* (1984), p. 143 and p. 53—see pp. 51–5 for the story of this attractive and generous personality.

25 Hughes, p. 94.

26 Margaret Wade Labarge, *Women in Medieval Life* (1986), pp. 3–4.

27 Raymond Hill and Thomas G. Burgin (eds.), *An Anthology of the Provençal Troubadours* (1941), p. 96.

28 Denis de Rougemont, *Passion and Society* (1956), p. 96. Note that the radical assertion of courtly love that women's love was certainly as strong as men's, and usually stronger, was still a live issue in the nineteenth century—see the climactic Chapter 23 of Jane Austen's *Persuasion* (1818), and Henry James's Lord Warburton in *Portrait of a Lady* (1881): "It's for life, Miss Archer, it's for life!"

29 Viola Klein, *The Feminine Character: History of an Ideology* (1946), p. 91.

30 O'Faolain, p. 202.

31 The first extract was written by Hélisenne de Crenne, author of the first psychological novel in French, *Les Angoysses qui procèdent d'Amour, contenant trois parties composées par dame Hélisenne de Crenne laquelle exhorte toutes personnes a ne pas suivre folle amour* (Painful Tribulations occasioned by Love, comprising three parts

composed by Lady Hélisenne de Crenne, who exhorts everyone not to follow the madness of love) in 1538. The second is taken from Jeanne de Flore (pseud. Jeanne Galliarde), *Contes Amoureux, touchant la punition que faict Vénus de ceux qui condamnent et mésprisent le vray amour* (Amorous tales, regarding the punishment by Venus of those who condemn and scorn true love), addressed "to noble ladies in love" in 1541. The third comes from the *Débat de Folie et d'Amour* (Debate of Folly and Love) by Louise Labé. All are cited by Evelyne Sullerot in *Women on Love: Eight Centuries of Feminine Writing* (1980), pp. 92–3.

32 Christine de Pizan, *Treasure of the City of Ladies*, trans. B. Anslay (London, 1985), Bk. I, Ch II.

33 This and a large number of similar views are expressed by the Abbot Antronius in Erasmus' dramatized colloquy on reactionary and progressive attitudes to women's education—see *Colloquies of Erasmus*, tr. N. Bailey (3 vol., 1900), II, 114–19.

34 Agrippa D'Aubigny, *Oeuvres Complètes*, E. Réaume and F. de Caussade (Paris, 1873), I, 445.

35 Joseph Besse, *A Collection of the Sufferings of the People Called Quakers* (2 vols., 1753), I, 84 ff.

Chapter 7 **Woman's Work**

1 For Joan of Arc, see Marina Warner's splendid *Joan of Arc: the Image of Female Heroism* (1982). Other dates and events are taken from *The Times Atlas of World History*.

2 For Parnell, see Burford, p. 74. This is of course a pseudonym, "Parnell" being a recognized name for a prostitute and "Portjoie" boasting of her professional ability to "bring pleasure". For Eva, see MacCurtain and Ó'Corrain, p. 22; and see Alice Kessler-Harris, *Out to Work: A History of Wage-Earning Women in the United States* (New York, 1982), and Ruth Milkman, *Gender at Work* (Urbana, University of Illinois Press, 1987).

3 W. I. Thomas, p. 124.

4 The working women of Greece are described by Homer, Aristotle, Plato, Demosthenes, Xenophon and many others; those of Rome by Ovid, Horace, Plautus, Martial, etc. For a useful digest and list of source materials, see the *Oxford Classical Dictionary*, pp. 1139–40. A fascinating discussion of the women musicians of ancient Greece is to be found in Yves Bessières' and Patricia Niedzwicki's *Women and Music, Women of Europe* Supplement No. 22 (Commission of the European Communities, October 1985); figures taken from p. 9.

5 Lewenhak, p. 33.

6 For the heavy work of women, including this portering episode, see Lewenhak, pp. 49, 77, 88 and 122–3.

7 Erasmus, *Christiani Matrimonii Institutio* (1526); O'Faolain, p. 194.

8 Lewenhak, p. 111.

9 O'Faolain, p. 272.

10 Jean de la Bruyère, *Oeuvres Complètes*, ed. J. Benda (1951), p. 333.

11 Klein, p. 9.

12 Jacques de Cambry, *Voyage dans la Finistère* (1799); O'Faolain, p. 272; and statistics of laborers' pay, pp. 266–7.

13 For women's much lower wages, see A. Abram, *Social England in the Fifteenth Century* (1909), p. 131 and Alice Clark's magisterial survey, *The Working Life of Women in the Seventeenth Century* (1919), pp. 65–6.

14 J. W. Willis Bund, *Worcester County Records,* (Worcester, 1900), I, 337.

15 O'Faolain, p. 273.

16 M. Phillips and W. S. Tomkinson, *English Women in Life and Letters* (Oxford, 1927), p. 76.

17 Lewenhak, pp. 42–3.

18 *Proverbs* 31, 13–27.

19 O'Faolain, pp. 265–6.

20 *Libro di Buoni Costumi* (The Book of Good Customs), ed A. Schiaffini (Florence, 1956), pp. 126–8.

21 Gies, p. 60; and see Patricia Franks, *Grandma Was a Pioneer* (Canada, 1977), p. 25.

22 Le Grand Aussy, Voyage d'Auvergne (Paris, 1788), p. 281.

23 Edwardes, p. 250.

24 Lewenhak, p. 124.

25 *Le Livre de la Bourgeoisie de la Ville de Strasbourg 1440–1530*, ed. C. Wittmer and C. J. Meyer (3 Vols., Strasbourg and Zurich, 1948–61), I, 443, 499, 504, 822, 857, 862, 1071.

26 With very rare exceptions: one woman from the North of England, Mariona Kent, rose to become a member of the council of a guild, the York Merchant Adventurers in 1474–5. In other guilds women could occasionally inherit a membership from a deceased husband, and even more interestingly *transfer* that coveted membership to a second husband, but such membership never gave women the full rights and privileges enjoyed by men. France and Italy boasted some all-women craft guilds, but their influence was necessarily limited.

27 Diane Hutton, "Women in Fourteenth-Century Shrewsbury" in Lindsay Charles and Lorna Duffin, *Women and Work in Pre-Industrial England* (1985).

28 Margaret Alic, *Hypatia's Heritage: A History of Women in Science from Antiquity to the late Nineteenth Century* (1986), pp. 54–7.

29 J. Q. Adams, *The Dramatic Records of Sir Henry Herbert* (New Haven, Oxford and London, 1917), p. 69.

30 Society, especially that section of it writing books about prostitution (see *The Oldest Profession: A History of Prostitution* by Lujo Basserman, 1967, and *The Oldest Profession: An Illustrated History of Prostitution* by Hillary Evans, 1979, and many others) insist on calling this the "oldest profession" of women. It is a perfect paradigm of the degradation of women that the exact opposite is true. The oldest profession of women was the priesthood, when they served the Great Goddess and later her phallic supplanters. Prostitution by contrast did not evolve until the stage of urban organization. The idea that the first real employment women ever had was to minister to the needs of men makes, however, a very satisfactory historical fiction.

31 Hilary Evans, p. 73.

32 Burford, p. 115.

Chapter 8 **Revolution The Great Engine**

1 Roger Thomson, *Women in Stuart England and America: A Comparative Study* (1974), p. 106.

2 Charles Royster, *A Revolutionary People at War: The Continental Army and the American Character 1775–1883* (Chapter Hill, North Carolina, 1979), pp. 30–1 and pp. 35–6.

3 Sarah's poignant and expressive letters are discussed by Robert Middlekauf in *The Glorious Cause: The American Revolution 1763–89* (New York and Oxford, 1982), p. 537. Sarah was luckier than many women—the husband for whom her "heart aked" finally came home to her and their children, in one piece.

4 Royster, pp. 296–7.

5 Royster, p. 166.

6 For the record of the women's activity, and further discussion, see William P. Cumming and Hugh Rankin, *The Fate of the Nation: the American Revolution through Contemporary Eyes* (1975), pp. 28–9.

7 For Lady Harriet Acland, see Mark M. Boatner, *Enclopaedia of the American Revolution* (New York, 1973), p. 4. Baroness Riedesel wrote her own story in what has become an invaluable source book, *The Voyage of Discovery to America* (1800). "Pitcher Molly" Hays is described in Cumming and Rankin, p. 215.

8 B. Whitelock, *Memorials of English Affairs* (1732), p. 398. The women's petition was finally presented to the House of Commons on May 5, 1649. A decent, dignified document arguing cogently for women's rights on the basis of both law and natural justice, it anticipates later feminist insistence that women's rights are only the human rights due to every member of society.

9 Lady F. P. Verney, *Memoirs of the Verney Family during the Civil War* (2 vols., 1892), II, p. 240.

10 Antonia Fraser, pp. 192–7.

11 James Strong, *Joanereidos: or, Feminine Valour Eminently Discovered in Westerne Women* (1645).

12 John Vicars, *Gods Ark Overtopping the Worlds Waves, or, the Third Part of the Parliamentary Chronicle* (1646), p. 259.

13 Edward Lytton Bulwer-Lytton, *The Parisians* (1873), Book 5, Chapter 7.

14 Christopher Hibbert, *The French Revolution* (1980), pp. 96–105.

15 Hibbert, p. 99.

16 Basserman, p. 213.

17 Edmund Burke, "Letter to the Hon. C. J. Fox," October 8, 1777.

18 Basserman, p. 215.

19 Hibbert, p. 139.

20 A. Le Faure, *Le Socialisme pendant la Révolution Française* (Paris, 1863), pp. 120 ff.

21 Marie-Jean de Caritat, Marquis de Condorcet, *Essai sur l'Admission des Femmes au Droit de la Cité* (Paris, 1790).

22 Olympe de Gouges, *Déclaration des Droits de la Femme et la Citoyenne* (1791), and see Jane Abray, "Feminism in the French Revolution," *American Historical Review* (1975), 80, pp. 43–62.

23 The whole masculine tenor of Mirabeau's meaning is clear from the context of this statement of June 1789: "History has too often recounted the actions of nothing more than wild animals, among which at long intervals we can pick out some *heroes* . . ." (Hibbert, p. 63).

24 C. Beard, *The Industrial Revolution* (1901), p. 23.

25 Anne Oakley, *Housewife* (1974), p. 14.

26 These comments are taken from a Factory Commissioners' report on working conditions, and from the Hansard record of the ensuing debate in parliament—see Ivy Pinchbeck's pioneering study *Women Workers and the Industrial Revolution 1750–1850* (1930), p. 94.

27 Pinchbeck, pp. 195, 190, 188, and 189.

28 J. L. Hammond and Barbara Hammond, *The Rise of Modern Industry* (1939), p. 209.

29 E. Royston Pike, *Human Documents of the Industrial Revolution in Britain* (1966), pp. 60–1, pp. 192–3 and p. 194.

30 Pike, p. 80 and p. 133.

31 The horrors of the mine work performed by the British women of the Industrial Revolution are very well documented. For the details cited here, see Pinchbeck, pp. 240–81, and Pike, 245–78.

32 Pike, p. 257–8.

33 Report of the parliamentary commissioners; see the testimony of Sarah Gooder, age eight: "I'm a trapper [trap-opener] in the Gawber pit . . . I have to trap without a light, and I'm scared . . . I don't like being in the pit, I would like to be at school far better . . ." (Pinchbeck, p. 248).

34 Pike, p. 124.

35 Pike, pp. 129–30.

36 T. S. Ashton, *The Industrial Revolution 1760–1830* (1948), p. 161.

37 Pinchbeck, pp. 2–3.

Chapter 9 **The Rod of Empire**

1 A. James Hammerton, *Emigrant Gentlewomen* (1979), p. 54 and p. 57.

2 Kay Daniels and Mary Murnane, *Uphill All the Way: A Documentary History of Women in Australia* (Queensland 1980), pp. 117–18.

3 James Morris, *Pax Britannica* (1969), p. 74.

4 Anne Summers, *Damned Whores and God's Police: the Colonisation of Women in Australia* (Ringwood, Vic., 1975), p. 12.

5 Dee Brown, *The Gentle Tamers: Women of the Old Wild West* (New York, 1958), p. 81.

6 Thompson, p. 84 and 88.

7 C. M. H. Clark, *Select Documents in Australian History 1788–1850* (Sydney, 1965), p. 48.

8 Frederick C. Folkhard, *The Rare Sex* (Murray, Sydney, 1965), p. 69.

9 Michael Cannon, *Who's Master? Who's Man?* (Melbourne, 1971), p. 55; *Report of the Select Committee on Transportation* (1837), evidence of James Mudie.

10 T. W. Plummer to Colonel Macquarie, May 4, 1809, *Historical Records of New South Wales*, VII, 120.

11 Brian Fitzpatrick, *The Australian People 1788–1945* (Melbourne, 1946), p. 108.

12 The sufferer "in torments" was Sir Malcolm Darling, *Apprentice to Power: India 1904–1908* (1966), p. 26. The *burra mem* was Annette Beveridge, described in her son William Beveridge's *India Called Them* (1941), p. 201.

13 Iris Butler, *The Viceroy's Wife* (1969), p. 164.

14 Eve Merriam, *Growing Up Female in America: Ten Lives* (New York, 1971), pp. 179–81.

15 Dee Brown, pp. 41–2.

16 Merriam, p. 195.

17 Dee Brown, pp. 51–2.

18 Butler, p. 101.

19 Butler, p. 111; Darling, p. 129.

20 Edna Healey, *Wives of Fame: Mary Livingstone, Jenny Marx, Emma Darwin* (1986), p. 14.

21 Beveridge, p. 60.

22 M. M. Kaye (ed.), *The Golden Calm: an English Lady's Life in Moghul Delhi, Reminiscences by Emily, Lady Clive Bayley, and by her Father, Sir Thomas Metcalfe* (Exeter, 1980), p. 213.

23 These lines are taken from the famous hymn, "I vow to thee my country," by Cecil Spring-Rice, which performed invaluable service during the empire and the First World War in inducing young men to volunteer to be killed. Its second verse subsequently afforded the title for the film *Another Country*.

24 Healey, p. 24. It is worth recording that Mary Livingstone was not totally submissive to her demanding husband—when he wanted to call the baby boy Zouga after the river beside which he was born, Mary refused point-blank.

25 Kaye, p. 215.

26 Kaye, p. 49; Beveridge, p. 240.

27 Joanna Trollope, *Britannia's Daughters: Women of the British Empire* (1983), p. 148; see also D. Middleton, *Victorian Lady Travellers* (1965).

28 Ziggi Alexander and Audrey Dewjee (eds.), *The Wonderful Adventures of Mrs Seacole in Many Lands* (1984), p. 15.

29 *The Insight Guide to Southern California* (1984), p. 243.

30 William Bronson, *The Last Grand Aventure* (New York, 1977), p. 166.

31 James (1962), p. 85.

32 For a discussion of La Malinche and a feminist reworking of her myth, see Cheris Kramarae and Paula A. Treichler, *A Feminist Dictionary* (1985), p. 245.

33 Trollope, p. 52.

34 Mayo, pp. 103–4.

35 Healey, p. 8.

36 F. Ekejiuba, "Omu Okwei: A Biographic Sketch," *Journal of the Historical Society of Nigeria* iii, (1967).

37 R. Miles, *Women and Power* (1985), p. 82; Susan Raven and Alison Weir, *Women in History: Thirty-Five Centuries of Feminine Achievement* (1981), p. 14.

38 Ronald Hyam, *Britain's Imperial Century, 1815–1914: A Study of Empire and Expansion* (1976), pp. 224–5.

Chapter 10 **The Rights of Woman**

1 For Cecilia Cochrane's case, see A. Dowling, *Reports of Cases argued and determined in the Queen's Bench Practice Courts* (1841), VIII, p. 630 ff. For Dawson, Addison and Teush, see O'Faolain, p. 333.

2 de Cambry, II, p. 57.

3 Louise Michele Newman (ed.), *Men's Ideas, Women's Realities: Popular Science, 1870–1915* (New York and London, 1985), pp. 192–3.

4 Klein, p. 24.

5 Queen Victoria's instructions to her secretary are to be found in Trollope, p. 29.

6 Beatrice Webb, *My Apprenticeship* (1926), p. 92.

7 Olive Schreiner, *Woman and Labour* (1911), p. 50.

8 Hubbard and Lowe, p. 48; and see their Chapter 4, "The Dialectic of Biology and Culture," for full discussion of the idea that white male dominance was legitimately based on mental superiority, "one of the most tenacious ideas of the last 100 years."

9 Darwin's ranking of the mental faculties is discussed at length in *The Descent of Man, and Selection in Relation to Sex* (1871). For a detailed critique of these ideas and their relation to modern feminism, see the work of Rosalind Rosenberg, in particular "In Search of Woman's Nature, 1850–1920," *Feminist Studies* 3 (Fall, 1975), pp. 141–153, and *Beyond Separate Spheres: Intellectual Roots of Modern Feminism* (New Haven, 1982).

10 George J. Engelmann, "The American Girl of Today," the President's Address, *American Gynecology Society* (1900).

11 Herbert Spencer, *Education: Intellectual, Moral, and Physical* (1861); and see Newman pp. 6–7 and p. 12 for full discussion.

12 The first speaker in this House of Lords debate was the Earl of Halstead—see Hansard vol. 175, 4th Ser. (1907), col. 1355. The second was Lord James of Hereford, Hansard (above), col. 1362.

13 J. Christopher Herold, *The Horizon Book of the Age of Napoleon* (New York, 1963), pp. 134–7. Strictly, the punishment for an adulterous male was to be forbidden to marry his mistress, but it is hard to see how this could have come as anything but a relief to many men. For the Code's other specific restrictions on women, see articles 213, 214, 217, 267, and 298, among many others.

14 De Riencourt, p. x and p. 306.

15 Edwin A. Pratt, *Pioneer Women in Victoria's Reign* (1897), p. 123.

16 "The Emigration of Educated Women," Social Science Congress in Dublin, 1861—see Klein, p. 22.

17 "Votes for Women" (1912), April 9, p. 737.

18 "General" Tubman's campaign took place in the Port-Royal region of South Carolina, with action on June 2, 1863—see Kramarae and Treichler, p. 31, and E. Conrad, *Harriet Tubman* (1943).

19 Kate Millet, *Sexual Politics* (1969), Chapter 3, "The Sexual Revolution, First Phase," and see H. Pauli, *Her Name was Sojourner Truth* (1962).

20 Roger Fulford, *Votes for Women: The Story of a Struggle* (1958), p. 16.

21 Quotations here are taken from the 1929 edition of the *Vindication*, edited by Ernest Rhys, pp. 21–3.

22 Flora Tristan, *L'Union Ouvrière* (Paris, 1843), p. 108.

23 Fulford, p. 24.

24 A. Angiulli, *La Pedagogia, lo Stato e la Famiglia* (Naples, 1876), pp. 84 ff.

25 Phillips and Tomkinson, p. 184.

26 Thomas Huxley, *Life and Letters of Thomas Huxley* (2 vols., New York 1901), I, p. 228.

27 Raven and Weir, p. 218, and see Mary Roth Walsh, *Doctors Wanted, No Women Need Apply: Sexual Barriers in the Medical Profession 1835–1975* (New Haven, Yale, 1977).

28 Raven and Weir, pp. 73 and 86.

29 Anne B. Hamman, "Professor Beyer and the Woman Question," *Educational Review* 47 (March 1914), p. 296.

Chapter 11 **The Body Politic**

1 Newman, p. 105. And see Daniel Scott Smith, "Family Limitation, Sexual Control and Domestic Feminism in Victorian America," in M. Hartman and L. Banner (eds.), *Clio's Consciousness Raised* (New York, 1974).

2 J. M. Allan, "On the Differences in the Minds of Men and Women," *Journal of the Anthropological Society of London* 7 (1869), pp. cxcvi–cxcviii.

3 Dr. Mary Scharlieb, *The Seven Ages of Woman* (1915), pp. 11–12, and 51, extols the joys of "Motherhood," Allan (above) argues that womanhood is an illness; and Dr. Howard A. Kelly, in *Medical Gynecology* (1909), pp. 73–4, warned of the danger of the "pelvic organs".

4 For a fuller consideration of the revolting saga of modern genital mutilation of females, see G. Barker-Benfield, "Sexual Surgery in Late Nineteenth-Century America," in C. Dreifus (ed.), *Seizing Our Bodies* (New York, 1978). Useful extracts from contemporary documents discussing this mutilation in Britain are to be found in Pat Jalland and John Hooper (eds.), *Women from Birth to Death: The Female Life Cycle in Britain 1830–1914* (1986), pp. 250–65.

5 The Japanese recipes and barrier methods are taken from Mandel, pp. 44–5. The Egyptian references come from Elizabeth Draper, *Birth Control in the Modern World* (1965), p. 75; Casonova's specifics from pp. 77–8.

6 Burford, p. 34.

7 Soranus's *Gynaecology*, tr. Owsie Temkins (Johns Hopkins, 1956), pp. 62–7.

8 Burford, p. 173.

9 Draper, p. 69.

10 De Riencourt, p. 281; for the parallel American experience, see Judith Walzer Leavitt, *Brought to Bed: Childbearing in America, 1750–1950* (New York, 1986).

11 Jalland and Hooper, p. 276.

12 G. Bruckner (ed.), *Two Memoirs of Renaissance Florence*, tr. J. Martines (New York, 1968), pp. 112 ff.

13 Madame de Sévigné, *Lettres de Marie de Rabutin-Chantal, Marquise de Sévigné, à sa fille et ses amis* (Paris, 1861), I, pp. 417 ff. and II, pp. 17 ff.

14 Herbert R. Spencer, *The History of British Midwifery from 1650 to 1800* (1929), pp. 43 and 51. For a full discussion of these issues see Anne Oakley, *The Captured Womb: A History of the Medical Care of Pregnant Women* (Oxford, 1985).

15 Jalland and Hooper, p. 121, and pp. 165–86 for the chloroform controversy.

16 Mayo, pp. 97–8.

17 F. Engels, *Condition of the Working Classes in England* (1892), pp. 148 ff.

18 Christabel Pankhurst, *Plain Facts about a Great Evil (The Great Scourge, and how to end it)* (Women's Social and Political Union, 1913), p. 20.

19 A. Sinclair, *The Emancipation of American Woman* (New York, 1966), p. 72.

20 Francis (sic) Swiney, *Women and Natural Law* (The League of Isis, 1912), p. 44 and *The Bar of Isis* (1907) p. 38. Interestingly, Swiney foresaw the link between unprotected sexual intercourse and cervical cancer.

21 L. Fiaux, *La Police et Les Moeurs en France* (Paris, 1888), p. 129.

22 Sheila Jeffreys, *The Spinster and Her Enemies: Feminism and Sexuality 1880–1930* (1985), p. 88.

23 Lillian Faderman and Brigitte Eriksson (tr. and ed.) *Lesbian Feminism in Turn-of-the-Century Germany* (Weatherby Lake, Missouri, 1980), pp. 23–32. See also Faderman's magisterial *Surpassing the Love of Men: Romantic Friendship and Love between Women from the Renaissance to the Present* (1981).

24 *The Well of Loneliness*, Chapter 56, section 3.

25 C. H. F. Routh, *The Moral and Physical Evils likely to follow practices intended as Checks to Population* (1879), pp. 9–17. It will be recalled that many of these diseases were also supposedly attendant upon higher education for women. For Francis Place, see Derek Llewellyn Jones, *Human Reproduction and Society* (1974), p. 228.

26 Eva Figes, *Patriarchal Attitudes: Women in Society* (1970), pp. 27–8.

27 Bleier, pp. 170–1.

28 Juliet Mitchell, *Woman's Estate* (1971), p. 164.

Chapter 12 Daughters of Time

1 M. N. Duffy, *The Twentieth Century* (Oxford, 1964), pp. 1–2.

2 Mata Hari's conviction has always been a matter of controversy. She herself claimed to be a double agent working for the French all along. It is possible that her real

guilt was fraternizing with the hated Germans—see S. Wagenaar, *The Murder of Mata Hari* (1964).

3 Richard Grunberger, *A Social History of the Third Reich* (1971), pp. 322–3 for this, and the Goebbels remark.

4 Vera Laska, *Women in the Resistance and the Holocaust* (Connecticut, 1983), p. 181.

5 Edward Crankshaw, *Gestapo* (1956), p. 19.

6 J. Henderson and L. Henderson, *Ten Notable Latin American Women* (Chicago, 1978), p. xv.

7 Macksey, pp. 56–7.

8 See M. Bochkareva and I. D. Levine, *My Life as a Peasant Officer and Exile* (1929).

9 V. Figner, *Memoirs of a Revolutionist* (1927), and V. Liubatovich, *Memoirs* (1906); also B. Engel and C. Rosenthal, *Five Sisters: Women Against the Tsar* (1975).

10 Leghorn and Parker, p. 83.

11 Llewellyn Jones, pp. 239–40.

12 *Planned Parenthood of Missouri v. Danforth*, 428 US 52; 49 L. Ed 788 (1976), records the US 1973 decision. For the British case, see *Paton v. Trustees of BPAS* [1978] 2 All ER 987 at 991. For these and a fascinating retrospective of the history of legal attitudes to abortion, see O'Donovan, pp. 87–92.

13 Betty Friedan, *The Feminine Mystique* (1963) p. 15.

14 Bleier, p. 167. Koedt's much-discussed paper was important because it challenged head-on Freud's key concept of *two* female orgasms, clitoral and vaginal, one "mature," the other "immature," and asserted that Freud's theory to "cure" women's supposed "frigidity" actually ensured lack of orgasm by requiring women to have sex in the way it is most difficult to reach orgasm. This issue of sexuality thus became both symbol and proof of women's need to take the management of their lives into their own hands and no longer allow male "experts" to explain their bodies to them.

15 This extract comes from the very earliest manifesto of women's liberation, drawn up by a New York women's group calling themselves the Redstockings—see Anna Coote and Beatrix Campbell, *Sweet Freedom: The Struggle for Women's Liberation* (1982), p. 15.

16 De Riencourt, p. 339.

17 *International Herald Tribune*, August 24, 1970.

18 *Kommunist*, Moscow, November 1963.

19 R. Fuelop-Miller, *The Mind and Face of Bolshevism* (New york, 1965), p. 173.

20 Susan Strasser examines this phenomenon in *Never Done: A History of American Housework* (New York, 1982).

21 Leghorn and Parker, p. 14.

22 Tuttle, *Encyclopedia of Feminism* (New York, 1986), p. 42; and see Bell Hooks, *Feminist Theory: From Margin to Center* (Boston, 1984).

23 Tim Hodlin, "Veil of Tears," the *Listener* June 12, 1986.

24 Selma James (ed.), *Strangers and Sisters: Women, Race and Immigration* (1985), p. 85.

25 Lerner, p. 13; see also Lerner's *The Majority Finds Its Past* (New York, 1979) and Gayatri Chakravorty Spivak, *In Other Worlds: Essays in Cultural Politics* (New York, 1987).

26 Tuttle, p. 42.

BIBLIOGRAPHY

Abram, A., *Social England in the Fifteenth Century* (London, 1909)

Abray, Jane, "Feminism in the French Revolution," *American Historical Review* (1975)

Adams, J. Q., *The Dramatic Records of Sir Henry Herbert* (New Haven, Oxford & London, 1917)

Alexander, William, *The History of Women* (2 vols., London, 1782)

Alexander, Ziggi and Dewjee, Audrey (eds.), *The Wonderful Adventures of Mrs Seacole in Many Lands* (London, 1984)

Al-Hibri, Azizah, *Women and Islam* (London, 1982)

Alic, Margaret, *Hypatia's Heritage: A History of Women in Science from Antiquity to the Late Nineteenth Century* (London, 1986)

Allan, J. M., "On the Differences in the Minds of Men and Women," *Journal of the Anthropological Society of London* 7 (London, 1869)

Angiulli, A., *La Pedagogia, lo Stato e la Famiglia* (Naples, 1876)

Apuleius, Lucius, *The Golden Ass:* see Graves, Robert (tr.)

Ardener, Shirley (ed.), *Defining Females: The Nature of Women in Society* (London, 1978)

Ardrey, Robert, *African Genesis: A Personal Investigation Into the Animal Origins and Nature of Man* (London, 1961); *The Hunting Hypothesis: A Personal Conclusion Concerning the Evolutionary Nature of Man* (London, 1976)

Armstrong, Karen, *The Gospel According to Woman* (London, 1986)

Ashton, T. S., *The Industrial Revolution 1760–1830* (London, 1948)

Bachofen, Johann Jakob, *Das Mutterrecht* [The Mother-Right] (London, 1861); *Myth, Religion and Mother-Right* (Princeton, 1967)

Baker, Michael, *Our Three Selves: A Life of Radclyffe Hall* (London, 1985)

Bassermann, Lujo, *The Oldest Profession: A History of Prostitution* (London, 1967)

Beale, Dorothea, *A Report on the Education of Girls* (London, 1869)

Beard, C., *The Industrial Revolution* (London, 1901)

Bermant, Chaim, *The Walled Garden: The Saga of Jewish Family Life and Tradition* (London, 1974)

Berryman, John, *Homage to Mistress Bradstreet* (London, 1956)

Besse, Joseph, *A Collection of the Sufferings of the People Called Quakers* (London, 1753)

Beveridge, William, *India Called Them* (1941)

Bickley, F. B., (ed.), *The Little Red Book of Bristol* (Bristol, 1900)

Branch, Lesley, *Pavilions of the Heart: the Four Walls of Love* (London, 1974)

Bleier, Ruth, *Science and Gender—A Critique of Biology and its Theories on Women* (New York & Oxford, 1984)

Boatner, Mark M., *Enclopaedia of the American Revolution* (New York, 1973)

Bochkareva, M., & Levine, I. D., *My Life as a Peasant Officer and Exile* (London, 1929)

Bodin, Jean, *De la Démonomanie des Sorciers* (Paris, 1580)

Bose, Pramatha Nath, *A History of Hindu Civilisation During British Rule* (London, 1894)

Boulding, Elise, *The Underside of History: A View of Women through Time* (Colorado, 1976)

Box, Christine, & Arnold, Erik, *Smothered by Invention* (London, 1985)

Brandon, S. G. F., *Creation Legends of the Ancient Near East* (London, 1963)

Branston, Brian, *The Lost Gods of England* (London, 1974)

Brazell, Karen (tr.), *The Confessions of Lady Nijō* (London, 1975)

Briffault, Robert, *The Mothers* (3 vols., New York, 1927)

Brink, L., (ed.), *Female Scholars* (London, 1980)

Bronson, William, *The Last Grand Adventure* (New York, 1977)

Brown, Dee, *The Gentle Tamers: Women of the Old Wild West* (New York, 1958)

Brown, J. C., *Immodest Acts: The Life of a Lesbian Nun in Renaissance Italy* (Oxford, 1986)

Bruckner, G., (ed.), *Two Memoirs of Renaissance Florence*, tr. J. Martines (New York, 1968)

Bulwer-Lytton, Edward Lytton, *The Parisians* (London, 1873)

Burford, E. J., *Bawds and Lodgings: A History of the London Bankside Brothels c. 100–1675* (London, 1976)

Burke, Barbara, "Infanticide," from *Science 84*, 5:4 (May), 26–31 (London, 1984)

Burton, R. F. (Sir Richard), *Personal Narrative of a Pilgrimage to Al-Madinah and Meccah* (2 vols., London, 1855–6)

Butler, Iris, *The Viceroy's Wife* (London, 1969)

Butterfield, Herbert, *Man On His Past* (London, 1955)

Calder, Nigel, *Timescale* (London, 1984)

Camhi, Jane Jerome, *Women Against Women: American Anti-Suffragism 1880–1920*, Ph.D. Dissertation, Tufts University (1973)

Campbell, Joseph (ed.), *The Masks of God: Occidental Mythology* (New York, 1970); *Man and Transformation: Papers from the Eranos Yearbooks* (Vol. V, 1964)

Cannon, Michael, *Who's Master? Who's Man* (Melbourne, 1971)

Carpenter, Edward, *Love's Coming of Age* (Manchester, 1896)

Carr, E. H., *What is History?* (London, 1961)

Carter, Jan, *Nothing to Spare: Recollections of Australian Pioneering Women* (Victoria, 1981)

Chadwick, Nora, *The Celts* (London, 1970)

Charles, Lindsey & Duffin, Lorna, *Women and Work in Pre-Industrial England* (London, 1985)

Clark, Alice, *The Working Life of Women in the Seventeenth Century* (London, 1919; reissued 1982)

Clark, C. M. H., *Select Documents in Australian History 1788–1850* (Sydney, 1965)

Coles, John, *The Archaeology of Early Man* (London, 1969)

Collier, Mary, *The Woman's Labour: An Epistle to Mr. Stephen Duck: In Answer to his Late Poem called The Thresher's Labour* (London, 1739)

Conrad, E., *Harriet Tubman* (London, 1943)

Constable, J., *The Neanderthals* (London, 1973)

Coote, Anna & Campbell, Beatrix, *Sweet Freedom: the Struggle for Women's Liberation* (London, 1982)

Cumming, William P., & Rankin, Hugh, *The Fate of a Nation: the American Revolution through Contemporary Eyes* (London, 1975)

Daly, Mary, *The Church and the Second Sex* (London, 1968); *Beyond God the Father: Towards a Philosophy of Women's Liberation* (London, 1973)

Daniels, Kay & Murnane, Mary, *Uphill all the Way: a Documentary History of Women in Australia* (Queensland, 1980)

Darling, Sir Malcolm, *Apprentice to Power: India 1904–1908* (London, 1966)

Dart, Raymond, "The Predatory Transition from Ape to Man", *International Anthropological and Linguistic Review*, Vol. 1, No. 4, (London, 1953)

Darwin, Charles, *On the Origin of Species by Means of Natural Selection* (London, 1859); *The Descent of Man* (London, 1871)

Davidson, Basil, *Africa in History: Themes and Outlines* (London, 1968)

Davis, Elizabeth Gould, *The First Sex* (London, 1971)

d'Aubigné, Agrippa, *Oeuvres Complètes* (Paris, 1873)

d'Aussy, Le Grand, *Voyage d'Auvergne* (Paris, 1788)

de Beauvoir, Simone, *The Second Sex* (London, 1949, first English edition, 1953)

de Bourdeille, Pierre, & de Brantome, Abbé, *Les Vies des Dames Galantes* (London, 1961)

de la Bruyère, Jean, *Oeuvres Complètes* (London, 1951) ed. J. Benda

de Cambry, Jacques, *Voyage dans de Finistère* (London, 1799)

de Caritat, Marie-Jean, *Essai sur l'Admission des Femmes au Droit de Cité* (Paris, 1790)

de Crenne, Hélisenne, *Les Angoysses qui procédent d'Amour contenant trois parties composées par dame Hélisenne de Crenne laquelle exhorte toutes personnes a ne pas suivre folle amour* (London, 1538)

de Flore, Jeanne (pseud. J. Galliarde), *Contes Amoureux, touchant la punition que fait Vénus de ceux qui condamnent et mésprisent le vray amour*

de Gouges, Olympe (pseud.), *Déclaration des Droits de la Femme et de la Citoyenne* (London, 1791)

De Gournay, Marie Le Jars, *Egalité des hommes et des femmes* (London, 1622); *Grief des Dames* (London, 1626)

de Pisan, Christine, *Cité de Dames* (1394)

de Riencourt, Amaury, *Women and Power in History* (London, 1983)

de Rougemont, Denis, *Passion and Society* (London, 1956)

de Sevigné, Madame, *Lettres de Marie de Rabutin-Chantal, Marquise de Sévigné, à sa fille et ses amis* (Paris, 1861)

Diner, Helen (pseud. Bertha Eckstein-Diener), *Mothers and Amazons: The First Feminine History of Culture* (London, 1932)

Dingwall, Eric John, *The Girdle of Chastity* (London, 1931)

Dodwell, H. H., *The Cambridge History of India*, 7 vols., (Cambridge & New York, 1932)

Dowling, A., *Reports of Cases Argued and Determined in the Queen's Bench Practice Courts* (1841)

Draper, Elizabeth, *Birth Control in the Modern World* (London, 1965)

Dreifus, C., (ed.), *Seizing Our Bodies* (New York, 1978)

Duffy, M. N., *The Twentieth Century* (Oxford, 1964)

Durry, Marcel (ed.), *Eloge Funèbre d'une Matrone Romaine: Eloge dit de Turia* (Collection des Universités de France, 1950)

Edwardes, Allen, *The Jewel in the Lotus: a Historical Survey of the Sexual Culture of the East* (London, 1965)

Eke, Jiuba, F., "Omu Okwei: A Biographical Sketch", *Journal of the Historical Society of Nigeria*, iii (London, 1967)

El Saadawi, Nawal, "Women in Islam," in Al-Hibri (London, 1982), q.v., pp. 193–206

Engel, B., & Rosenthal, C., *Five Sisters: Women Against the Tsar* (London, 1975)

Engelmann, George J., The President's Address, *American Gynecology Society* (London, 1900)

Engels, F., *Condition of the Working Classes in England* (London, 1892)

Engels, F., *The Origin of the Family, Private Property and the State in the Light of the Researches of Lewis H. Morgan* (London, 1884, 1st English edition 1942)

Erasmus, Desiderius, *Christian Matrimonii Institutio* (London, 1526)

Etienne, Mona & Leacock, Eleanor (eds.), *Women and Colonisation* (London, 1980)

Evans, Sir Arthur, *The Palace of Minos at Knossos* (4 vols., London, 1921–1935)

Evans, Hilary, *The Oldest Profession: An Illustrated History of Prostitution* (London, 1979)

Evans, Jean, *Index to the Palace of Minos* (London, 1936)

Evans, Mary, (ed.), *The Woman Question: Readings on the Subordination of Women* (London, 1982)

Evans, Richard L., (eds.), *Dialogue with Erik Erikson* (New York, 1967)

Faderman, Lillian, *Surpassing the Love of Men: Romantic Friendship and Love Between Women from the Renaissance to the Present* (London, 1981)

Faderman, Lillian, & Eriksson, Brigitte (tr. & ed.), *Lesbian Feminism in turn-of-the-century Germany* (Weatherby Lake, Missouri, 1980)

Fagan, B. M., *People of the Earth: An Introduction to World Pre-History* (London, 1980)

Fagniez, G., *Documents Relatifs à l'Histoire de l'Industrie et de Commerce en France* (Paris, 1899–1900)

Farb, Peter, *Man's Rise to Civilisation as shown by the Indians of North America, from Primeval Times to the Coming of the Industrial State* (London, 1968)

Le Faure, A., *Le Socialisme Pendant la Révolution Française* (Paris, 1863)

Ferguson, John, *The Religions of the Roman Empire* (London, 1970)

Fiaux, L., *La Police des Moeurs en France* (Paris, 1888)

Figes, Eva, *Patriarchal Attitudes: Women in Society* (London, 1970)

Figner, V., *Memoirs of a Revolutionist* (London, 1927)

Firestone, Shulamith, *The Dialectic of Sex: the Case for Feminist Revolution* (London, 1970)

First, R., & Scott, A., *Olive Shreiner* (London, 1980)

Fisher, Elizabeth, *Woman's Creation: Sexual Evolution and the Shaping of Society* (New York, 1979)

Fitzgerald, C. P., *China: A Short Cultural History* (London, 1961)

Fitzpatrick, Brian, *The Australian People 1788–1945* (Melbourne, 1946)

Folkhard, Frederick, C., *The Rare Sex* (Murray, Sydney, 1965)

Franks, Patricia, *Grandma was a Pioneer* (Canada, 1977)

Fraser, Antonia, *The Weaker Vessel: Woman's Lot in Seventeenth-Century England* (London, 1984)
Frazer, Sir James, *The Golden Bough* (London, 1922)
Freeman, Jo (ed.), *Women: A Feminist Perspective* (Palo Alto, California, 1979)
French, Marilyn, *Beyond Power: Men, Women and Morals* (London, 1985)
Friedan, Betty, *The Feminine Mystique* (New York, 1963)
Friedrich, Paul, *The Meaning of Aphrodite* (Chicago & London, 1978)
Fuelop-Miller, R., *The Mind and Face of Bolshevism* (New York, 1965)
Fulford, Roger, *Votes for Women: the Story of a Struggle* (London, 1958)

Gage, Matilda Joslyn, *Woman, Church and State: The Original Exposé of Male Collaboration Against the Female Sex* (London, 1893)
Gallichan, Walter, M., *Women Under Polygamy* (London, 1914)
Gattey, C. N., *Gauguins's Astonishing Grandmother* (London, 1970)
Geoffrey of Tours, *Historia Francorum Libri Deum* (1120)
Gies, Joseph & Frances, *Life in a Medieval Castle* (New York, 1974); *Women in the Middle Ages* (New York, 1978)
Gilman, Charlotte Perkins, *Women and Economics* (London, 1898)
Gorean, A., *Reconstructing Aphra* (London, 1980)
Grant, M., *Elizabeth Blackwell* (London, 1974)
Graves, Robert, *The White Goddess* (London, 1948); *The Greek Myths* (London, 1960); (ed.) *The New Larousse Encyclopaedia of Mythology* (London, 1959); (tr.) *Apuleius: The Golden Ass* (London, 1950)
Greene, Graham, *Lord Rochester's Monkey: Being the Life of John Wilmot, Second Earl of Rochester* (London, 1976)
Greer, Germaine, *The Female Eunuch* (London, 1970); *The Obstacle Race: The Fortunes of Women Painters and their Work* (London, 1979)
Griffiths, Elisabeth, *In Her Own Right: The Life of Elizabeth Cady Stanton* (Oxford & New York, 1986)
Grunberger, Richard, *A Social History of the Third Reich* (London, 1971)

Haggard, Sir Henry Rider, *King Solomon's Mines* (London, 1886)
Hall, Radclyffe, *The Well of Loneliness* (London, 1928)
Hamer, F., *Théroigne de Méricourt: a Woman of the Revolution* (London, 1911)
Hamman, Anne B., "Professor Beyer and the Woman Question," *Educational Review* 47 (March, 1914)
Hammerton, A. James, *Emigrant Gentlewomen* (London, 1979)
Hammond, J. L., & Hammond, Barbara, *The Rise of Modern Industry* (London, 1939)
Harding, M. Esther, *Woman's Mysteries, Ancient & Modern, A Psychological Interpretation of the Feminine Principle as Portrayed in Myth, Story and Dreams* (New York, 1955)
Hartley, C. Gascoigne, *The Position of Women in Primitive Society* (London, 1914)
Hawkes, Jacquetta, *Dawn of the Gods* (London, 1958); *Prehistory* (New York, 1965); *The First Great Civilisations* (London, 1975)
Healey, Edna, *Wives of Fame: Mary Livingstone, Jenny Marx, Emma Darwin* (London, 1986)
Henderson, L. & J., *Ten Notable Latin American Women* (Chicago, 1978)
Herold, J. Christopher, *The Horizon Book of the Age of Napoleon* (New York, 1963)

Hibbert, Christopher, *The Roots of Evil: A Social History of Crime and Punishment* (London, 1966); *The French Revolution* (London, 1980)

Hill, Raymond & Burgin, Thomas G. (eds.), *Anthology of the Provençal Troubadours* (London, 1941)

Holden, Pat, *Women's Religious Experience* (London, 1983)

Hooks, Bell, *Ain't I a Woman: Black Women and Feminism* (Boston, 1981); *Feminist Theory: from Margin to Center* (Boston, 1984)

Horney, Karen, *Feminine Psychology,* ed. Harold Kelman (New York, 1967)

Hosken, Fran, *The Hosken Report—Genital and Sexual Mutilation of Females* (Autumn 1979, Women's International Network News, 187 Grant St., Lexington, Mass. 02173, USA)

Hughes, Pennethorne, *Witchcraft* (London, 1965)

Humphreys, M. E., Beggs, Gregor Hugh, and Humphreys, Darlow, *The Industrial Revolution* (London, 1976)

Hurt-Mead, Kate, C., "Trotula," Isis, 14 (London, 1930), pp. 349–69

Hutton, Diane, "Women in Fourteenth-Century Shrewsbury," in Charles L., and Duffin L., q.v.

Huxley, Thomas, *Ethics and Evolution* (London, 1893); *Life and Letters of Thomas Huxley* (2 vols., New York, 1901)

Hyam, Ronald, *Britain's Imperial Century 1815–1914: a Study of Empire and Expansion* (London, 1976)

Isaac, G., & Leakey, R., *Human Ancestors* (London, 1979)

Jalland, Pat & Hooper, John (eds.), *Women from Birth to Death: the Female Life Cycle in Britain 1830–1914* (London, 1986)

James, E. O., *The Cult of the Mother Goddess: an Archaeological and Documentary Study* (London, 1959); *Sacrifice and Sacrament* (London, 1962)

Jeffreys, Sheila, *The Spinster and her Enemies: Feminism and Sexuality 1880–1930* (London, 1985)

Johanson, Donald C., and Edey, Maitland A., *Lucy: The Beginnings of Humankind, The Dramatic Discovery of Our Oldest Human Ancestor* (London & New York, 1981)

Jones, Derek Llewellyn, *Human Reproduction and Society* (London, 1974)

Kaye, M. M., *The Golden Calm: an English Lady's Life in Moghul Delhi, Reminiscences by Emily, Lady Clive Bayley, and her Father, Sir Thomas Metcalfe* (Exeter, 1980)

Kaye, Melanie, *Nice Jewish Girls,* ed. Evelyn Torton Beck (Mass., 1982)

Kelly, Dr. Howard A., *Medical Gynecology* (London, 1909)

Kerenyi, C., *Eleusis: Archetypal Image of Mother and Daughter* (New York & London, 1967)

Kessler-Harris, Alice, *Out to Work: A History of Wage-Earning Women in the United States* (New York, 1982)

Klein, Viola, *The Feminine Character: History of an Ideology* (London, 1946)

Koedt, Anne, *The Myth of the Vaginal Orgasm* (New York, 1969)

Kramarae, Cheris & Treichler, Paula A., *A Feminist Dictionary* (London, 1985)

Labarge, Margaret Wade, *Women in Medieval Life* (London, 1986)

Labé, Louise, *Débat de Folie et d'Amour* (London, 1595)

Ladurie, Emmanuel Le Roy, *The French Peasantry 1450–1660,* tr. Alan Sheridan, (London, 1986)

Lane, Anne S. (ed.), *Mary Ritter Beard: A Sourcebook* (New York, 1977)

Langdon-Davies, John, *A Short History of Women* (London, 1928)

Lantier, Jacques, *La Cité Magique* (Paris, 1972)

Laska, Vera, *Women in the Resistance and in the Holocaust* (Connecticut, 1983)

Leakey, R., & Lewin, R., *Origins* (New York, 1977); *The Illustrated Origin of Species*, ed. R. A. Leakey (1979)

Leavitt, Judith Walzer, *Brought to Bed: Childbearing in America, 1750–1950* (New York, 1986)

Lee, R. B., & De Vore, Irven, *Man the Hunter* (London, 1968); (eds.) *Kalahari Hunter-Gatherers* (Harvard University Press, 1976)

Lefkowitz, Mary R., *Women in Greek Myth* (London, 1986)

Leghorn, Lisa, & Parker, Katherine, *Woman's Worth: Sexual Economics and the World of Women* (1981)

Leroi-Gourhan, André, *The Art of Prehistoric Man in Western Europe* (London, 1969)

Leslie, Julia, "Essence and Existence: Women and Religion in Ancient Indian Texts", in Holden (London, 1983) q.v., pp. 89–112

Lewenhak, Sheila, *Women and Work* (London, 1980)

Liubatovich, V., *Memoirs* (London, 1906)

Livingstone, W. P., *Mary Slessor of Calabar: Pioneer Missionary* (London, 1916)

Lorenz, Konrad, *On Aggression* (London, 1966)

Lowe, Marian, & Hubbard, Ruth, *Woman's Nature: Rationalisations of Inequality* (New York & Oxford, 1983)

Lucas, Angela M., *Women in the Middle Ages: Religion, Marriage & Letters* (London, 1983)

Luquet, G-H., *The Art and Religion of Fossil Man* (Oxford, 1930)

Luther, D. Martin, *Kritische Gesamtausgabe*, Vol. III. *Briefweschel* (Weimar, 1933)

Lyell, Charles, *Principles of Geology* (London, 1830)

MacCurtain, Margaret & Ó Corrain, Donna, (eds.), *Women in Irish Society: The Historical Dimension* (1986)

Macksey, Joan, *The Guinness Guide to Feminine Achievement* (London, 1975)

McLean, Scilla, *Female Circumcision, Excision and Infibulation: the Facts and Proposals for Change* (Minority Rights Groups Report No. 47, December 1980)

Maitland, Sara, *A Map of the New Country: Women and Christianity* (London, 1983)

Mandel, Gabriel, *A Poem of the Pillow: the Japanese Methods* (Fribourg, 1984)

Markdale, Jean, *Women of the Celts* (Paris, New York, London 1982)

Mayo, Katherine, *Mother India* (London, 1927)

Mead, Margaret, *Male and Female: A Study of the Sexes in a Changing World* (New York, 1949)

Mernissi, Fatima, *Beyond the Veil: Male-Female Dynamics in a Modern Muslim Society* (New York, 1975)

Merriam, Eve (ed.), *Growing Up Female in America: Ten Lives* (New York, 1971)

Middlekauf, Robert, *The Glorious Cause: The American Revolution 1763–1789* (New York & Oxford, 1982)

Middleton, D., *Victorian Lady Travellers* (London, 1965)

Miles, R., *Women and Power* (London, 1965)

Milkman, Ruth, *Gender at Work* (Urbana, University of Illinois Press, 1987)

Millett, Kate, *Sexual Politics* (London, 1970)

Mitchell, Juliet, *Women's Estate* (London, 1971)

Montague, Ashley, *Sex, Man, and Society* (New York, 1969)

Morgan, Elaine, *The Descent of Woman* (London, 1972)

Morris, Desmond, *The Naked Ape* (London, 1967)

Morris, James, *Pax Britannica* (London 1969)

Morris, J., *The Lady was a Bishop* (New York, 1973)

Murdock, George P., *Our Primitive Contemporaries* (New York, 1934); *Social Structure* (New York, 1949); "World Ethnographic Sample," *American Anthropologist*, (London, 1957); "Ethnographic Atlas: A Summary," *Ethnology* 6, No. 2, pp. 109–236

Murray, Margaret, *The Witch-Culture in Western Europe* (Oxford, 1921)

Musurillo, Herbert, *The Acts of the Christian Martyrs* (London, 1972)

Nefwazi, Shaykh, *The Perfumed Garden*, tr. Sir Richard Burton (London, 1963)

Neumann, Erich, *The Great Mother: An Analysis of the Archetype* (New York & London, 1955)

Newman, Louise Michele, *Men's Ideas: Women's Realities: Popular Science 1870–1915* (New York & London, 1985)

Ní Chuilleanáin, Eilean (ed.), *Irish Women: Image and Achievement—Women in Irish Culture from Earliest Times* (London, 1985)

Nicholson, John, *Men and Women: How Different Are They?* (Oxford, 1984)

Niedzwiecki, Patricia, *Women and Music, Women of Europe*, Supplement No. 22, (Commission of the European Communities, October 1985)

Nijō, Lady, *Confessions*—see Brazell, Karen

Oakley, A., *The Captured Womb: A History of the Medical Care of Pregnant Women* (Oxford, 1985); *Housewife* (London, 1974); *Subject Woman* (Glasgow, 1982)

Oakley, Kenneth, *Man the Tool-Maker* (London, 1947)

O'Donovan, Katherine, *Sexual Divisions in Law* (London, 1985)

O'Faolain, Julia & Martines, Laura, *Not in God's Image: Woman in History* (London, 1973)

O'Neill, John, *The Night of the Gods* (2 vols., London, 1893)

O'Neill, Lois Decker (ed.), *The Woman's Book of World Records and Achievements* (New York, 1979)

Pankhurst, Christabel, *Plain Facts About a Great Evil (The Great Scourge and How to End It)*, (Women's Social and Political Union, London, 1913)

Parent-Duchatelet, A. J. B., *De la Prostitution dans la Ville de Paris* (2 vols., Paris, 1857)

Parker, Rozsika, & Pollock, Griselda, *Old Mistresses: Women, Art and Ideology* (London, 1981)

Parrinder, Geoffrey, *Sex in the World's Religions* (London, 1980)

Patai, Raphael, *The Hebrew Goddess* (New York, 1967)

Pauli, H., *Her Name was Sojourner Truth* (London, 1962)

Petrie, Glen, *A Singular Iniquity: the Campaigns of Josephine Butler* (London, 1971)

Phillips, M., & Tomkinson, W. S., *English Women in Life and Letters* (Oxford, 1927)

Pike, E. Royston, *Human Documents of the Industrial Revolution in Britain* (London, 1966)

Pinchbeck, Ivy, *Women Workers and the Industrial Revolution 1750–1850* (London, 1930, reprinted 1969)

Pratt, Edwin A., *Pioneer Women in Victoria's Reign* (London, 1897)

Rae, I., *The Strange Story of Dr. James Barry* (London, 1958)

Ranelagh, E. L., *Men On Women* (London, 1985)

Raven, Susan & Weir, Alison, *Women in History: Thirty-Five Centuries of Feminine Achievement* (London, 1981)

Read, Carveth, *Origins of Man* (London, 1925)

Reed, Evelyn, *Woman's Evolution: from Matriarchal Clan to Patriarchal Family* (New York, 1975)

Reichard, Gladys, *Navajo Religion: A Study of Symbolism* (New York, 1950)

Reiter, Rayna (ed.), *Towards an Anthropology of Women* (London, 1975)

Rennie, Susan, & Grimstad, Kirsten, *The New Woman's Survival Catalog* (New York, 1973)

Riedesel, Baroness, *The Voyage of Discovery to America* (London, 1800)

Ripley: E.M. Denise, *"Am I That Name?": Feminism and the Category of "Women" In History* (London, 1988)

Roberts, J. M., *The Hutchinson History of the World* (London, 1976)

Robinson, Victor, *Pioneers of Birth Control in England and America* (New York, Voluntary Parenthood League, 1919)

Rosenberg, Rosalind, *Beyond Separate Spheres: Intellectual Roots of Modern Feminism* (New Haven, 1982); *Feminist Studies 3* (Fall 1970)

Rothery, G. D., *The Amazons* (London, 1910)

Routh, C. M. F., *The Moral and Physical Evils Likely to Follow Practices Intended as Checks to Population* (London, 1879)

Royster, Charles, *A Revolutionary People at War: the Continental Army, the American Character 1775–1783* (Chapel Hill, North Carolina, 1979)

Rugg, W. F., *Unafraid: a life of Anne Hutchinson* (London, 1930)

Rule, Jane, *Lesbian Images* (New York, 1982)

Russell, Bertrand, *History of Western Philosophy, and its Connection with Political and Social Circumstances from the Earliest Times to the Present Day* (London, 1946)

Sabbah, Fatna A., (pseud.), *Woman in the Muslim Unconscious* (London, & New York, 1984)

Sandars, N. K., (tr.), *The Epic of Gilgamesh* (London, 1960)

Scharlieb, Mary, *The Seven Ages of Woman* (London, 1915)

Schiaffini, A., (ed.), *Libro di Buoni Costumi* (Florence, 1956)

Schimmel, Annemarie, "Women in Mystical Islam," in Al-Hibri (q.v.)

Schmidt, Master Franz, *A Hangman's Diary* (London, 1928)

Schneider, J. A., *Flora Tristan* (London, 1980)

Schreiner, Olive, *The Story of an African Farm* (London, 1884); *Woman and Labour* (London, 1911)

Scot, Reginald, *The Discovery of Witchcraft*, ed. B. Nicholson, (London 1886)

Scott, G. R., *Phallic Worship: A History of Sex and Sex Rites in Relation to the Religion of all Races from Antiquity to the Present Day* (New Delhi, 1975)

Seltman, Charles A., *Women in Antiquity* (London, 1956)

Shackley, Myra Lesley, *Neanderthal Man* (London, 1980)

Shuttle, Penelope, & Redgrove, Peter, *The Wise Wound: Menstruation and Everywoman* (London, 1978)

Sicherman, Barbara; Monter, E. William; Scott, Joan Wallach; and Sklar, Kathryn Kish; *Recent United States Scholarships of the History of Women* (Washington, D.C., American Historical Association, 1980)

Sinclair, A., *The Emancipation of the American Woman* (New York, 1966)

Slocum, Sally, "Woman the Gatherer: Male Bias in Anthropology," (London, 1971), in Reiter (q.v.) and Evans (q.v.)

Smith, Daniel Scott, "Family Limitation, Sexual Control and Domestic Feminism in Victorian America," in M. Hartman and L. Banner (eds) *Clios's Consciousness Raised* (New York, 1974)

Smith, F. M., *Mary Astell* (London, 1916)

Solanas, Valerie, *S.C.U.M. Manifesto* (New York, 1968)

Soranus, *Gynaecology*, tr. Owsie Temkins, (Johns Hopkins, 1956)

Spencer, Herbert, *Education: Intellectual, Moral and Physical* (London, 1861); *Principles of Biology* (London, 1864–7)

Spencer, Herbert R., *The History of British Midwifery from 1650 to 1800* (London, 1929)

Spivak, Gayatri Chakrovorty, *In Other Worlds: Essays in Cultural Politics* (New York, 1987)

Sprenger, Jacob, *Malleus Maleficarum* (1484)

Stanton, Elizabeth Cady, *Eighty Years and More: Reminiscences 1815–1897* (New York, 1898)

Stanton, Elizabeth Cady; Anthony, Susan B.; Gage, Matilda Joslyn; *The History of Woman Suffrage* (New York, 1876–85)

Stone, Lee Alexander, *The Story of Phallicism* (Chicago, 1927)

Stone, Merlin, *The Paradise Papers* (London, 1976); *Ancient Mirrors of Womanhood* (London, 1979)

Storr, Anthony, *Human Aggression* (London, 1968)

Strong, James, *Joanereidos: or Feminine Valour Eminently Discovered in Westerne Women* (London, 1645)

Summers, Anne, *Damned Whores and God's Police: the Colonisation of Women in Australia* (Ringwood, Vic., 1975)

Suttie, Ian D., *The Origins of Love and Hate* (London, 1960)

Swiney, Francis, *Women and Natural Law* (League of Isis, 1912); *The Bar of Isis* (London, 1907)

"T.E." (anon), *The Lawes Resolution of Women's Rights* (London, 1632)

Tax, Sol (ed.), *The Evolution of Man, Evolution After Darwin* Vol. II (University of Chicago, 1960)

Thomas, W. I., *Sex and Society: Studies in the Psychology of Sex* (London, 1907)

Thompson, Roger, *Women in Stuart England and America: a Comparative Study* (London, 1974)

Thorndike, Lynn, *A Short History of Civilisation* (London, 1927)

Tomalin, Claire, *The Life and Death of Mary Wollstonecraft* (London, 1978)

Tristan, Flora, *Pérégrinations d'une Paria* (London, 1838); *L'Union Ouvrière* (Paris, 1843)

Trollope, Joanna, *Britannia's Daughters: Women of the British Empire* (London, 1983)

Tuttle, Lisa, *Encyclopedia of Feminism* (New York, 1986)

Uglow, Jennifer S. (ed.), *The Macmillan Dictionary of Women's Biography* (London, 1982)

Vaerting, Mathilde & Mathias, *The Dominant Sex: a Study in the Sociology of Sex Differences* (London, 1923)

Verney, Lady F. P. (ed.), *Memoirs of the Verney Family During the Civil War* (2 vols., 1892)

Vicars, John, *God's Arke Overtopping the World's Waves, or the Third Party of the Parliamentary Chronicle* (London, 1646)

Wagenaar, S., *The Murder of Mata Hari* (London, 1964)

Walsh, Mary Roth, *Doctors Wanted, No Women Need Apply: Sexual Barriers in the Medical Profession (1935–1975)* (New Haven, Yale, 1977)

Warner, Marina, *Joan of Arc: The Image of Female Heroism* (New York, 1982)

Washburn, S., & Lancaster, C. S., "The Evolution of Hunting," in Lee & De Vor (q.v.)

Webb, Beatrice, *My Apprenticeship* (London, 1926)

Webster, Paula, "Matriarchy: A Vision of Power," in Reiter (q.v.)

Weideger, Paula, *History's Mistress* (London, 1985)

Wells, H. G., *The Outline of History* (London, 1930)

Whitelock, B., *Memorials of English Affairs* (London, 1732)

Wittmer, C., & Meyer, C. J. (eds.), *Le Livre de la Bourgeoisie de la Ville de Strasbourg 1440–1530* (Strasbourg & Zurich 1948–61)

Wolf, Josef & Burian, Zdenek, *The Dawn of Man* (London, 1978)

Wollstonecraft, Mary, *A Vindication of the Rights of Women* (London, 1792)

Woolley, Hannah, *The Ladies' Directory* (London, 1661); *The Gentlewoman's Companion* (London, 1675)

Wu Chao (ed.), *Women in Chinese Folklore,* Women of China Special Series (Bejing, China, 1983)

INDEX